Praise for the Book

Written in an engaging style with scores of fascinating stories, *Gifts of an Uncommon Life* shows us the ways and means to change our lifestyles so that we can live our lives to the fullest and become agents of God to change the world that is into what God wants it to be.

> *Tony Campolo, Professor Emeritus of Sociology, Eastern University, St. David's, Pennsylvania*

Christianity is inherently a prophetic faith in that it seeks not only to soothe but also to challenge in light of its vision of God's future. This lively book is an exploration of how an awareness of being unsettled is creative, healing, and brings us closer to God

> *Dr. Iain Torrance, President of Princeton Theological Seminary*

Howard Friend proves to be both a faithful pilgrim and a fearless scout into the hills and valleys of an authentic life. He offers compelling reminders that real life, the life that ultimately matters, happens when we dig deep in the soil of ordinary moments. In the daily surprises, we are given what we need for building a truly "uncommon life" together, a way of being that can embolden us to become the people God needs for the challenges of these days.

> *Gordon Cosby, founding pastor, Church of the Savior, Washington, D.C.*

Gifts of an Uncommon Life is a book for all followers of Jesus in the Western world at this point in time. It calls us to let go of the old with hope in order to find deeper and truer embodiments of grace for the healing of the world today.

> *J. Philip Newell, former warden at Iona Abbey in Scotland, leading author and teacher of Celtic spirituality*

Howard Friend has invited us to accompany him on a wise and insightful personal and professional faith journey. He will be your advisor, your coach, your teacher, your prophet, your personal trainer, your spiritual director, your confidant, and your friend.

> *Bishop Claire Burkat, Southeastern Pennsylvania Synod, Evangelical Lutheran Church of America, and author of* Transformational Regional Bodies

Gifts of an Uncommon Life joins the growing chorus of writings that integrate the inner and the outer, the contemplative and the activist, wisdom and intellect, right brain and left brain, East and West in a synthesis of the whole. It is a gem waiting to be discovered.

> *Walter Wink, Professor of Biblical Interpretation, Auburn Theological Seminary*

The skill to shape the passages of life in congregations is held by some spiritual adepts, as is the skill to tell these stories with vitality and passion. *Gifts of an Uncommon Life* is a testimony to the life-renewing and story-telling skills of Howard Friend.

   Rabbi Arthur Waskow, author of Godwrestling, Round 2 *and co-author of* The Tent of Abraham

With a simple and dynamic style, Howard Friend invites his readers to leave their inertia behind and passionately serve our unjust, cynical, yet beautiful world. This is a book of wisdom for life that stimulates the humanization of society, the church, and ourselves. In a world where our humanity is bought and sold, a book like this becomes indispensable for everyone.

   Elsa Tamez, Professor of Biblical Studies, Universidad Bíblica Latinoamericana, San José, Costa Rica; author of The Amnesty of Grace, Jesus and the Courageous Women, *and* The Scandalous Message of James

This collection of essays touches the furthest reaches of my soul. What does it mean to be faithful in the heart of empire? Dare we dream of a new—or perhaps renewed—community of followers of Jesus? These are essays for those of us who know our church is complicit with the powers and principalities, and who wonder how we might rediscover the Way.

   Rick Ufford-Chase, Moderator, 216th General Assembly of the Presbyterian Church (USA), Director, Presbyterian Peace Fellowship

The attraction of the physical world spawns idolatry—an obsession with externals—so tragically, how we look takes precedence over who we are. Physicality trumps spirituality. We obsessively choose the fleeting and temporal and neglect the eternal. Contemplative activism invites us toward our deepest self and to oneness with a just and loving God.

   Shaykh T. A. Bashir, Asst. Secretary General of the African Council of Imams in America, President and Board Chair, House of Peace, New Sanctuary Movement

Howard Friend brings the two poles of contemplation and activism into a creative tension. He raises the bar for effective ministry and does so simply by pointing us to the example of Jesus Christ. *Gifts of an Uncommon Life* affirms that creative ministry still needs Jesus as its anchor—a message that many of us need to hear and implement.

   Wallace Charles Smith, President, Palmer Theological Seminary of Eastern University, Pastor, Shiloh Baptist Church, Washington, D.C.

GIFTS OF AN UNCOMMON LIFE

GIFTS OF AN UNCOMMON LIFE

The Practice of Contemplative Activism

HOWARD E. FRIEND, JR.

THE
ALBAN
INSTITUTE
Herndon, Virginia
www.alban.org

The Alban Institute
2121 Cooperative Way, Suite 100
Herndon, VA 20171-5370

Unless otherwise noted, all Scripture quotations are from the New Revised Standard Version of the Bible, copyright © 1989, Division of Christian Education of the National Council of the Churches of Christ in the United States of America, and are used by permission.

Scripture quotations marked GNT are from the Good News Translation - Second Edition, Copyright © 1992 by American Bible Society. Used by Permission.

Scripture quotations marked RSV are from the Revised Standard Version of the Bible, copyright © 1952 [2nd edition, 1971] by the Division of Christian Education of the National Council of the Churches of Christ in the United States of America. Used by permission. All rights reserved.

Original cover art by Bo Bartlett, www.bobartlett.com.

Interior art by Bonnie Gross.

Library of Congress Cataloging-in-Publication Data

Friend, Howard E.
  Gifts of an uncommon life : the practice of contemplative activism / Howard E. Friend, Jr.
     p. cm.
  Includes bibliographical references.
  ISBN 978-1-56699-374-6
  1. Christian leadership. 2. Friend, Howard E. I. Title.

BV652.1.F75 2008
253--dc22
                                        2008036030

        12   11   10   09   08   VP   1   2   3   4   5

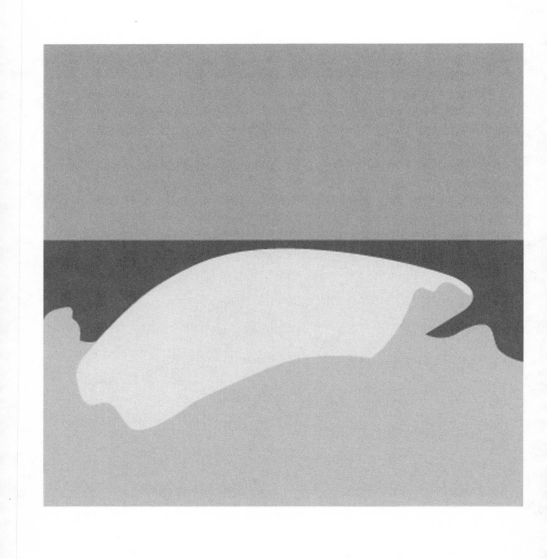

Contents

FOREWORD

C hristianity worldwide has come to have an often negative public image. The Christian religion no longer naturally connotes people who serve the world, people who care about others, other nations or religions, poverty and injustice, or even people who are very happy. In fact, our common image is often exactly the opposite.

How did we get to this impossible place, after placing ourselves in the following of Jesus who described himself as "gentle and humble of heart" (Matthew 11:29) and whom the Samaritan woman saw as the "Savior of the world" (John 4:42)? Now we often appear tribal, territorial, and timid—a strange combination of defensive and offensive—in the name of the one who was none of these.

My own opinion, and clearly shared by Howard Friend, is that we lost the contemplative mind in favor of partisanship, paranoia, power politics, and often aggressive apologetics. You can no longer be contemplative when you need to win too badly, defeat others, prove yourself right or others wrong. These are the unnecessary concerns of the soul because it has already won once and for all. These are all needs of the ego self, what Jesus calls the self "that has to die", and are of no interest to the true self or "The Life that we have, hidden with Christ in God" (Colossians 3:3).

I founded the Center for Action and Contemplation here in Albuquerque, New Mexico in 1987 after being an itinerant Franciscan preacher around the world for 15 years at that point. We gave ourselves that long, cumbersome title to hold ourselves to our always central task, the integration of our inner work and our outer work. It is the great art form, and always will be. When people debate about the most important word in that title, or which should be first, I say that the important and first word is "and"! It is such an "and" that Howard is seeking here in this fine work so rightly named from "an uncommon life".

The much more "common life" is invariably that we act out of personal preference and temperament. Some of us are better at doing, and some prefer to help by thinking, talking, considering, or even praying. Some go outside first, some go inside. We must do both. Neither of them are necessarily the contemplative midpoint, where we act as one—one with God, one with all the different parts of ourselves, and even one with the supposed enemy or the opposition. You can see why that integration is the work of a lifetime, many failures and many graces. It is the life of a saint.

I hope you will find as much wisdom, inspiration, common sense, and uncommon sense, as I myself found here. Doing good things will change the world a bit, contemplative doing of good things will change both you, those around you, and therefore the world—but it will not just be fruit, but now "fruit that will last" (John 15:16).

Richard Rohr, O.F.M.
Center for Action and Contemplation
Albuquerque, New Mexico

PREFACE

A Place to Start

$\mathcal{W}$hat is popularly known as the "hundredth monkey" story—based on research by four Japanese scientists, reported by zoologist and anthropologist Lyall Watson,[1] and popularized by author Ken Kesey[2]—remains controversial as credible science; but the account is nonetheless thought-provoking and compelling.

MONKEYS AND PEACEFUL REVOLUTIONARIES

Koshima is the largest of a cluster of islands off the northern coast of Japan, each inhabited by a troop of monkeys that had been observed in the wild for thirty years. In 1952 scientists, concerned about the growth of the monkey population and the scarcity of food, began to air-drop sweet potatoes, which settled undamaged into the sandy soil, providing a simple, highly nutritious source of nourishment. The moneys appeared to find this new food tasty—except for the grit that clung to the potato skin.

One day a young female monkey, dubbed "Imo" by research observers, plucked a sweet potato from the ground and paused before taking a first bite. Wandering to a nearby stream, she gingerly washed the sweet potato clean. Though the precise details can only be imagined, it seems reasonable to assume that Imo alerted her family, her playmates, and others living nearby; and soon a whole neighborhood of monkeys were washing their sweet potatoes, the expanding practice chronicled by the team of scientists. Slowly but steadily across five years, the practice spread, though only among a tiny minority of the monkey population. Then one autumn day in 1958, something startling happened. At daybreak there were, at least in Kesey's telling, ninety-nine monkeys washing their sweet potatoes. Sometime later that morning a hundredth monkey caught on. By sunset all the monkeys on Koshima Island got it! They were all washing their sweet potatoes—a stunning development that seemed all the more amazing when scientists found that monkeys on adjacent islands separated from Koshima by turbulent waters, were washing their sweet potatoes as well.

There are plenty of critics to join whatever skepticism this story stirs in you—as it did and does in me! Was the research embellished? Was it reputable in the first place? But in the four decades since this phenomenon was reported, an explosion of evidence has surfaced suggesting that changes of consciousness, culture-wide tipping points, and paradigm shifts occur well before a majority is reached. What was true for those monkeys appears to be true for humans. Once a critical mass is reached, a distinct minority number, there is a sudden spread to universal practice. I choose to believe that to be true, and hear within that truth an invitation to become part of a momentum toward creative change, per chance a movement. I want to be part of the movement!

THE PEACEFUL REVOLUTIONARIES

The Old Testament spoke of the remnant, that tiny minority whose faithfulness carried the divine message and movement forward across the generations, transforming the consciousness of God's people and readying them for seasons of awakening and renewal. The New Testament speaks of leaven and the reign of God within, which empowered a faithful minority to carry a divine message and movement worldwide. The departure of the British from India, the fall of the Berlin wall, the end of apartheid in South Africa, the non-violent and history-changing revolutions in five Eastern European countries in a single year, 1989—all these events of the 20th century illustrate the power of a minority to turn the tide. Analysts suggest that the Romanian revolution was not only reported but organized by television, the Philippine revolution by transistor radios, and the nonviolent Thai revolution by portable telephones, and that the Chinese student resistance was set in motion by fax.[3]

But these ultimately seismic changes unfolded across decades. In 1928 satyagraha, nonviolent protest or "truth force," as Gandhi called it, inspired thousands to face machine-gun fire until the es-teemed British Rifle Brigade stopped shooting; they thereby risked arrest, penalties, even life imprisonment.[4] In 1930 the Gandhi-led Dharasana Salt March mobilized tens of thousands of peasants to march four abreast, offering no resistance or retaliation, as they were bludgeoned into unconsciousness or death; the protest continued until British soldiers could lift their truncheons no more. Indepen-dence, however, was not achieved until 1947.[5] At what moment in those twenty years did the tipping point occur? What nameless "hundredth monkey" turned the tide? How did those claimed by a dream of freedom and committed to peaceful resistance keep their bearings, stay the course, and proceed with hope and confidence? Transformation takes time and patience.

No history book or tombstone names the last man to col-lapse under the blows of the militia at Dharasama, a "hundredth monkey," the one whose courage halted the brutality. The brave housewife who walked cautiously and courageously to the nearby shore to harvest salt illegally, or the 80,000th peasant jailed for nonviolent direct action remains unknown and unnamed as the hundredth monkey whose actions led to the repeal of the hun-dred-year-old Salt Act. What man, woman, or child, a hundredth monkey, was the last to fall from that indiscriminate gunfire before the rifles went silent?

On January 5, 1968, Alexander Dubček came to power in Czechoslovakia, initiating the short-lived "Prague Spring," a season of daring reform finally crushed by the invasion of Soviet tanks on August 21. A thirty-two-year-old poet and playwright named Václav Havel, expelled from his career in the theater for seditious activity, became a political dissident. Constantly harassed, barred from education and work, imprisoned for seven years, he became president in the "Velvet Revolution" of 1989, which brought a bloodless end to communism in his country.[6] Transformation takes time and patience.

The "hundredth monkey phenomenon" is more formally observed and named—physicists call it "critical mass theory" or the "theory of dissipative structures"; those who study changing social dynamics dub it "paradigm-shifting."

The Chinese word for crisis overlays the word-pictures for danger and opportunity. In these essays you will meet people and organizations summoning the courage to name and face the reality of a planet in peril and a human family at risk, the face of awesome and potentially overwhelming danger. These same people—realistic, unwilling to yield to denial, unpersuaded by blind optimism or simplistic solutions—lay claim to opportunity.

These essays profile individuals and organizations, Christians and churches among them, that tenaciously believe God is doing a new thing among us, that we are living in a transformative moment in history. The revolution is quiet, and its heroes are largely nameless— those who have been claimed by a vision, animated by a spirit, emboldened and empowered. Most define themselves as rooted in Scripture, but some are inspired by other sacred texts— spiritually grounded, but motivated by differing faith traditions. Most call themselves Christian, some more simply "followers of Jesus"; still others are followers of other faiths, and a significant number are part of what author Jim Wallis calls America's fastest-growing "denomination"—spiritual, but not religious. Their stories, interwoven with my own and now passed on to you, have filled me with hope, joy, and determination.

AND THE ELEPHANTS

On a visit to Thailand, en route to work as volunteers with Mother Teresa and the Sisters of Charity in Calcutta, my wife, Betsy, and

I attended an elephant show, impressed, of course, by the animals' enormous strength. At one point I joined fifty volunteers who tightened our grips on a mammoth rope tethered to the harness of a particularly immense elephant. The flag dropped, and we began to pull, inching backward. We were winning—until the elephant decided, "Enough of that!" Calmly, effortlessly, with annoying nonchalance, the elephant strode backward, as we lurched forward, muscles straining, veins standing out on our necks, our feet bouncing awkwardly in front of us.

After the show a young Thai unharnessed the elephant, looped a green cord about the diameter of clothesline around its rear ankle, drove a small stake into the ground, and tied the cord to the stake. I thought aloud: "You could attach a chain to that elephant's leg and fix it to the side of a building, and if the elephant had a stroll in mind, he'd take the building with him!" The young man, who spoke a little English, explained that newborn elephants, unlike humans, can stand upright in a day or two but lack strength for lateral movement. A small green cord, just like this one, is strong enough to tether a baby elephant in place. So when this elephant, now full grown, looks down and sees the small green cord, he assumes that he is unable to move! The question raised is unavoidable: "What little green cord is tied around my ankle—or yours?"

Abraham complained that he was too old, and Timothy protested that he was too young. But when the Spirit is poured out, "Old men dream dreams and young men see visions." Isaiah felt hopelessly doomed by sinfulness, Jeremiah insisted he didn't know what to say, and Ezekiel was afraid—but God touched their lips, and they spoke and acted with clarity, boldness and authority. Paul reminded Timothy that he was "called not to a spirit of timidity, but a spirit of power and might." All these were unremarkable people doing remarkable things, everyday people called to an extraordinary mission. There are five-talent, two-talent and one-talent people—but no "no-talent" people! There are different gifts—but all are gifted. There are greater and lesser parts of the body of Christ, but all are members of that body. All are called—and then gifted.

From time to time a passage comes alive, released from the bondage of inaccurate assumptions. I've never much liked "Blessed are the meek." The doormats, the spineless, the pushovers, it seemed to say, until I learned that "meek" comes from a root word that images "bridling the raw strength of an animal" or "harvesting the powerful energy of wind or water."

PARTNERS ON THE WAY

Writing as one who has sought to be a faithful journeyer, numbered perchance among the remnant or leaven, I have needed companions, circles of encouragement and support—"the beloved community," as Martin Luther King, Jr., called it. I write in that spirit, with you, as reader, a companion close at hand. I want to cut whatever tethers me to doubt, discouragement, or disabling attitudes. I want to dream impossible dreams.

I have been blessed throughout my life with mentors and models, those who have inspired and challenged me, who have walked the talk and invited me along. Betsy, first Betsy, my sweetheart still, wife of soon a half-century, my lover and companion, colleague and friend. Our sons, David and Erik; their wives, Linda and Griselda; and four rousing and robust grandsons, Drake, Todd, Garrett, and Rodrigo. My dad, Howard, who has known and loved me the longest; and my mom, Mary, who has enriched me with deep Catholic devotion and natural ecumenicity; my mother, Marjorie, whose death when I was fourteen, after a lengthy season of struggle with loss and grieving, awakened my compassion and charted my course into ministry.

Faces tumble by from congregations I have served as pastor—Montauk and Gladwyne, Honey Brook, Union, and Trinity—who welcomed and deepened my gifts, loved and nurtured me, and were tolerant and patient with me as well. Ken, George, and Ken, who stood with me in cap and gown at seminary graduation, holding a single diploma. Some said we deserved only one! Dave and Gail, Susie, Mark, and Rya; Arnie, Newt, and Bob; Terry and Barbara;

Tom, Carol, Betsy, and Barry; Doug, George, and Victor. Richard Bass, who encouraged me to coax another book forward. Rochelle Melander, who has been a skilled and devoted, encouraging and demanding content editor, and Jean Caffey Lyles, who has artfully brightened and sharpened the text. And others who will keep coming to mind long after I have completed this list.

A Franciscan Benediction

May God bless you with *discomfort*
at easy answers, half-truths, and superficial relationships,
so that you may live deep within your heart.

May God bless you with *anger*
at injustice, oppression, and exploitation of people
so that you may work for justice, freedom, and peace.

May God bless you with *tears*
to shed for those who suffer from pain, rejection, starvation, and war,
so that you may reach out your hand to comfort them and turn their pain into joy.

And may God bless you with enough *foolishness*
to believe that you can make a difference in the world,
so that you can do what others claim cannot be done to bring justice
and kindness to all our children and the poor. Amen.[7]

I've Lost My Last Excuse
Not To Tell The Truth

The Gift of Integrity

*J*ust a month or two after I'd drawn my first pension check, someone casually asked me, "What does retirement mean to you?" A response popped into my mind and out my mouth before I had given it much thought: *"It means I've lost my last excuse not to tell the truth."*

I've always viewed myself as a truth-speaker, even when silence, or at least a muted or edited version of the truth as I saw it, might have seemed more prudent. Sure, I can say how lovely I find a rather atrocious outfit, fingers crossed behind my back. I have chosen silence when speaking would be unduly hurtful or poorly timed. But when the only argument for silence seems tactical or manipulative, I'd rather err on the side of candor.

I have spent a lot of time with churches—pastors, lay leaders, and people in the pew—over my four-plus decades of ministry, especially during the last twenty years when the focus of my work has been serving as a congregational consultant. Four drawers of a file cabinet bulge with folders from more than 150 churches, nonprofits, and a scattering of corporate clients—files on leadership training and organizational structuring; visioning, goal-setting, and strategic planning; staff development and team-building; biblically based and spiritually grounded congregational development; asset-based management and outcome mapping; small groups and innovative program planning—and all too often, conflict intervention. Torn between feeling mystified and embarrassed, I am overwhelmed at how quickly and easily, in many cases habitually, even instinctively, church communities generate conflict and how harshly and hurtfully it manifests.

But nothing is more depressing than the boredom, the obsession with trivia, and the listlessness that characterize far too many congregations. I ask a church's leaders what they think Jesus had in mind when he envisioned the church, those who would carry forward his message and movement. As often as not, this important and urgent question draws looks of bewilderment and awkward silence. You can imagine how uncomfortable things become when I ask what they discern God has in mind for *their* church.

I am often asked in various contexts the pointed question: *Why don't you just give up on the church?* I never answer quickly, because I ask the same question of myself. Looking into many churches is like looking into a tomb with no Lazarus in sight. Too many congregations have raised boredom to an art form. A "cult of coziness," as I sometimes call it, prevails. As a congregational consultant, I see it over and over again: the "comfortable and familiar, but ineffective" seems to prevail over the "uncomfortable and unfamiliar, but new and promising." Yet, as persuasive as the argument to give up becomes, I seem to be imprinted with a relentless, resilient, even defiant commitment to the church. As much as it saddens, perplexes, and infuriates me, a given Sunday finds me sitting in my home church pew or donning my robe as a guest preacher. I fight the temptation to become cynical and sarcastic. At times I would prefer to jettison the whole thing. But here I am, writing as persuasively and passionately as I can muster, to churches, their leaders and members. Giving up on the church just does not seem an option for me.

LET ME INTRODUCE MYSELF

My mother died when I was fourteen, and Mother Church took me under her wing in tender and nurturing ways. A year later a woman who had become a mother figure asked me what I wanted to be when I grew up, and I replied, to her surprise and mine, "A minister." I went to college and on to seminary and then to serve the church, and have had few doubts, across four decades of ministry, about the wisdom wrapped in that unexpected answer. I have formed my closest friendships, forged my personal faith, and found myself most profoundly touched and healed within the walls of a church. Baptized, confirmed, and married in a sanctuary, I will surely end my life as it began, as part of a faith community, given a church funeral. Disgruntled, discouraged, even disillusioned as I may feel, the church has laid, it seems, a lifelong claim on me. What I most deeply want and need—where I am most in need of personal renewal and healing, how God is calling me to manifest love in the world—has been, and I hope will be, most overwhelmingly known and made manifest through the church.

A Contemplative Activist

I will refer to myself as a *contemplative activist,* which, if you unpack the word *contemplative,* is a redundancy. A *contemplative*—one who wants to manifest the image of God within, yearning to welcome Christ into a home in his heart, desiring to be Christlike, however flawed and human, longing to see and celebrate divine presence immersed in all creation—is inevitably, intrinsically an *activist* as well. The mystical contemplative masters write of a paradox that mingles understanding and mystery, an artful, faithful blend of *effort* and *grace.* If you are curious, read Teresa of Avila or John of the Cross, Carmelites from Spain; Juliana of Norwich or the anonymous author of *The Cloud of Unknowing* from the British Isles; Meister Eckhart or Hildegard of Bingen from Germany. Spiritual journeying blends utter determination with unrelenting effort, tapping deeply every ounce of stamina and the fullness of human *effort,* while, in a dance of delicate balance, is fully dependent on *grace,* surrender, letting go, and yielding to reliance on

God. These are among the spiritual mentors who guide me still along my way.

My personal theology, and with it my theology of church, has become increasingly clear and compact: *vocation* and *stewardship*. Discernment of *vocation* is a delicate art. I continually ask myself what gifts God is calling forth in me just now (the word for gift being "charismata" in Greek, the manifestation, *mata*, of grace, *charis*). How is God *calling* me just now (*kaleo* in Greek, the root of *ekkaleo* meaning church, those called out into community)? What personal mission, focus and direction, clarity of *purpose* is God coaxing from me? Where is my *passion* to serve? This side of certainty, open to daily correction, I choose to embrace and be embraced by *vocation,* flawed and incomplete as my discernment may be.

And then *stewardship*: I seek to expend my finite time and energy in alignment with *vocation.* There is always more I *could* do than I realistically *can* do, endless possibilities vying for a place on my calendar. Schedules quickly fill up. My commitment to stewardship guides *how* any particular thing makes its way onto my calendar. "First come, first served" could be an organizing principle, surely fair and logical, but hardly a discipline of faithfulness. "Make a to-do list and get to work, dutifully scheduling and addressing each item in order"—that seems sensible, but what creates the list? *People make requests and I respond:* I want to be—or at least I ought to be, some voice inside insists—constantly available and responsive, so if someone asks, that person has a right to claim my time, while weariness and resentment build. There's a constant momentum toward losing control. I used to feel as if I handed my calendar to the world, the world filling in its demands, giving it back with most time slots, surely the prime ones, gone.

Now I try to hold a steady, faithful routine. When there is any request for my time, to claim a spot on my calendar, I defer responding for forty-eight hours, and I tell the requester so. I need time to discern and pray. Would this expenditure of time and energy serve my sense of vocation? Would it be an act of faithfulness? I do not like to be fatigued and depleted, but I love to feel "spent." Stewardship is the conscious spending of myself.

A Maverick, Some Say

I am, I think, more than a just a bit "odd," even if that is an odd way to put it—unorthodox, outside the box, even heretical, on many, maybe most fronts. Though isn't anyone's belief system by definition, if held with vigor and integrity, *orthodox*, truth as one discerns it? I hold my faith in an unabashedly eclectic way. I am nurtured by Buddhism and Baha'i, Islam and Judaism, Sufism and New Age spirituality, shamans and indigenous spirituality, yet I am deeply rooted in Scripture, a lover of Jesus, unapologetically Christian. Naming myself as a *contemplative activist* puts me outside mainstream Christianity. I am a *psychotherapist,* but just as eclectic in that arena. I am captivated by cutting-edge thinking, research in body/mind dynamics, the elusive nature of time and space, the likes of crop circles and soul travel. I can raise eyebrows in almost any circle. I am a *thinker,* holding and expressing my opinions in a vigorous and persuasive way. Yet I am non-ideological, willing to be unapologetically illogical, rarely tightly aligned with anyone. I am an "equal-opportunity offender," able to annoy "right-to-lifers" as well as "pro-choice" folks, fundamentalists and radicals, right-wingers and left-wingers. I am, as a mentor long ago urged me to be, a *critical lover* of any and all faith perspectives. There is loneliness in that. I have no "camp," I am "in, but not of" almost any grouping. An article once called me a "maverick minister," unmasking my affection, even attachment, to this "oddball" persona. I pay a price for unorthodoxy—and yet, I love it!

Above All, Hopeful

I am convinced that something's trying to happen in our midst, a new consciousness emerging, a *positive, hopeful, grassroots, life-affirming, power- and self-interest-challenging people's movement* gaining momentum. I sense deep truth in a remarkable consensus of native peoples and coalescence of native wisdom and lore—from First Nation people in Canada to our own Native Americans, to indigenous peoples throughout Central and South America—that we are living in a time of transition between a long, sweeping historical era ending and a new era rising. I am persuaded that people longing to live by a different set of values and to follow principles different from those currently guiding our country, ready to march to a different drummer, are greater in number than we think, and nearing critical mass. I believe that life is as you dream it—and we are being challenged to live into a new dream. I believe that envisioning that new dream, "seeing it" in our mind's eye, thinking and feeling it, being grateful for it in advance, advances it. If any of this is true, I want to invest myself and my life, my time and energy, in alignment with it.

A Bible Always Close at Hand

In my early years as a pastor, scrambling to produce a sermon every seven days, it was not uncommon for me to write a sermon and then choose the biblical text. As time passed, I became a consistent biblical preacher, the scriptural text the soil out of which a given sermon grew. My experience at the monastery, which I will profile in detail, birthed a covenant of daily devotional discipline, including biblical reflection with no other purpose than my own spiritual nourishment. And my favorite study Bible, now tattered, amply underlined across forty years of use, has been within arm's reach as I have written these essays.

One of my doctoral students, reflecting on competing theologies of inspiration of Scripture, and confessing that infallibility or inerrancy just did not work for him, suggested a compelling alternative, that Scripture is *unfailing*. That word caught my eye. Since I am convinced that all truth—even truth posited as objective, revealed, divinely inspired—is inevitably *subjectively* received, poured into truly earthen vessels, I nodded agreement with his proposal. All that is written in the following pages has been informed and shaped by my engagement with the biblical narrative.

I bring a particular approach to Scripture that I tried to explain in a Sunday sermon not long ago. You need to employ your imagination, so you can see what I tried to share with my congregation, because I want to share it with you as well. Imagine holding an open Bible in your left hand, as you might when preaching or speaking. If you gesture, the movement and energy of your right hand is likely *upward and outward* above the surface of the text. Symbolically, that's where biblical scholarship resides, above the text. Commentaries, systematic theologies, and Sunday sermons tend to *lift from* the text whatever might be taught and applied. Good interpretive work is crucial.

I am more interested, however, in what lies *down under* the text—where real people living everyday lives resided, and where engagement with everyday life came to be seen as encounter with divine presence. That divine meeting was a source of illumination and guidance, healing and forgiveness, affirmation and challenge—experiences so powerful and life-giving they had to be shared, the birthplace of Scripture. And *down there*, under the text, though separated by centuries and living in extraordinarily different contexts, I find people struggling with self-esteem, living in relationship, finding meaning, overcoming guilt, making decisions, discerning moral choices—as I do! It's *down there* where their stories and mine can interweave, their quest for redemption joining mine, their laughter echoing and their tears mingling with my own, their liberation inspiring mine, as we become fellow pilgrims on the way.

When I need companionship in my struggle to be a loving and forgiving brother, when I let resentments linger and cause division, I consult with Joseph and his brothers, or Jacob and Esau. When I mute or silence my crying out to Christ, I invite Bartimaeus to urge me to call out. When I hesitate to bring my heartfelt question to Jesus, I look to Nicodemus to nudge me out of the shadows. When I am shying away from a hard word I am being called to speak with courage, I look for Jeremiah to nod encouragement. When I feel stumbling and halting in leading a congregation, I seek an appointment with Moses or Paul.

There is hardly a page in what follows that does not invite you to such a biblical encounter. I rarely use a passage simply to illustrate or prove a point, but to invite you *into* a biblical story, *down under* the text where its players speak from an lived experience of engagement with deep truth, perchance the divine.

TRUTH AS DISCOVERY—A PEDAGOGICAL BIAS

My wife, Betsy, and I teach a course in a doctor of ministry program that equips students to employ *experiential education methodology,* a bit of a mouthful, in designing and leading marriage and family events. At first this approach feels unfamiliar and awkward, students report. Most of their lifelong classroom experiences, like mine, entailed traditional educational models (sometimes called *deductive learning*), a four-step process in which (1) a teacher (preacher, writer) presents a *body of information*, basic concepts, a presentation organized around a topic or theme, theoretical propositions; (2) the presenter offers additional *explanation* together with data to support and substantiate theories proposed, followed by (3) *illustrations* of those theories at work; and finally (4) potential *applications* of that thesis in the learner's life are offered. A time for questions and answers may provide opportunity for further interpretation and application. This method is teacher-centered, one person speaking and others listening. Educator and missionary Paolo Freire, whose educational methods evolved out of his work with literacy education in Brazil, terms this the *banking method* of education where a teacher makes a *deposit* in the head of a largely passive student, from which that student can *spend* the wisdom—a process, he argues, that is static, inevitably accepting and supporting the status quo. He offers, as an alternative, what he calls problem-posing or *liberating education*, with an emphasis on narrowing the teacher/student distinction, initiating a mutual exploration toward insight and creative response.[1] I think Freire is right.

Fully respecting and honoring that time-tested approach, Betsy and I offer what can seem a radical alternative (sometimes called *inductive learning*), a four-stage process that virtually reverses the prior order: (1) lived *experience* is the initial focus, everyday life, present or remembered experience, (2) upon which one *reflects:* watching for patterns, noticing positive and negative outcomes, observing relational dynamics, after which teacher and learner, working in partnership, (3) *draw possible insights,* craft hypotheses about both how life *is* and how it might *become,* based on observation and reflection, finally (4) identifying *new ways of behaving* in the future that the reflection process yielded, variously called circle of praxis, discovery-based learning, partnership education, or process-based learning.

Bring to mind a moment when you *learned,* truly learned. Savor the memory. Appreciate those present who contributed to that learning. Pause to let the experience sink in. Then revisit it with a more discerning eye. What *criteria* did you employ to distinguish it as an experience of true learning? What *elements* blended to create that moment? Who were the *players?* A designated leader, others in the scene, you yourself—*who* did *what* to coax the potentiality into reality?

When we invite this kind of recollection in class, common themes emerge:

- "I felt open and safe," a class member will say, adding that there was an atmosphere of trust.
- "Everyone participated," someone will add. "It was a collaborative effort."
- "Truth was discovered more than taught," another person will note, the result of mutual exploration.
- "The teacher facilitated more than taught," helping to set a tone, encouraging everyone's investment and involvement.

- One student offered a curious phrase: "My mental furniture got re-arranged." He offered a biblical anecdote: Nicodemus came to Jesus seeking *new thoughts* and went home with a *new way of thinking.*
- Someone suggests that true learning demands *change*—the person changes, ways of thinking change; there are new choices available in the future.

This educational bias saturates the pages that follow. I typically begin with stories—not hesitating to suggest messages implicit within them, lessons to learn from the narratives, possible applications, but as often as not I will leave that work to you. I write as one committed to be a *continual learner,* as unsettling as that can be, one willing to change. I invite you to read with the same commitment.

THESE ESSAYS AND MY OWN CONTINUING JOURNEY

Doesn't a landscape artist behold a magnificent vista, fix it in his mind's eye, and then paint it onto a blank canvas? Doesn't a novelist craft characters, project a plot line, then spread it across blank pages? Sometimes. Sometimes not. "The canvas has a life of its own," says my friend Bo, a fine artist, "in lively dialogue with my palette, brush, and me. The final canvas, though it bears only one signature, belongs to both of us."

A popular novelist speaking at a library forum shared how recalcitrant characters may plot and scheme to rewrite the text, collude to craft unanticipated turns in the narrative, take the story into their own hands.

Eric is a songwriter, his best-known piece a Grammy nominee a decade ago that "just arrived" one night, as he puts it. "I woke up, amped up my guitar, turned on the recorder, and sang the song in its entirety, words and music, not a word or note altered," he reports, his eyes still alive with the mystery of it. I understand!

When I undertook this writing project, I was sure that I would complete it in a month or two—an understandable but clearly naive assumption. I've logged four-plus decades of experience, read extensively, attended endless seminars, sat at the feet of mentors, and I know myself to be brimming with bright ideas. I'd just tilt my head and pour it all onto the page. Piece of cake. In my sleep. *NOT!* The process had a life of its own. I rewalked old terrain with new eyes, revisiting the joys and struggles. I was launched into new explorations, uncharted territory, without MapQuest or global positioning—a more daunting, even grueling effort than I had anticipated.

I am a work in progress. I am a permanent pilgrim. I am pressing on toward an upward call. I believe; help my unbelief. If you want certainties spoken with certainty, you've got the wrong guy. If you want a companion, a partner, a fellow traveler, we just might have something going.

WHAT DO YOU WANT?

I heard a story some years ago of a young journalist who undertook what seemed an enormous task with a disarmingly simple process, her goal to "put a finger to the pulse of the American people." She traveled from coast to coast, north and south, visiting big cities and rural towns, meeting young and old, rich and poor, including a broad sweep of people of various racial and ethnic groups, randomly selected as anyone accepted the invitation to respond to her three-question survey. Sitting on a park bench, in a shopping-mall entrance, even strolling side by side, she'd ask her questions, requesting fifteen or twenty minutes of her subject's time. *"What do you want?"* was the first question. Typically initial hesitation gave way to hearty response, the content most often a wish list of things, some basic change in one's circumstances, often material in focus. As speaking ebbed, she'd ask her second question, *"What do you want?"* "But that was the first question" was the predictable reaction, followed by a fresh flow of words. This time the words came in a more measured and quiet way, from what seemed a more pensive and reflective place. When it came time for the third question, many said, "I bet you're going to ask me again what I want." "Indeed," the journalist gently replied, and was touched by how much closer to the heart of things, more intimate, more heartfelt the responses were this last time, some speaking as tears glistened in their eyes or coursed down their cheeks.

Before she moved on, last words were often shared. Almost all her respondents expressed *appreciation* for being asked the question, remarking that they were rarely asked, "What do you want?" other than in a perfunctory way. They wished it were otherwise. Many added that they rarely asked *themselves* that question! They confided that in the rush of their lives, often frenzied and unbalanced, there was no time to reflect on what they truly, most deeply wanted from life. And finally, many predicted that the interview would have a *significant effect* on their lives.

How Much Do You Want It?

Preparing a lecture on Jesus's healing ministry, I noticed something that had never caught my eye before, and it seems to blend with that journalist's experience: *with one possible exception, Jesus did not heal at his own initiative.* He seemed to look for signals of readiness—Zacchaeus climbing a tree, Bartimaeus shouting insistently, a woman stretching to touch the hem of his garment, the faith of a paralyzed man's companions—a signal of lives available and receptive. Those who are doggedly determined, persistent, and insistent in their quest to be whole catch Jesus's eye or ear, capture his undivided attention, and mobilize his healing power. Jesus asked Bartimaeus directly, "What do you want?" (Mark 10:51), having noticed already how much he wanted it.

What constitutes this *readiness* Jesus looked for? Our pastoral and leadership experience may offer more frequent illustrations than we'd guess. Sarah called, with more than a hint of concern in her voice, requesting an hour to talk. She settled into a chair, eager to begin. "I want to do something about my marriage." Her opening sentence sounded clear and assertive. But then her words and tone became halting and hesitant. "It sort of gets me down," she continued. "Maybe I ought to think about what I might do," she added. And finally, "My friends are pushing me to do something. I think they're really the reason I came."

I knew immediately what I wanted to say, though unsure whether it would be fair or sensitive. Integrity trumped thoughtfulness, so risking being unduly abrupt, I proposed that we end our conversation. "But you promised an hour, and I know you'll listen and help me," she objected. "Sarah," I replied, "being 'sort of down' and 'maybe ought to do something' rarely mobilizes change." Obviously annoyed, but also curious, she asked me to explain. "Sarah, I trust you know I care about you and hope for your best future, but I think you are not ready to make the changes you've talked about. You're not feeling enough discomfort—maybe *pain* is the better word. You lack a clear and compelling *vision* of that better future. I don't think you *want* it enough. I don't think you'll mount the *stamina* to follow through." We exchanged awkward smiles as she left. She returned three months later, acknowledging the resentment she had felt after our last meeting, but expressing appreciation for my forthrightness. "You cared enough about me to tell the truth," she confessed. And she was ready this time to begin the work.

A consultant interview makes a similar point in an organizational context. As I drove toward a church to meet with its official board, a hypothesis formed in my mind as a question: *do I presume a congregation's readiness to change based on too little input?* I had no idea that an opportunity to test that hypothesis lay so close at hand. Why was I here? Only two votes had been cast! The pastor issued the invitation, urged by a denominational executive, assuring me the board was ready to undertake a church-growth process. My curiosity about my hypothesis was sharpened.

The meeting was crisp and businesslike. Two members reported in clear and decisive language that the broad expanse of farmland that had surrounded their village church since its founding would soon become home sites—one development fully occupied and two more under construction. They wanted surefire, tried-and-tested, fully guaranteed strategies for church growth. I replied just as succinctly, profiling the qualities that characterize growing churches, and the kinds of changes demanded of churches ready to grow.

My hypothesis became a hunch, as I sensed reluctance beneath the expressed readiness to move forward. Barely into our allotted time, I found myself surprised at how directly and forcefully I interrupted: "You have told me that you *want* to grow. You say that you believe that healthy, faithful churches *should* grow. Your pastor and denomination assure you that you *could* grow. But at a deeper level I think you *do not want* to grow. And, may I add, why would you? You already have a stable, even slightly growing membership. There is no financial urgency. You are comfortable with what you do and how you do it. My guess is, if we pursued a partnership with the goals you have voiced, you'd be the first to resist the forward progress."

"Thank you," sighed the president of the board, after an awkward silence, followed by nods around the circle. "That's hardly what I expected from a consultant interviewing for a contract," said a longtime member. During that last hour, talking more among themselves than with me, they concurred that, truth be known, they were just not ready to undertake any serious program with church growth as a goal. They expressed their appreciation, though the pastor wasn't sure, and the judicatory official was, I think, a little miffed.

How often do we, whatever our role, spend time helping people or congregations that are unready to be helped? How might firm, even blunt honesty help encourage readiness? How can we summon the courage to speak more clearly, with bolder integrity? Even Jesus, in the face of uninterest, could "do no deed of power there" (Mark 6:5). When you encounter unreadiness or resistance, he counseled his disciples, move on.

Across the years I've tried to resist the temptation to rush home from a conference, or to rise from reading the "latest and best" in congregational-revitalization literature, itching to put it into immediate action. Surely the people will welcome it all with eager enthusiasm. I blithely, unthinkingly assume to know what they want, or *should* want. Such ardent but blind intensity diminishes our presence, dulling our listening and blurring our seeing, and, in the process, mindlessly preempts the community's sharing their yearning and longings, naming what they urgently and passionately want, voicing their heart's desire. A rich and vital source for fresh vision and awakening, from the people, is lost in the process.

THE LOGICAL NEXT QUESTION

Reader, what do *you* want? Really, profoundly, urgently want? Personally and professionally? What is your "pearl of great price," the "hidden treasure" you search for tirelessly? What do you yearn for? Long for? I find that those very words—*yearning* and *longing*—stir something in me. May I gently invite you to take a break from your reading to respond? You are presently investing precious time and energy reading these essays. What do you want from these paragraphs? This reading is nestled—maybe squeezed is a better word—amidst your ample list of "things to do" today. What do you want from today? From life? For a moment, let these questions probe deeper.

INEVITABLY PERSONAL AND SUBJECTIVE

Much of what lies ahead will be laced with personal stories from my own journey. It seems to me self-evident that whatever is known is known by a *knower*, in this case *this* knower, making sheer objectivity a myth. I am convinced that the only God I know is the God *I* know. We can share our understandings but always as *personal* theologies, fascinated and intrigued by the exchange while aware of our similarities and differences, minimal or profound. *Questions unite, answers divide* seems wise counsel to me. I prefer pencil to pen, the eraser well worn. My beliefs, even those foundational and firmly held, are provisional, tentative, and open to reflection. I speak my truth of today. Ask me again tomorrow.

Some years ago I attended a lecture followed by a question-and-answer session. The speaker warned that he would answer each question with confidence and an air of authority, and then offered this disclaimer: *It is only an estimate, of course, but I would guess that half of what I say is highly reliable, logical and sound, worthy of reasoned consideration. The other half is suspect at best, misleading or misguided, best left behind. The problem is that I do not know the difference between the two.* He spoke for me!

On a visit to the Holy Land I watched a woman separating wheat and chaff, sitting on a hillside near the site of the house of Mary, Martha, and Lazarus in Bethany. She held a large ring, a thin wooden band forming a circle with cloth stretched across the middle, a mix of wheat and chaff piled in the center. She shook the ring briskly back and forth, and then flipped the mix into the air, as though tossing a giant pancake. The wind, just as Jesus described it, carried the chaff away, as the wheat fell back onto the cloth. I will offer ample wheat and chaff as we explore together—separating the wheat and chaff falls to you!

A CONFESSION PERHAPS BETTER NOT MADE

Twenty years ago I was pastor of a congregation that I then believed (and still do believe) was uniquely innovative and effective. Fifteen years ago I set sail on a voyage to bring that model to any congregation that would offer me a mooring. Ten years ago I remained optimistic that this model, or whatever adaptation a given church evolved, would become transformational and life-giving. Five years ago that confidence began to teeter and then collapse. Today I am simply unsure.

That there may have been flaws in my trusted model, basic inadequacies in my role as coach and consultant, does not elude my awareness. My confidence may have been unduly ego-driven, even arrogant. I am not assigning blame. And writing this is, oddly, neither upsetting nor depressing. Explanation resides between two poles of possibility—it may be that I have failed as a companion toward congregational revitalization, or that congregations, consciously or unconsciously, have little real interest in revitalization. I am strangely comfortable leaving the answer floating in ambiguity.

This book of essays is my last conscious and concerted effort to address the church and churches. It is an effort made with abandon, unfettered and uncontrived. I choose to be neither measured nor tactical.

FORGING A WRITER/READER PARTNERSHIP

Might we forge a covenant? Though I am writer and you are reader, might we frame a dialogue? If so, I want our exchange to be robust and lively, your concurrence and disagreement equally hearty and animated. My intention and hope are to be illuminating and clarifying, inspiring and empowering, direction-giving and equipping, though you'll find me at times to be annoying, even infuriating; audacious, even arrogant; unorthodox, even heretical. *I've lost my last excuse not to tell the truth!*

These essays began as an article submitted to *Congregations* magazine, whose editor passed it on to the book editors at the Alban Institute, who invited me to submit a book proposal, and a contract arrived. Ego and elation sent me searching for a pen. Faithfulness reminded me of that forty-eight hour discipline. Writing is demanding. My wife had warned me that if I ever wrote another book, she'd divorce me. I prayed and talked to Betsy! I signed the contract. Vocation and stewardship concurred. Now this book has made it into your hands. May I suggest a forty-eight hour discipline? You've read this introductory essay. Thumb through the others. Does it seem good stewardship of your time to read them?

WHAT LIES AHEAD

You can choose to read these essays in an order that seems logical to you. Each blends personal and congregational stories, interspersed and interwoven with biblical narrative, with my reflections and exposition as literary glue. Each essay carries a subtitle identifying a personal and leadership gift. Even in larger churches where job profiles may be focused and specific, leaders are generalists, holding in their person and role a tapestry of qualities and competencies. Tap even more deeply and richly the gifts you have already claimed, and gently nurture new gifts yet to fully manifest themselves.

The first two essays highlight two foundational gifts, bedrock qualities upon which what follows might rest: a capacity to be fully present and a readiness to embrace paradox. The next four blend personal qualities with leadership skills to encourage congregational revitalization: cultivating receptivity to solitude and silence as an approach to congregational renewal; fostering patience that blends assertiveness and a gentle pace; cultivating a style and developing strategies that are empowering; and mounting the courage to let go. The final three essays, admittedly and intentionally more provocative, encourage robust and deeply rooted hopefulness, reclaiming the prophetic voice, becoming ever more comfortable feeling and expressing outrage, and joining the people of God in activism that rejoices in the collaboration of God's people (perchance including the church) in working to save a planet in peril.

A HEARTFELT MONOLOGUE AS DIALOGUE

Some years ago, before Pope John Paul II, Morris West wrote a novel titled *Shoes of the Fisherman*. The story line evolves from the election of a non-Italian pope, a young Russian prelate named Kiril. Though devoted and committed to this awesome call, he remains more comfortable walking the streets as a country priest than living amid the pomp and circumstance of the papacy. Whenever he has the opportunity, he dons his simple robes, slips out a side door past the Swiss Guard, and wanders unrecognized among the people. He has a lovely gift. Whenever a circle of people gathers about him, they feel somehow safer; the space he nurtures is inviting and engaging. People speak with openness and love, and listen with sensitivity and compassion. Kiril finds himself saying, as he watches this communication edging toward communion, "When heart speaks to heart, the sound our voices make as we speak are, perchance, a whisper of the voice of God."[2]

I have "heart speaking to heart" in mind as I write—my heart speaking to your heart, this leader's heart whispering to yours, this believer's conviction seeking resonance with yours—daring to believe that, in this partnership, we will be renewed and inspired personally; revitalization, even reinvention in the church may erupt and we may contribute to the healing of our planet.

You may want to read my prior book, more specifically focused on congregational revitalization, *Recovering the Sacred Center: Church Renewal from the Inside Out*. And I'd welcome dialogue via e-mail. You can contact me at hfriend@prodigy.net.

2

RIDE YOUR DONKEY BACKWARDS

The Gift of Presence

enerations ago, itinerant wise men in China made their way from town to town, on foot or astride a donkey, chatting with those waiting at the gate, teaching those who gathered in small circles under the shade of a tree, or sharing among welcomed guests at a family cottage in the village. One of them, a spirited sage with a particular zest for life, a sense of adventure, and an obvious sense of humor, was known to arrive on his donkey *riding backwards!* When asked why, he replied that he felt at risk of focusing so much on the road ahead, so attentive to later today or tomorrow, that he was not fully present to the moment. Wisdom, he added, gives itself to those fully present, undistracted by what lies ahead, or what has gone before.[1]

What if that Chinese sage is right, that wisdom arises as we are fully present with each other? My teacher and mentor Pat Middleton, a neurologist and psychiatrist, would say repeatedly in a course she taught in pastoral psychotherapy, "Do not forget. Presence heals." She'd get more specific. She coached us in forming trust-based relationships; how to be discerning diagnosticians; how to project a treatment plan; and, how to make artful and timely interventions. "But if you ever find your work as a therapist distracting you from being present, stop," she'd say pointedly, "and become fully present again." She offered Jesus as a model. Surrounded by a crowd bumping and jostling its way through the marketplace in Jericho, Jesus offered Bartimaeus his undivided attention. In the same setting, likely on the same day, when Jesus gazed up into a twisted, stunted sycamore tree, there was Zacchaeus. When Jesus turned to see who had touched the fringe of his robe in that dense crowd, there was only that woman. And Jesus was seldom in a rush. Even the robust and hearty narrative of Mark speaks of a Jesus often at rest, off by himself, with the three, on R & R with the Twelve in Caesarea Philippi. Urged by his disciples to make haste for Bethany, he waited two days. With a woman caught in adultery at his feet, the crowd restlessly awaiting him to authorize execution, Jesus bent silently to write in the sand with his finger. Wanting, it appears, to respond rather than react, discerning and following divine leading and not merely his own instincts, he paused.

In 1993 my spouse, Betsy, and I spent two weeks with Mother Teresa and the Sisters of Charity in Calcutta, India. Mother Teresa invited our circle of eight to meet with her for an hour one sweltering Calcutta afternoon. Short, bent, and wrinkled, she was a "woman fully alive." She shared a bit of her story, the work of her order around the world, and responded to our questions. After she left, we reflected on the gift of time with this remarkable person. One woman in our group hesitantly said, "During the hour I think she looked at *me* the most." A man in the circle spoke up: "Funny you should say that. I thought she looked at me the most!" We went around the circle, and each of us shared the same feeling. When you were "looked at" by Mother Teresa, "taken in" by her gaze, you were truly, fully, timelessly "looked at." *Presence heals.*

NOT AS SIMPLE AS I EXPECTED

To be present is to be still and centered, undistracted by whatever might vie for my attention, open to the fullness of myself, ready to be transparent and authentic. To be present requires dropping my guard, letting go of pretense, becoming quiet and focused. The longing to be present, to engage in genuine and trusting dialogue, seems balanced by uneasiness and anxiety, activating subtle strategies of resistance and avoidance. Any movement toward being more fully present seems countered by a just as persuasive moving away. Being present evokes the same inner mixed feeling that entering silence does.

My primary support group, a circle of five that gathers monthly for two and a half hours, has been meeting for more than twenty years. We began a recent meeting as we usually do, with a time of extended silence that ends as someone feels led to speak a first word. Carol spoke that first word one week, with a comment that she acknowledged to be paradoxical. "Part of me wished the silence would fill our entire time; yet another part of me was becoming increasingly agitated," she confessed, "as if something within me was protecting me from the silence." We began to explore the silence we had just shared and other silences we remembered. The connection between becoming silent and seeking to be more present became more vivid as we shared. We spoke first of an unqualified appreciation of silence. "Why don't we welcome its gifts more often?" we asked. We agreed that silence calms our bodies and minds, evokes a sense of safety and tranquility, sharpens awareness and attentiveness. When Barry said that silence helps him find confidence in the face of self-doubt and clarity amid confusion, we nodded agreement. "But I often feel sadness when I am silent," Betsy said quietly, "and anxious at times, now that I think about it." Others spoke of their feelings—often strong feelings, some they had been consciously suppressing—that silence released. "Maybe our resistance to silence is trying to protect us," Tom added. For all the gracious gifts of silence, it also softens our defenses, stirs what we've been trying to ignore or hide, and brings to awareness what we try to keep secret, from others and from ourselves.

FOUR DISCIPLINES

Reflecting on my own desire and commitment to being present, I offer four guidelines, four disciplines, for becoming freer for fuller presence. Life is not simple and orderly, so they are suggestive rather than definitive, grist for the mill of your own reflections: (1) be real, (2) slow down and do less, (3) embrace your shadow, and (4) focus your attention.

1. Be Real, the Masterpiece You Are

Some years ago Betsy and I were visiting the Metropolitan Museum of Art in New York City. We had barely commenced our tour when we came upon a broad section of a downstairs gallery cordoned off with yellow tape, "no passage" clearly indicated. My curiosity was piqued. Against the far wall hung a very large canvas, brightly illuminated by a series of lights atop stanchions, and there stood a man working intently, his face just inches from the surface. Squinting, I saw that he held no palette. He clearly wasn't painting, yet he was working with intense concentration. I could not contain myself. I slipped under the tape, clearing my throat as I approached. His welcoming smile set me at ease. From that vantage point I was puzzled to see that the upper two-thirds of the canvas seemed to be a different painting from the lower third. "Let me explain," said the man, noting my confusion. He was working, he told me, with a set of scalpels. He was removing paint! He had completed the lower third; the upper two thirds remained to be addressed. The painting he was removing, worthy of purchase and display by the Metropolitan, had not been painted on a fresh canvas, but painted over a prior work. An unknown, struggling artist, needing money for food, had sold his painted canvas for reuse. That struggling artist came to be recognized as a master, but later in his life. On a hunch, someone had guessed that one of his paintings lay beneath the existing painting. "Ironic," the worker said, "beneath a fine piece of art a masterpiece!"

Endless theories of individual development and the dynamics of human interaction tell a similar story to the hidden masterpiece, Eric Berne's theory as clear as any. Berne, the author of *Games People Play: The Basic Handbook of Transactional Analysis*, speaks of a "life script" that begins to form between ages five and seven.

A five-year-old, largely unconsciously, watches the "players" on the "stage" of his or her young life speak their "lines" and notices the "stage directions." There is dialogue, plot, and drama. This child begins to discern the "script" of this play, with its recurring themes, patterns, and outcomes. And, most poignantly, the child begins to learn his or her "part," what "lines" he or she is to speak and what "stage directions" to follow. The child becomes an increasingly good actor and less and less an authentic person. Decades go by and the child grows into adulthood, but continues to behave as a producer-director, recruiting players, assigning roles, and directing outcomes—all to replicate and perpetuate the "script" learned years before. The original masterpiece begins to disappear.

We become like those computer-driven, amazingly real robots at Disney World. Those life-size characters were first programmed by running wires from a real person to the corresponding body part of a robot. The real person speaks and gestures, synchronized with the recording of the speech, which activates and programs the same motions in the robot. A computer "remembers" the words and gestures and is then able to reproduce them.[2]

Tragically, such robotic characters are everywhere we look. Liz was beautiful and fragile, with a face that could either dance with delight or betray deep anxiety, even paranoia. A supportive husband and a circle of friends had kept her stable for over a year, but the death of a special cousin unsettled her equilibrium. She rebuffed advice to cancel a planned cocktail party. I was taking my turn standing at her side at the party to lend moral support, when, taking my arm, she invited me to glance around the room crowded with guests and noisy with conversation. She spoke rapidly, sounding frantic: "Howard, look, they're all talking at once. They're nodding and gesturing as if they're listening. But they're not! They try to look as if they care. But they don't! They're all talking, but no one is saying anything. And for sure no one is listening. Can't you see it? I can!" Two days later Liz was admitted to a nearby psychiatric hospital. Her doctors said she'd lost touch with reality. I harbored the haunting feeling that she had actually come too close to reality!

Watching players on a stage playing a role, following a script in tailored suits and designer dresses, their masterpieces buried, was more than Liz could handle.

Visit for a moment with a spiritual support group that has been gathering monthly for a year, its members becoming increasingly open and trusting. Listen in as they talk together about gathering the courage to become more authentic, about taking the next steps toward deeper intimacy, becoming even more open with one other. Hear them confess that even as they long for such authenticity, they oddly resist it. A middle-aged man speaks with disarming candor: "Actually, as I think about it more carefully, I'm afraid to tell you who I really am." Several others nod in agreement, as a younger woman asks why. Thinking for a moment, he responds in a steady and measured way, "What if you don't like who I am? It's the only 'me' I've got." "Me too," an older man chimes in, almost immediately. "You know what I think I do? Maybe I've always done it. I present 'another me' in place of the real me. No, that's not quite right. I sort of make up a 'me.' It's not really dishonest. But it isn't very real. I say what I think you'll like. I act in a way you'll accept."

The conversation that follows is fascinating. "Yeah," adds the youngest in the circle, leaning forward in her chair. "If you like the 'me' I make up, the sort of concocted me, I can polish her up and you'll like her ever more the next time. And it you don't like her," she continues, her eyes dancing and her words racing, "I can come up with still another version of 'me.' And the real me remains in hiding, perfectly safe." An odd but palpable relief settles in, as if shared honesty itself is opening new pathways of intimacy. They'd "fessed up," as one of them names it; it is out in the open, and their circle of safety seems to broaden.

The word "hypocrite," which Jesus used repeatedly as he confronted the Pharisees, means "actor," and costuming in the theater of Jesus's day focused on the actor's using a mask to take on a role.[3] Jesus's intent was less accusation of some intrinsic badness than the unmasking of inauthenticity. The Pharisees feigned benevolence, piety, and generosity—a mask, a facade, the tragedy being that they

became inaccessible to Jesus's wisdom and love, which his conclud-
ing words affirm: "How often would I have gathered your children
together as a hen gathers her brood under her wings" (Matt. 23:37
RSV).

I recently conducted a funeral for Kevin, who died in a construction accident at age thirty-seven. At first glance, one would
think that Kevin had not led a very successful life. His brother
had become a physician, and his sister was completing graduate
school, but Kevin had moved from job to job, never quite finding
his niche. Seventy-five chairs were set up for his service—more than
enough, the family was sure. But 250 people crammed into a series
of adjoining rooms. Those gathered were offered an opportunity
to share spontaneously, Quaker-style, and no one became restless
as person after person spoke, dozens in all, choking back tears and
speaking in remarkably heartfelt ways. A common theme emerged
in the words shared, a celebration of how real Kevin was, without
pretense, disarmingly present. Kevin had failed as a mask-maker,
that failure an odd gift to Kevin and those who knew and loved
him. He had no titles and took on no roles. He played from no
script and followed no choreography. What you saw was what you
got. The mourners loved him as audiences loved Tom Hanks in
Forrest Gump and Jim Carrey in *The Truman Show*.

A workshop facilitator in a high-powered leadership seminar on
excellence and optimum personal performance invited participants
to write down the roles they played, one each on a set of ten three-
by-five cards. He instructed us to stack the cards in priority order,
the most important on top. Speaking slowly to set a tone for the
next direction, he invited us, peeling from the bottom, to remove
a card, ponder it for a moment, and then lay it on the floor, mindful of how we felt as we placed it there. We continued, one card
at a time, slowly enough to be fully aware of our feelings as each
slipped from our hand. "How does it feel, now that all the cards,
your roles, are at your feet, sitting with empty hands, without any
roles for a moment?" the leader asked, allowing several minutes for
reflection. The final instruction was more flexible. He instructed
each of us to pick up the cards, with the option of leaving some

on the floor, conscious of how we felt in deciding to leave a role unretrieved. We could place any of the picked-up cards in a different order if we chose. As we sat quietly with cards back in our hands, he asked us one more time to be conscious of what we noticed, what we were thinking and feeling.

It took well over an hour to share around the small circle; each response was unique, but common themes emerged. We expressed surprise how each role, as it was set aside, evoked clearly differing feelings, and still different feelings as we retrieved them, or decided not to. We were conscious of how dramatically some of us reordered the roles when we picked them up, roles related to family and relationships closer to the top. But the most poignant sharing revolved around our thoughts and feelings when our hands were empty, role-free for a time. Most of us expressed feelings of relief, joy, even exhilaration, feeling liberated from those roles. Yet we also acknowledged discomfort, a distinct anxiety, a disarming emptiness. We wondered aloud how we might live freer of roles.

No romanticizing here. We need our costume closets and masks, our roles, scripts, and choreography. We set them aside astutely, as we are able, or let them become more translucent, even transparent. We set them aside only in clearly trustworthy settings, where it is a joy and gift to do so. The risk lies in becoming *identified* with our outer selves in ways that lead us to lose connection with our inner selves, making them less and less available to our world. Being present demands the courage, as fully as we are able, to be real.

2. Slow Down and Do Less

As the pastor of the same church for twenty-three years, preaching well over a thousand sermons, I was bound to repeat myself. Loving storytelling, and believing a good story best carries the message, some of my stories became familiar to the congregation. None was more requested for repetition than what came to be known as the *file folder story*. Let me tell it briefly. My office always looked "lived in." Some thought "chaotic" would be a better description.

But always visible and close at hand were two items: my calendar and my "important and urgent" file. Any pastor's important and urgent file is fullest in September, as the church year begins. One September Monday I arrived to find my calendar, but could not locate that essential file folder. I scoured the office, sorted through each carefully stacked pile of stuff, and checked the trash cans, even the ones outside. Gone! It was really, truly gone—until eight months later, as the end of the church year approached. Here's the story: I typically placed my calendar and the "important and urgent" file on that little pull-out shelf peculiar to older desks. Thus, I did not use the skinny drawer underneath. One day in May, I opened that drawer—and there was the file folder! In my haste the Friday before that September Monday, I must have unconsciously dropped the file in the drawer, rather than laying it on the shelf. But here's the real story: of, say, fifteen items carefully tucked into the file designated as "important and urgent," I realized that I had actually completed half, if that. And, I am embarrassed to say, as I looked back across those months in between, I could discern no fallout, none at all, for what had gone undone! Embarrassing as telling the story remains, there is its lesson.[4]

The Chinese form their words by a series of mini-drawings, sometimes a word formed by the overlay of other words. The word for "busyness" combines the words for "heart" and "killing." The word for "leisure" overlays "spaces" and "sunshine." I think it was educator and author Parker Palmer who said a glance at an average pastor's calendar offers evidence of "functional atheism." We preach justification by grace on Sundays but live justification by works through the week. We forget that presence heals.

Neurological research, reflecting on the mental functioning activated in the communication process, sheds light at two levels. When I interact with another person, the engagement invites me to be both receiver and sender, involving two levels of brain functioning. The basic, more primitive brain level, sometimes differentiated as reptilian and mammalian, engages automatically and instinctively, without reflection or choice. The neocortex is the conscious and reasoned brain level, capable of creativity and imagination, of pondering and choosing. The lower brain function, which we share with crocodiles and house pets, can only *react*. The higher brain, unique to the human species, can *respond*. As the pace of interaction accelerates, lower-brain influence increases, producing *reaction;* as the pace slows, the higher brain is activated, creating the possibility of *response.*

I make that choice with every interaction. Betsy begins a conversation over supper, the content and length of what she will say unknown to me. After she has spoken a sentence or two, maybe less, my brain begins to *react*, beneath my consciousness, promptly *deciding* what she is going to say, well before she has completed her thoughts. This internal process steals my attention. I may keep nodding, offering gestures of attentiveness and active listening, but a part of me has *gone inside*. My brain, blithely confident that it knows what Betsy will say, scans my cerebral cortex, synapses rapidly closing, noting what I am *thinking* in response to what she is saying. Simultaneously, my limbic system checks my body sensations, noting and naming my *feelings* in response, other synapses closing. Before Betsy finishes speaking, even if it is relatively brief, my brain has produced my *reaction*, what I will say and do when she has finished.

This mental process is automatic and immediate, largely unconscious and, most important, incomplete: *receive—think—feel—send* in a virtual instant. It has produced, to return to the distinction at hand, a reaction, but not a response. Whatever I say or do when she has completed her thought will be nothing more than a replication of how I have reacted in the past, in a prior situation akin to this one. We are about to have an exchange we've had many times before. Same old, same old. There's nothing new under the sun.

So what to do in light of this neurological information? Try this: As you find an important interaction speeding up, slow your reactions down. Sigh. Breathe. Place a "meditative pause" between stimulus and response. Interrupt the cycle. Then consciously and intentionally revisit *all* of what was said. Paraphrase what you heard that other person say until she nods agreement that you have fully heard her. Revisit your inner domain of thought, aware of the broader range of thinking, including the more subtle or unchosen thoughts, claiming and choosing from a broader range of thinking. Revisit the product of your limbic system for the more subtle or unchosen feelings, a broader range of emotional possibilities. Finally, revisit the decision made more *for* you than truly *by* you, and explore the possibility of different responses.

Why did Jesus write in the sand with his finger, an enigmatic gesture without a hint of his motivation, as the woman caught in the act of adultery lay sprawled at his feet? The request from the leering Pharisees was simple enough: just a gesture would do, rabbinic permission to proceed with the stoning. Did he want to respond, not react? To be fully present in a way that heals? Is that why Jesus, even the Jesus of the Gospel of Mark, robust and hearty, his actions preceded forty-two times by the word "immediately," chose so often to be alone, off with the three, or the Twelve? "Very early the next morning, long before daylight . . . Jesus went out of town to a lonely place, where he prayed" (Mark 1:35 GNT). "Let us go across to the other side of the lake" (4:25 GNT). "Let us go off by ourselves to some place where we will be alone and you can rest awhile" (6:51 GNT). "He went into a house and did not want anyone to know he was there" (7:24 GNT). Was it to be fully present, to respond and not react, that Jesus, knowing his friend was deathly ill, lingered for two days before journeying to Bethany?

This principle has organizational implications. The reorganizing process a Quaker community undertook some years ago proved more challenging and potentially disruptive than anyone anticipated. The process brought to the surface issues long held beneath the surface. Resentments, quietly harbored across the years, emerged. Differing opinions were strongly held and vigorously expressed. Interpersonal frictions edged toward antagonism. In a typically quiet and gentle Quaker way, tensions mounted and conflict simmered.

A special meeting was called to address the issues and to deliberate the reorganization plan. As members filed in, nodding graciously to each other, a quieter-than-usual hush betrayed the gravity of the evening, their anxiety more about the process than the outcome. Civility and personal regard, diligent listening and high respect, and confidence in consensus-seeking are at the heart of Quakerism. The clerk stood and began the meeting with these words: "As you know, we usually begin our meeting with thirty minutes of silence, sitting quietly and rising to speak as the Spirit leads. But, given the length of our agenda and the broad spectrum of opinions we bring, may I suggest that we take *forty-five minutes* this evening." The meeting continued past eleven, the dialogue hearty, as each spoke urgently and persuasively, and then listened patiently and attentively. Differences began to narrow, shared focus emerged and, yes, consensus commenced to form. Rooted in the gifts of that longer-than-usual time of quietness, reflection and sharing at the outset nourished an abundant flowering and a rich fruit-bearing harvest. The pace remained slow and unhurried, marked by meditative pauses, gracious space allowed between speakers.

3. *Embrace Your Shadow*

Three generations ago a one-man show won unanimous and unqualified acclaim in cities all across Europe—an acrobat, juggler, clown, and comedian named Garibaldi. His performances in concert halls, auditoriums, or stadiums always sold out. The day his show was to open in a particular city a downcast, depressed, almost suicidal man knocked at a pastor's door. No counsel, no word of encouragement seemed able to lift his spirit. "Go see Garibaldi," the pastor finally urged as a last hope. "I *am* Garibaldi," the man forlornly replied. *Garibaldi could not escape his shadow.*

Intimidation was my instinctive response when I learned that a frequent visitor to the church I was serving belonged to Marble Collegiate Church in New York and knew its minister personally. Norman Vincent Peale was her pastor! Quietly apologetic for the sermon I'd just preached, surely not up to her expectations, I mumbled something about what a privilege it must be to know him personally. "Yes, he's just delightful," she said, "when he's not depressed!" "D-d-d-depressed," I am quite certain I stammered, "did you say depressed?" "Yes, he struggles with it constantly," she went on. *Norman Peale kept his shadow a secret.*

Thomas Merton, widely revered and imitated for his monastic discipline, has always been a hero of mine. He'd simply close his eyes, I assumed, quiet his body, and be in instant, intimate communion with God. In the quietness of that intimacy his discernment was surely clear and certain. Imagine how comforted I felt listening to tapes of late-afternoon conversations with novices in his hermitage at Gethsemani, hearing him say in his uniquely soothing and humble way, "Just in case you think I only have to close my eyes and there I am, resting in the heart of God, let me be honest. If I have logged a grand total of thirty minutes across my lifetime in true intimacy with God, I am being generous with myself." *Thomas Merton was honest about his shadow.*

I have always struggled with my shadow, my dark side. Should I be honest about it, or keep it a secret? I constantly wrestle with that choice. People find me articulate and compassionate, honest and trustworthy, generous and forgiving, which I am—in part. After all, my name is *Friend*, so graciousness and affability are expected. I am *Reverend Doctor* Friend, clearly one of solid faith and steady prayerfulness. I am those qualities—and I am not. But I'd rather keep that other part a secret.

My Christian upbringing didn't help. Biblical heroes were always presented as pure and flawless, models of perfection, mine to imitate—Moses and David, Isaiah and Jeremiah, Peter and Paul. They loomed as standards beyond reach, more intimidating than inspiring, setting a bar I could never clear. Their stories evoked more guilt than encouragement. I remember with vividness the day I learned that Moses had murdered an Egyptian soldier, and David, driven by lust, had arranged the battlefield death of Uriah. No one told me that Rebecca had helped Jacob deceive his father and cheat his brother. I gasped when I heard about a victorious general promising as a thank-offering to God to sacrifice the first person he meets returning home—only to be greeted at the gate by his daughter! I was devastated at first, but then awkwardly delighted. The more I learned, the freer I became.

These stories encouraged me to fully claim my dignity and giftedness, my blessedness and high calling, yet freed me as well to embrace my blemishes and flaws, my clumsy humanity, my glaring failings. No sin I had committed or would later commit was without biblical precedent. I was in good company, endless biblical characters making the same point: Abraham and Isaac, Jacob and Joseph, Moses and Joshua, Peter and Paul, human just like me. "Blessed are you, Simon bar Jonah" and "get thee behind me, Satan"—Jesus addressing Peter. "You are precious to me, I love you and give you honor" and "I can't stand your New Moon festivals, your Sabbaths, and your noisy religious gatherings"—affirmation and repudiation spoken by Isaiah. "Imitate me" and "there is nothing healthy in me"—Paul's candid self-awareness. "Woe is me, a man of unclean lips" and "here I am, send me"—confession and commitment a part of Isaiah's call. We are the apple of God's eye, held in the hollow of God's hand; surrounded by the everlasting arms, and beloved of God. We are masterpiece. And, as the Buddhists would remind us, a complete range of thoughts and feelings, every possible act of human behavior, creative and destructive, resides within us.

I pass on some good news I learned just a few years ago, that Jesus could not have said "Be ye perfect," a verse that haunted me for decades. Consistent with the Hebrew understanding of being human, there was no word in the language Jesus spoke for "perfect" as it relates to persons. "Be ye loving, be ye compassionate" are possibilities. Or "Be ye ones made clean by forgiveness." Perhaps closest is "Be ye whole." Beloved of God, we are yet "ransomed, healed, restored, forgiven," as a familiar hymn frames it.

Finally, embracing our shadow is primarily an *inner* discipline, the courage to welcome all within me who sit at my inner family table, all who live in me. As Jesus held that epileptic boy, we can embrace even the troubled and troublesome within us. But *disclosing* our shadow is a different, more delicate and artful matter. Sharing my imperfections and revealing my flaws must maintain appropriate boundaries. Yet the cost that hiding my shadow exacts, the energy drain that hiding claims, any anxiety that hiding tactics might fail, compromises my authenticity and diminishes my capacity to be present.

4. Focus Your Attention

I once said in a sermon, or so I was recently told, that *the opposite of love is distraction.* I don't remember saying it, but I believe that statement to be true. I offer myself as primary evidence. My younger son, Erik, who recently turned forty, has been my teacher since he was in preschool. Young enough that he still held my hand as we walked in the woods near our home, he'd gently tug on my arm when he knew I'd "disappeared" into a sermon idea that had beckoned from a corner of my mind, a possible strategy for tonight's meeting that intruded from another corner, or the sudden awareness that I had forgotten to make a phone call. "Dad, look at the buds on these wild flowers . . . listen to the birds singing in the pine trees . . . can you see the pirate ship in that cluster of clouds?" Or worse yet, sometimes the tug reminded me that I had tuned out in the middle of a question he was asking. I'm a slow learner. Just months ago, decades later, as his own toddler played at our feet, he stopped in the midst of our conversation, sensing I had tuned out. "You still do it, Dad," he said lovingly, but firmly.

When I meet a friend for lunch, I choose a chair facing a wall. If I am facing outward, my mind inevitably leaps out of my control, and distraction stirs. Do I know that fellow waiting to be seated? Is the waitress at the far table the one we had last time? The woman in the tweed jacket reminds of Jill, whose husband is having surgery next week. What a lovely painting between those windows. The distracters are legion, inside my head and out. Being present is hard work for me.

That eccentric Chinese sage, riding his donkey backwards, was likely a Buddhist, an adherent of a faith tradition from which I draw spiritual nurturance and guidance. At the heart of Buddhist practice is *mindfulness,* a spiritual discipline that encourages one to be awake, conscious, and fully alive to the present moment. Thoughts may rise and fall, feelings come and go, the agenda of the future or memories of the past may stir, but Buddhism counsels, "No grasping, no pushing away." Let it all mingle calmly in the preciousness of the present moment. Peace and compassion, quietness and well-being, clarity and wisdom are the fruits of mindfulness.

A compelling, oddly titled book, *Be Here Now*, written by a spiritual teacher named Baba Ram Dass, opens with an enigmatic slogan, "no matter where I go, there I am."[5] Cute, but hardly profound. Who else can I be but *me?* Where located in space and time but *here* and *now?* It appears to be infinitely more difficult than that, more complex and complicated, if my life is any testimony. What is so difficult about allowing ourselves to be simply who we are? Here? Now?

The Personal Orientation Inventory[6] offers a psychological profile, what it calls a time/ratio, of how we tend to orient, to "distribute ourselves" in time—how we typically divide our focus: past, present and/or future. A painting by French artist Marcel Duchamp comes to mind, titled "Woman Descending a Staircase." In a large, ornate, formal hallway with circular walls, on the far side winds a staircase, which a woman is descending. Using the modernist's touch, the artist has painted the woman on the top step, and on the third step down, and on the eighth, and at the bottom of the stairs *all at the same time.* Feel familiar? To become present, fully present, I may have to "call back" that part of me that has rushed ahead, and "wait for the arrival" of that part of me that is lingering behind.

Jesus employed all his senses in disciplined, focused attentiveness and presence. The noise level in the bustling marketplace must have been deafening—the shriek of the competing merchants, the cries of animals herded through the town square, the voices of endless conversations growing louder just to be heard—yet Jesus *heard* the cry of Bartimaeus, the urgency in his shouted words. He had to be alert to navigate passage through the swelling crowd surging this way and that along the narrow road, visual distractions on every side—yet Jesus *saw* Zacchaeus, perched on the tree branch, readiness etched on his face. The path near the lake was narrow, thick with travelers coming and going, bumping and jostling; the messengers from Jairus pressed to his side and the crowding became more intense—yet Jesus *felt* the subtle touch of that woman at the hem of his garment, and felt the healing power go out of him. The stench wafting from the tomb was as acrid as they warned—yet Jesus caught the *scent* of renewed life and called Lazarus out to be unwrapped.

Endless biblical stories reverberate in my mind, competing for telling. Ponder just a few. A conniving mother and an aging father collude to drive a wedge between brothers who had been struggling since before their birth. The birthright stolen, Jacob flees the murderous rage of Esau. For twelve years they live in lands far apart, but brothers are not meant to live in fear and resentment. The drama builds, the outcome uncertain, their armies at hand lest the reunion goes awry. The distance between them narrows, and they embrace. "To *see* your face is like seeing the face of God" (Gen. 33:10), Jacob declares.

Jesus encouraged alertness, focused awareness, fuller presence with those he taught, most often focused on seeing. As Simon's luncheon with Jesus on the terrace was interrupted by a weeping woman who washed Jesus's feet with her tears, Simon looked on, no doubt, with discomfort, even disgust. "Do you *see* this woman?" was Jesus's simple question, as if truly seeing might alter Simon's dismissing and demeaning gaze (Luke 7:44). Jesus, gasping with every word, chooses a single word to encourage John and his mother to care for one another: "Woman, *behold,* your son! Son, your mother" (John 19:26–27 RSV). "Behold," simply "to see," as if from a commitment to truly see all else will emerge.

Peter and John, startled by a lame beggar as they rush toward the temple, remember Jesus's promise that they too could heal in his name. Peter and John "looked intently at him" and then said, "Look at us" (Acts 3:4), Luke reports, and only then gave the command to rise and walk. The looking was part of the healing process. Paul, noticing a lame man listening intently, seeing readiness to be healed etched across his face, "looked straight at him and said in a loud voice, 'Stand up straight on your feet!'" (Acts 14:8–11 GNT). And he did.

THE GIFTS OF PRESENCE

The *gifts* of presence are infinitely more profound and abundant than we could ever imagine. Three distinct, life-giving gifts of presence come into focus, but just as quickly reveal themselves as inextricably interwoven dimensions of a single reality: the healing gift of presence to *myself*, the relationship-deepening gift of presence *between us*, and the sacred gift of presence as *communion with God*.

Frequently the generative theme, woven through biblical journey stories, is a pilgrimage toward the discovery and embrace of *self*, often culminating in receiving a new name. Abram—leaving security and departing in trust, tussled with God and watched his patience tested, the promise finally fulfilled—became Abraham. Jacob—deceived his brother, lied to his father and fled in fear; wrestled all night with an angel and then reunited with Esau—with a new name, Israel. Simon—a mercurial, impulsive, surely unrock-like fisherman, wrong as often as right in his process of formation—evolved into Peter, the Rock. Saul—persecuted Christians with relentless fervor then was blinded by a piercing light, a courageous disciple helping the scales fall from his eye—emerging as Paul.

Presence builds and deepens *relationship*, forges community. Those in the early church, embraced by a truth and graced with a fullness of life they'd never experienced, searched and stretched their language for words to express a new reality—*koinonia*. Commonly translated as "share" or "community," the word suggests more dynamism than that, a threefold movement implied: *Koinonia* manifests when two people begin to *move toward* one another, or feel *beckoned toward* one another. This movement continues until the two *touch*, their lives tangent, making contact. This mysterious movement culminates as the two intertwine, lives interpenetrating, comingling, not unlike the "soul of David knit with the soul of

Jonathan." Echoes of the *mystical union* of husband and wife are declared in the wedding liturgy. Communication becomes communion, as being more fully present births true community.

The third distinct gift bestows *communion with God*. Paul, uncharacteristically, stumbles for words, stuttering and stammering as he affirms the reality of being "in Christ"—"I, yet not I, but Christ in me" . . . "Christ in you the hope of glory" . . . "Christ making his home in our hearts." *The Cloud of Unknowing*, by an anonymous fourteenth-century English monk, urges the spiritual pilgrim to proceed with tireless effort. But when effort has reached its limit, lay a "cloud of forgetting" over it, and simply stand, naked and alone, before the "cloud of unknowing," to be gathered into the very essence of divinity.

The deepest mystery lies not in the distinction but in the intertwining of these three, ultimately indistinguishable, part of a whole. It may require a mystic's intuition to fathom Jesus's prayer in the garden in John 17. The setting is quietly simple: Jesus is alone, the disciples are scattered, huddled in fear. Jesus prays—kneeling in an olive garden at the rim of a valley outside the city walls—praying to God at a distance, the form of his prayer implies, however one locates God. The paradigm of prayer suddenly shifts, Jesus declaring and celebrating oneness with his Father, distinction and distance yielding to mysterious, mystical unity. First communication, but now communion. Jesus asks that this oneness become all-inclusive—the disciples one with God, one with himself, and one with each other, all gathered into some single, all-embracing oneness. Indeed mystical literature speaks of this as the paradox of God's utter otherness and absolute oneness.

A LAST WORD

It all seems so simple. In some ways it is. "Wherever you go, there you are"—be there, fully present. "Show up"—awake, conscious and alert. "Be here, now"—focused, undistracted and attentive. Ride your donkey backwards. The gifts are extraordinary.

3

CELEBRATE UNCERTAINTY

The Gift of Paradox

*T*hey were the best of friends—Moshe, Reuben, and Jacob—as close as the closest brothers, together as often as possible. They'd tell stories and laugh until tears ran down their cheeks. They'd eat bagels and lox until they were stuffed, then eat some more. One day, so unusual it caught them all off guard, Moshe and Reuben got into an argument that rapidly escalated from hearty to heated to downright nasty. "Moshe! Reuben!" Jacob pleaded; "Please," but the exchange only got louder and more intense. At Jacob's insistence they quieted down, and Jacob suggested that they seek the guidance of the rabbi. The rabbi is fair and wise, they quickly agreed, and soon they found themselves knocking at his door.

The rabbi welcomed them with a broad, gracious smile, nodding toward a small circle of chairs where they could all sit comfortably. "Oh my, I can see how upset you are," he said in his deep, resonant, calming voice. "Yes," Jacob nervously replied, "they've had a terrible argument. They trust you can help them resolve it."

"Why don't you begin, Moshe," the rabbi said. So Moshe told his side, the words tumbling from his lips, his arms gesturing vigorously, making his case as forcefully as he could. The rabbi patiently waited until he was sure Moshe was finished. He paused, stroked his chin, leaned forward and said, "I think you're right."

"Wait a minute," Reuben complained, "you haven't waited to hear my side!"

"Speak, Reuben, please," the rabbi said gently. Reuben, matching Moshe in gesture and energy, pleaded his case just as loudly and demonstratively. When he had stated his case, the rabbi paused again and said, "I think you're right." Jacob, startled, indignant, unbelieving, leapt to his feet. "Rabbi," he virtually shouted, "they can't both be right." The rabbi turned, nodded, smiled and said, "I think you're right."

There's a crafty illogic to Jewish stories, a wise irony, a poignant paradox. The philosopher Hegel posed the matter in a more scholarly way, what he called the *theory of the dialectic*—people of different opinions, ideological adversaries, engaging in a process by which the very engagement brings them together toward a higher truth. A person proposes a *thesis,* a particular point of view, which is challenged by its apparent *antithesis*, a counterproposal, a divergent opinion. Antagonism may ensue; ideological collision may occur; an adversarial struggle may erupt. Hegel suggests an alternative. *Thesis* and *antithesis* may yield, when mutual respect is held and deep curiosity is mustered, to *synthesis*, a higher truth than either thesis or antithesis contains.

Jesus offers an example. As Jesus began his all-too-brief public ministry, at least four religious/political parties confidently awaited his arrival. Each had evolved a worldview, a set of practices and a lifestyle, and formed expectations about the awaited messiah. Each had crafted, over centuries, an integration of the political, social, economic, and religious realms. The *Pharisees* sought to live a diligently law-abiding life in the heart of a foreign culture, surrounded by but not co-opted by the lure of secularity, to faithfully demonstrate a pure and exemplary Jewish life. They hoped their highly visible faithfulness would inspire others. They were separatists, spiritually if not geographically. Oft maligned, their intention was noble. The *Sadducees*, by contrast, integrated more fully with the culture that surrounded them, their faithfulness more eclectic, perhaps realistic. The *Essenes* divorced themselves from the culture, which they viewed as corrupt and contaminating, living a rough and rustic separatist life, many in caves to the south. Finally, the *Zealots* were the revolutionaries, amassing caches of arms and awaiting the moment when military uprising, in the spirit of King David, would be timely. As different as these four groups were, each lived with an ideological and practical integrity worthy of respect. Each had framed a profile of the Messiah, what he would be like and what he would do, a profile they held as consistent with the deepest, truest Jewish tradition. Each fully expected the Messiah either to be one of them or to affirm their definition of faithfulness.

Simply stated, Jesus said to the Pharisees, Sadducees, Zealots, and Essenes: I think you're right! Indeed, Jesus seemed Essene-like when he frequently prayed alone or sought retreat with the three or the Twelve, and Pharisee-like when he boldly declared that not a jot or tittle shall pass from the law. He seemed Zealot-like as he brandished a whip of cords and drove out the moneychangers and overturned their tables, and Sadducee-like when he healed a Roman centurion's son or, reluctantly at first, talked with a Syro-Phoenician woman and healed her daughter. He clearly stated, just as boldly and emphatically, that each strongly held position, each ideological certainty, was incomplete. Each theological position and faith practice, offered as absolute and superior, was relative and flawed. Their self-righteousness, their delusion of absolute correctness, sadly, tragically, kept them from knowing Jesus for who he was.

WARNING: LIBERAL IN CAMP

Biblical narratives come most alive in my life when my story interweaves itself with the biblical story. An experience following Hurricane Katrina taught me more than I could have anticipated.

"What's wrong with this picture?" I complained to Betsy, shivering as I pumped a tank full of gas at a service station in northern Mississippi. We had left an unseasonably warm Philadelphia, watching the temperature dip steadily lower as we headed south toward Biloxi to work for two weeks as relief volunteers, just three months after Hurricane Katrina. The hastily assembled camp was near capacity, so we bunked in an aging Winnebago camper with windows that did not shut tight, on a night when the temperature dropped to 26 degrees.

The camp was overcrowded because two busloads of students from Grove City College had arrived the same day. Seven students joined Betsy and me for supper, squeezing around a table meant for six. The conversation turned immediately to matters of theology, biblical interpretation, and the relationship of faith and culture. I quickly surmised that these were enthusiastically evangelical young men and women. I sat back and listened as a curious pattern seemed to develop, around two apparent roles: "question-askers" and "answer-givers." As one usually in the thick of such exchanges, my quietness surprised me. A young woman finally caught my eye and asked what I was thinking. "You kids amaze me," I began, "with the rapidity with which you flop certainties onto the table. And most of you aren't even twenty. And I'm coming up on sixty-five. You hear half a sentence, before it fully reveals itself as a question, then promptly and swiftly provide an answer, spoken with confidence and certainty." I paused for a minute, but they seemed to be waiting for more. "I can only speak for myself, but certainties seem to be exiting the back door of my life at a furious rate. And precious few new ones come knocking at my front door. I think I'm running out of certainties!"

That same young woman spoke up quizzically, "I thought when you got older you had more answers, you believed more and more, more and more strongly, and were more and more certain. Doesn't that frighten you?" she added, a bit apologetically. "I used to think that too, until maybe ten years ago," I confessed. "And yes, at first, it was a bit unsettling. Even embarrassing. I am a minister, after all. And yes, frightening at first. But now, and I'm being honest, it's wonderful. It's liberating. And, oddly, I feel more secure in my faith. Closer to God than ever." Awkwardness set in, I think, as we cleared our dishes and wandered off.

The plot thickened. The next evening at a sharing time, with surely mixed motives at work, I announced that I was a liberal. That's unlike me. I don't like labels. And I suppose I'd prefer "progressive" to "liberal," now that I think about it. But I had a hunch, borne out by a professor who accompanied their delegation as a chaperone, that they knew a lot *about* liberals, but may have *known* few, if any, "up close and personal."

Then, wouldn't you know it, the next morning I was assigned crew chief for about fifteen of the students. Imagine, all day, with a liberal in charge! Here's what I found fascinating. From time to time, with remarkable frequency, always choosing a safe and private moment to protect their anonymity, one student and then another would wander over and ask if we could talk. "They told me that no one from any other religion, no matter how faithful they are, can go to heaven. What do you think about that?" a lanky, mop-haired sophomore in a faded sweatshirt asked. I paused, sensing anxiety in his question, seeing vulnerability in his eyes. I responded softly, unhurriedly, beginning with a question of my own, "What do *you* think?" Speaking haltingly, but seeming more relaxed, he responded, "Well . . . I'm just not sure. It's hard to imagine God just shutting someone out like that. I don't know what to think." "Thanks for feeling free to ask, Josh, and here's the scoop. I'm not sure either. And I think it's OK not to be sure." If it was an answer he was looking for, he must have left disappointed. But as he walked away, I think he looked relieved.

Within the hour, during a break from the harsh, sweaty, stinky work of mucking out a house that had been sealed up for the three-plus weeks since the storm, a vivacious blonde in a cheerleader's shirt found me in a safe place around a corner. "Gotta sec?" she asked. "Sure!" "They told me that every single word in the Bible is absolutely right. 'Infallible' they called it. And that I shouldn't ask any questions about that." She paused. I just cocked my head and nodded silently. "I don't know if I believe that," she continued, looking hesitant. "What do you think?" "Sandy," I said, "the Bible is the most important book in my life. I read it every day. It inspires me, guides me, comforts me, and gives me advice. It feeds me. Is every single word absolutely right? I have to be honest. I don't even think a lot about that. I just keep reading it." Her "thanks" as we went back to work came with a broad smile and a sigh of relief, I sensed.

Finally, after dinner the following day, someone asked the question I'd anticipated, and it came with a quiet defiance and more

than a hint of judgment: "Are you a born-again Christian?" I wasn't
proud of my answer, my penchant for sarcasm getting the best of
me, "Are you a give-away-all-you-own-to-feed-the-poor-and-fol-
low-Jesus Christian?" I countered. If he can assault me with his
favorite biblically based query, I have a right to launch my own.
What could possibly follow but tension, spilling out over others
who'd been listening in? I sighed self-consciously, releasing the
tightness that clenched my stomach and shoulders, and ventured
a subtle smile. He seemed to soften a touch as well. "Why don't we
get a cup of coffee and sit and chat?" I suggested. We headed for the
coffee urn, and so did the contingent of observers. "Zack, I'd love
to tell you what Jesus means to me. And learn more about what
he means to you. Born again? I can't think of a biblical story that
means more to me than Nicodemus encountering Jesus under the
cover of night. But, like that courageous Pharisee, faith deepening
takes time for me. I am so glad Jesus did not press him to make a
decision immediately, on the spot. I can tell you stories of how my
life has been transformed, made brand new, how I've been 'born
again,' I suppose." And tell stories we did, well into the night, each
in the circle sharing a story of when and how their faith had been
birthed or deepened.

As I was falling asleep that evening, the Nicodemus narrative
kept coming back. I could feel Nicodemus's shadowy, cautious
approach, hear the whispered clarity and urgency of his question,
and glimpse his bewildered look at Jesus's response, so mysterious
and enigmatic. I could sense his longing to understand, even as
understanding eluded him. The silence becomes awkward. Nothing more spoken, he slowly walks away. Nicodemus, like many
who approached Jesus with their questions, brought *answer-shaped
containers*—seeking clear, definitive, unwavering responses—and
Jesus responded, as he frequently does, with a metaphor, a symbol, a story, more riddle than propositional, leaving one such as
Nicodemus walking away scratching his head.

Then my imagination played an odd trick. No, I have not
unearthed any "lost verses of John," but suddenly I "saw" a new
character in my mind's eye and "heard" some fresh dialogue as the

familiar narrative continued. Beckoning from the darkness just a few yards away, a stranger catches Nicodemus's eye, and they fall into conversation. "My name is Aaron," he introduces himself, "a follower of Jesus. And, if I may, I want to apologize on his behalf. He's such a poet and mystic, he cannot resist responding to a question, even as clear and uncomplicated as yours, with images and symbols, stories and metaphors. He does it all the time. So, if you have a moment, I think I can explain, in clearer, more logical, simpler ways what he was trying to say."

The nightstand clock clicked soundlessly to 2:00 a.m. as a rude self-consciousness pierced my reverie. How many times had I played Aaron from endless pulpits to a collective Nicodemus in the pew? Since this inquisitive Pharisee is so captivating to me, I have preached dozens of sermons on John 3, each, I'd no doubt vigorously argue, an exegetically disciplined explanation and application of Jesus's exchange with Nicodemus. Was I trying, unawares, to "save" Jesus from the embarrassment of being so cryptic and obtuse? Was I inadvertently "saving" any Nicodemus present from a wrestling with the mystery Jesus so artfully initiated? Then a veritable onslaught of pointed critique descended. Jesus's parables came to mind, another typical response to a reasoned and reasonable questioner. How embarrassing! The audacity of my daring to "explain" what Jesus "really meant" by this story or that! I cringed with each memory of a sermon that confidently and methodically graced worshipers with an explanation of a story or metaphor, symbol or image Jesus employed. Finally, I fell asleep.

Those Grove City students, who may still pray for my salvation, have no idea how they affected my life. What is truth? Can we embody our faith in reliable propositions? Is certitude real, or reliable, or even available? I have a hunch about that. I know how restless I can become if an important, foundational, urgent question lingers unanswered too long. I prefer the shortest possible time lapse between question and answer; I want my answers airtight and unarguable. I don't like things to float in ambiguity, to linger in uncertainty. But what if our haste to proclaim truth, our rush to certainty, and our eager embrace of an answer is, in reality, more in the service of security than truth-seeking, more psychological than theological? What if the rush to beliefs serves primarily to relieve discomfort, to ease anxiety, to quell fear? However persistent our inner longing for the certain and unambiguous, fanned by that gnawing, escalating fear that can engulf us, is there greater "wisdom in insecurity"? Might the "delusion of understanding" block or detour our steady, if halting, journeying toward truth?

What sense do you make of Jesus's explanation in Mark 4:11–12 about why he teaches in parables? What is the "secret" or "mystery" of the kingdom of God given to the disciples (v. 11)? But even more perplexing, how do you understand words that seem so cryptic, "that they may indeed look, but not perceive, and may indeed listen, but not understand, so that they may not turn again and be forgiven" (v. 12)? Revisiting various commentaries on these verses has been less than satisfying. Clever, perhaps, but not illuminating. Give this idea some thought. When I think I understand something, I am apt to tuck it away in my "things I understand" file. I literally "set it aside." It goes off my radar screen, moving to some back corner of my mind. Exploration ceases. The yeasty work of germination and fermentation stops. I no longer wrestle. Creativity lapses. The last word spoken, new voices silenced, the lights go out.

What *did* Jesus wish for those he encountered—those who thronged on a hillside outside Capernaum or huddled at the seashore as he spoke from a borrowed boat; those he taught in the ordered quietness of a synagogue or on a noisy street corner; those who came under the shadow of night or to a well in the noonday heat; those who lowered a friend through a roof, cried out from their blindness, or climbed a sycamore tree? What were his hopes for those who left their nets, the tax collector's table, a place of prayer under a fig tree, or their home town of Bethsaida to follow him? John, unlike other biblical authors, shares what motivated his writing, that we might "believe," he said, and "believing, have life!" Jesus seemed to have abundant life in mind, healing and wholeness, freedom from religious and economic oppression, eternal life, a capacity for trust, an awakening of compassion and loving-kindness, forgiveness and forgivingness, a commitment to justice, evoking a faith that could make one well, overflowing joy and oneness with God. You add to the list. *Experience* appears far more important to Jesus than *explanation*.

Psychoanalyst, philosopher, and seminal thinker Carl Jung intrigued persons of faith of many traditions, including Christians. Near the end of his life he was interviewed by the BBC, and the commentator quietly asked, "Dr. Jung, do you believe in God?" In an answer that could seem arrogant, unless you could see the old man's face and hear his intonation, he said, "I think I *know* God." Echoes of Jesus's prayer in John 17: ". . . that they may be one as you and I are one . . . as you, Father, are in me, and I in you, may they also be in us . . . I in them and you in me that they may become completely one . . . that they may be one as we are one."

Biblical scholar Elaine Pagels writes of faith experience "beyond belief." A baccalaureate sermon spoke of "The God beyond Theology." Dietrich Bonhoeffer spoke of "the beyond in our midst." Karl Barth, theological giant of a generation ago, after four days of erudite lecturing at a prestigious seminary, when asked to summarize his theology in a sentence or two, smiled and said, "Jesus loves me; this I know, for the Bible tells me so."

Reading anything written by historian and Islamic scholar Karen Armstrong is worth the effort—she looks deeply, pondering the rich and deep complexity of things religious. Armstrong's book *Battle for God* is a classic, exploring the phenomenon of colliding fundamentalisms—Islamic, Jewish, and Christian—exploring deep historical roots, five centuries of interweaving and colliding of colonial expansion and indigenous tradition, inter- and intracultural intrigue. In the early chapters she makes a pivotal distinction that will illuminate and inform her analysis throughout the book—between what she calls *mythos* and *logos*. She notes that the enduring world religions—Buddhism and Hinduism, Confucianism and Taoism and Middle Eastern monotheism, soon to be followed by Christianity—emerged during what historians call the Axial Age (800 to 200 BCE). Widely diverse and broadly varied in belief and practice, these religions represent a profound shift in spiritual consciousness—from local deities, contained and controlled by primitive ritual, confined to sacred locations, to the "worship of a single universal transcendence and source of sacredness . . . internalized spirituality . . . and the importance of practical compassion."[1] These religions, she argues, were founded in *mythos*, glimpses of the mystical, mysterious and ineffable, of the infinite and eternal, of pure meaning, always beneath the grasp of rationality, eluding the farthest reach of language. *Mythos* is at the heart, the depth from which all else arises, sheer essence. The founding figures of these religions—Moses and the prophets, Zoroaster and Buddha, Confucius and Laotzu, Jesus and Paul—were graced with "entry into the mystery," receiving those glimpses, plumbing those depths, in mystically experienced *mythos*. Nothing inspired their teaching and writing like the profound and passionate desire to invite others to touch and be touched by that mystery as well.

Sacred texts were written, collections of teachings of the masters, employing the only vehicle at hand, language. Peruse any of these ancient and revered writings and you will find them brimming with story and metaphor, symbol and simile, just like Jesus. All, nonetheless, are held in linguistic containers, what Armstrong calls *logos*—as important as *mythos*, but different and distinct in its role in the religious quest. *Logos* is rational and reasoned, seeks to be exact and precise, scientific and logical, empirical and practical. After the Enlightenment, the Age of Reason, *logos* eclipsed *mythos*, dismissing it as primitive and superstitious. Christian mystery began to be displaced by doctrinal precision and creedal formula in the time of Irenaeus, when Christianity, conveniently available as glue to the collapsing empire that had once persecuted it, relinquished its rich multiplicity of form and practice and yielded to a centralizing momentum toward right belief and right practice. The emergence of systematic theology and crafting of the fundamentals of Christianity in the eighteenth and nineteenth centuries solidified that shift. In a phrase, *mythos* was turned into *logos*, or at least in the imagination of religious orthodoxy, including Christianity.

Parables, and the ones who tell them, invite us deeper into *mythos*, a glimpse of mystery, a brush with divinity. Sermons interpreting parables remain necessarily, inevitably *logos*; reasoned, but contrived logic; comforting, but synthetic clarity. I like the simplicity of that familiar phrase, "don't look at the finger pointing, but at the moon to which it points." Any parable—the apparent illogic of Jesus's discourse with Nicodemus, the horticultural allusion inviting one to *abide* in me (John 15), Jesus's insistence that the kingdom of God can only be known in simile and metaphor, as *like unto*—beckons us inward and downward, upward and outward, ever deeper, beyond the edges of language and into the inevitable silence, beyond *knowing about* into sheer *knowing* itself.

Paul, usually articulate and precise, gropes for the words, delightfully tongue-tied, when he tries to name the wondrous phenomenon by which Christ and a person become one, with echoes of Jesus's prayer in the garden—"it is no longer I who live, but it is Christ who lives in me" (Gal. 2:20), "Christ in you, the hope of glory" (Col. 1:27), "if anyone is in Christ, there is a new creation" (2 Cor. 5:17). I become similarly tongue-tied when you ask me if I am "saved" or "born again," and you must be patient and lend a most attentive ear if you want to know how I experience being one with Christ, how I know God; how I have, however faintly, touched and tasted divinity; how I have felt the guiding presence; how I have been held in the everlasting arms or nestled in the hollow of God's hand.

Did those Grove City students and I stumble upon some common ground where we could stand together? I came to welcome and respect the clarity and certainty with which those college students stated their faith—only after I quieted my immediate, hasty, and surely less generous impulse. I chose to look behind and listen into the familiar, predictable, and to date annoying biblically based phrases they employed, thus to discern ways in which their hearts and lives were being transformed by their faith. My "ears were opened," as Jesus urges; "scales fell from my eyes," as Paul described his new and deeper seeing after Damascus Road. The challenge to have "eyes to see" and "ears to hear" took on new, fresh, and utterly contemporary meaning. And those evangelical students, bless their hearts, set aside their assumptions about a "liberal in their midst" and focused with loving attention on how I shared my faith, and the unfamiliar way in which I spoke of it. They turned out to be different than I had, too hastily, assumed; and evidently the same was true of their view of me.

A final Biloxi anecdote: After evening devotions and a time of sharing the events and reflections of the day, always powerful and moving, having encountered people of astounding resilience and durability, victims of Katrina's devastation, a leader of the Grove City contingent suggested we sing some praise songs together, with time to read any passage of Scripture that "the Spirit leads you to share." I sat back, singing the songs I knew, appreciating those who felt moved to read, but hardly expecting to hear the sound of my voice. Then, inexplicably, mysteriously, unaccustomed to such things, a "voice" whispered from some quiet corner of my mind, "Isaiah 58:6–9." The voice was steady and insistent. I spotted a Bible on a table nearby, rather self-consciously opened to that passage, previewed its message to make sure I'd not be embarrassed by something clearly inappropriate, and read it aloud during the next space between songs. As I read the last words and closed the Bible, I became aware of a dozen faces looking my way, jaws ajar and eyes gazing widely. After the closing prayer a half-dozen of them gathered around, speaking almost in unison, "How did you know?" "Know what?" I responded with genuine innocence. "To read that passage? Did someone tell you?" Keith replied. My puzzled look spoke for me. "Months before we drove down here," Keith continued, "soon after we decided to make the trip to Biloxi, we decided to pray for a passage to be our beacon, our guiding word. We asked the Holy Spirit to reveal that passage to us. I felt led to a particular passage and, when we had our next meeting, there was immediate confirmation among our team. The passage was Isaiah 58:6–9!" Now my jaw dropped open and my eyes widened. "We didn't think liberals got those kinds of leadings," Sophia said incredulously. "Me neither," I quietly replied.

Nothing has saddened me more in recent years than the harshness and animosity that so quickly mobilizes when Christians of differing theological perspectives engage. Civility yields to coarse and brusque exchanges that tumble into sarcasm and disrespect. In the name of Christ, Christlikeness thins and evaporates. Someone has pointed out that *discussion* comes from the same root as "percussion" and "concussion," like *discurso* in Spanish, a clash of ideas, a debate, a win/lose battle; while *dialogue* combines *dia / through* and *logos / truth*, an exchange that seeks to journey through toward truth, differing ideas seeking companionship en route to deeper truth. Nothing has encouraged me more than my week in Biloxi with my evangelical mentors. We could have opted for tolerance, a better choice than hostility; or for rising above a verbal fray, a tactic of avoidance but not engagement. We could have bitten our tongues, but we'd have had little tongue left after a week in such close quarters. We chose—or, more likely, were led by a deeper graciousness, guided by higher wisdom—to meet each other, to work through rather than skirt around what threatened to divide us. I wish we had a deftly edited video that could have captured our pilgrimage. It just might be a gift to the churches.

WHY NOT QUIT WHILE YOU'RE AHEAD?

Prudence might counsel ending this essay right here, but integrity demands otherwise. My intent has been to challenge Christians to broaden common ground, meet under a broader tent, to relinquish certainty in a shared search for wisdom, to make faith sharing more like a poetry reading than an engagement of faith positions. But what of other faiths? Walk gingerly out onto some thinner ice with me.

Every third Saturday for nearly a year I have gathered for two hours in a circle that ranges from eight to twenty persons of differing faiths. Last month, for example, we were four Protestants, three Catholics, three Muslims, two Jews, three Baha'is, a Buddhist, and a Zoroastrian. We typically find our place in the circle in silence, meditative music from one of our traditions inviting us to settle, focus, and quiet within. Holy books from each tradition are on a table scattered around a vase of flowers, from which anyone can read as they are led. A leader for the day whispers "amen" in the language of their birth, and we briefly introduce ourselves, adding to our name and faith background whatever we feel led to share. The heart of the meeting is not a forum. An early meeting, where we tried sharing our faith's basic teaching or our founding teacher's basic instruction on a given theme or topic, proved disappointing. "We decided to share how our faith passes through our hearts rather than instructs our minds," a Muslim member recently stated it, interpreting to a newcomer what draws him back month after month. The leader may write a question to start the sharing, framed in a way that has become helpful to us, like: How does your faith comfort and support you? How does your faith help you understand and cope with adversity and suffering? How does your faith nurture your relationships, your friendships, your marriage and family life? How does your faith help you make decisions and give you guidance? How does your faith encourage you to respond to human need?

On a given Saturday Moses and Jesus, Muhammed and Baha'u'llah, Buddha and Zoroaster are frequently and unapologetically named and quoted, as the teacher and teachings that have most touched a given person's heart. We often end our time with each intoning a benediction from their tradition, each in our native language: Arabic and Hebrew, Farsi and English, Polish and Spanish, creating an unpredictable harmony where one might reasonably expect cacophony. Whether we nod, bow, or embrace as we depart, a weaving of hearts is richly felt and celebrated.

As I drove home from a gathering a month or two ago, I saw a bumper sticker that read, "No religion is big enough to embrace the fullness of God." It reminded me of another I had seen a few days earlier, "All religions are right, but mine is righter." If you'd have asked me a year ago for my thoughts about Christianity and other religions, I would have offered a cogent, reasoned, and persuasive opinion, with which you might have agreed or disagreed in varying measure. If you asked me now, I am rather unsure how I would answer. And, if I tried, I'd likely interrupt myself before you would. The faces of my third-Saturday friends would crowd my consciousness, my warm and loving feelings for them would arise, and my deep respect for them and the faith that defines and guides them would fill me. I have a name for the One others call Allah or Yahweh. Just God works for me. I know who my teacher is: Jesus, whom I know as Lord, Master, or Savior. I call my source of guidance the Holy Spirit. The holy text that nurtures, teaches, and instructs me is the Bible. But I know that, when our interfaith circle gathers, I will be gifted and guided, enriched and expanded by those who address God differently, follow a different teacher, use a different language, or hold different ideas.

Dreams, imaginings, story lines that weave themselves in some quiet corner of consciousness, ideas that "come" to us, which "pop into our minds," as we sometimes say, fascinate me. Where do they come from? They are products, psychology would say, of our unconscious, and may, as often as not, be best let to slide by. I have had this one on a now ragged and yellowed piece of paper for several years. You'll have to decide if I'd best let it slide by.

Maybe it was just happenstance, an overwhelming though totally unlikely coincidence, a chance meeting. Maybe one of the three took charge and set it up, arranged it, as anyone could argue was a prerogative and power each possessed. Providence, perhaps. Divine intervention. Anyway, there they were entering the same restaurant, at the same hour, on the same day, heading to the same table marked "reserved," a different server pulling back a chair and carefully unfolding and placing a napkin. Someone had penned name tags in sweeping calligraphy on linen stock: God, Allah, and Yahweh.

Lest anyone guess, even worry otherwise, their words of greeting in tone and gesture were warm and heartfelt. They were clearly delighted to share the moment. Not a hint of competition, let alone animosity. Others in the restaurant, unaware just who the guests at "that table" actually were, nonetheless felt it, though describing it was elusive. Warmer. Quieter. A touch lighter. Suddenly feeling safer, diners found their conversations more animated. Those with a decision to make felt suddenly clearer. Those arguing slowed their pace of exchange, speaking just as vigorously but with greater sensi-

tivity, listening more attentively and compassionately. Businessmen maneuvering, seeking to manipulate, blunting truth with strategic outcome in mind, found themselves speaking with disarming straight-forwardness and candor.

I'm not sure who spoke first, at that table of three, as the silence they shared was so rich and full. They discovered each had come to share what was clearly a common concern, a common anguish, a matter each had reasoned they could only resolve together. It had nothing to do, as one might have expected, with the truth as they embodied and taught it. Different as they may have been, they held each other only in the highest respect and regard. It was their follow-ers that brought them such pain, the ways they were using the truth as they knew it to assault each other. As they confessed their common lament, they shared a common hope, and made a common pledge. That they would do all that they could to transform the antagonism of their followers into the same respect and regard with which they held each other.

They left as quietly as they had arrived and the maitre d' beck-oned to a busboy to clear the table. There was only a single place setting.

The Gift of Paradox

Such an ironic dilemma, seeking to describe the indescribable, to capture in words what resides beyond the reach of words, to capture the inevitably elusive, to define *mythos* with the only tool of com-munication we have at hand, *logos*. The most important things we have to say cannot be said! When we depend on the reliability of our propositions and positions, do we rob ourselves of depth, and limit the gift of dialogue? Even as we long for certainty, is there value in valuing uncertainty? "I believe, help my unbelief," stammered that father, when Jesus said he would use *his* faith to heal his son. And it was faith enough. We are in good company!

4

Hearing the Silence

The Gifts of Solitude and Silence

et three brief quotes, from widely different persons, converge as a place to start, like the three panels of a triptych. Priest and author Henri Nouwen once said that *silence is the home of words.* Words arise from a silence that proceeds and settle back into a silence that follows. Even the syllables within a word are defined by the silence between them. When we are at home with silence, are not strangers to silence, our words reside closer to wisdom. When we are awkward with silence, do not welcome and cherish it, our words become hollow and shallow.[1] Choreographer George Balanchine said that *stillness is the home of movement.* A fine dancer's movement—subtle, gentle, and graceful, or leaping, sweeping, and robust—begins with stillness, and then returns to stillness.[2] Father William McNamara, founder of a community of Carmelite hermit monks, said *solitude is the home of community.* When we speak, enriched by words spoken with care and received with sensitivity, we deepen communication. But when we are "solitaries together," when we are, as the poet Rainer Maria Rilke wrote, "guardians of one another's solitude," we open to communion.[3] This chapter's themes are best summarized with this triptych of quotes. Consider the possibility that artful, timely, effective leadership is conceived, if not born, at the intersection of these three.

ONE MAN'S STORY

I have permission to tell this man's story. We'll call him Jake for now. Perhaps you'll find something of yourself in him. Seen by most as competent and self-confident, creative and resourceful, he was a typically driven Type-A personality, and his life had run a relatively smooth and undetoured course. He knew himself as motivated, unhesitant, and self-assured. But suddenly his confidence began to falter, his self-assurance waver, his emotional wheels began to wobble. Jake was shook! And that was unfamiliar. Vocation had never been an issue. He chose a profession while still in high school, completed college and graduate school on schedule, and pursued his career in successful and satisfying ways. Recently, he began to dread his trek to work. Formerly life-giving and rewarding tasks suddenly felt dull, even annoying. A "people person" in a "people-person's role," he found himself wanting to retreat behind his office door. He was rattled. Having met his wife when they were teenagers and wed as college students, he thought their marriage, as it entered its third decade, was strong and steady. But they began to fall into more frequent, then more heated, disagreements, becoming impatient, even testy, with each other. Word of attractions to other men or women leaked out in one encounter. Life was unraveling.

What to do? An extended leave of absence from his work seemed impossible. A formal separation from his wife did not seem a realistic or desirable choice. In a moment of serendipity and synchronicity, he ended up making an unlikely decision: he needed to learn to pray! This realization led to an even more out-landish decision, to use accrued vacation time to spend a month at a monastery in Canada with hermit monks who lived in a small community committed to solitude and quietness. The abbot accepted his application, and Jake quickly bought a plane ticket, before he lost his nerve.

An ancient four-wheel-drive Harvester International van, driven decisively by a robust sister of the Carmelite Order, wended its way forty miles from an already remote airport in Nova Scotia, the last twenty down roads likely impassable after a heavy rain. It bounced to a halt near the hermitage of the abbot as the sister pointed this would-be monk toward its rough and rustic front door. "Welcome, Jake," the abbot said warmly and nodded toward a chair by a roaring fireplace. "I want to learn to pray!" Jake blurted out, before the abbot said much of anything. The abbot smiled gently. "Let's go for a walk," he finally suggested.

They just walked at first, not speaking a word, Jake's pace awkward and hurried, constantly having to slow to match the measured, almost leisurely pace of the abbot. Finally the abbot stopped and gently asked, "What do you hear?" Absorbed in rumination, his annoyance mounting that teaching about prayer had yet to begin, he had, in reality, seen or heard nothing. "I hear birds, yes, I hear birds . . . singing," he finally said. "Good," the abbot said, a single word his only response, and he walked on. Though disappointed, Jake noticed his sense of urgency quieting a bit, his pace a touch slower as they continued along the forest trail. The abbot stopped again, posing the same question, "What do you hear?"

"I hear the wind, high in the pines, like a voice in the forest whispering," Jake said, with less hesitation. "Good," said the abbot, walking on. As they came to a clearing, the abbot stopped again, Jake anticipating the question, "What do you hear?"

"Ah, the brook. I hear the brook. Tumbling over the rocks," Jake exclaimed, feeling oddly comforted this time by the abbot's one-word response. They wandered on, Jake beginning to enjoy the deliberate, unhurried pace. The abbot stopped again, Jake's lips silently shaping the abbot's words as he spoke, "What do you hear?" The birds were still singing. The wind high in the pines still whispering. The muted sounds of the stream still audible. Jake stood quietly, the shuffle of his feet rustling the newly fallen leaves. "All I can hear is the silence," he finally muttered.

"Ah," said the abbot with a smile. "Now you are ready to begin to learn to pray!" They returned to the abbot's hermitage walking briskly and chatting in an easy and animated way.

Perhaps you've guessed that I am Jake. I had known myself as confident, competent, self-assured, and assertive. Feeling suddenly uncertain, hesitant, and anxious caught me by surprise. I had not anticipated this crisis of self-esteem.

Called to pastoral ministry as a teen, in the wake of the death of my mother, I finished high school to complete college, to attend seminary, to become ordained as a minister, and had served two congregations over nearly two decades with energy and joy. My call and commitment seemed steady and unwavering. Just as suddenly my vocational focus blurred, my personal faith began to falter and fracture, my sense of purpose and passion in free fall. And I panicked.

Betsy and I met a year after my mother's death, courted for five years, married, and seemed to be models of compatibility—boldly leading marriage workshops on communication skills, coping with conflict, deepening intimacy, and building mutual respect, and offering team counseling for couples in crisis. Just as suddenly we lost our step, started to "miss" each other, squabbles mounting into hurtfulness, a troublesome veering apart unarguable. We were giving classic definition, I suppose, to "midlife crisis."

I tried, and we tried together, to put the pieces back together. We worked to recapture what we once had and lost. It was a three-front battle for me—self-esteem, vocational clarity, and marital healing. It was almost overwhelming. An unexpected clarity began to slowly emerge. The work before us was to re-create, not recapture; to envision a new picture, not piece together an old one. New wineskins were in order. Though only thirty days, the time at the monastery was more than a month, substantially, significantly more. Time flows differently in the heart of solitude and silence.

My retreat offered our marriage what a six-month separation might have, I'd guess. I returned longing to recovenant with Betsy, more than merely renewing our vows but ready to commit myself to her in ways I suspect I never had. A therapist who helped us navigate the months before and after my time away had offered a rather paradoxical observation just before I left on retreat: "I want to help you two become more separate, so you can become more intimate." Our compatibility had more than trace elements of entanglement and enmeshment, a "togetherness" that blurred and stunted our individual gifts and strengths. As poet Kahlil Gibran, quoted at our wedding, said, "Let there be spaces in your togetherness." Healing for our marriage was birthed in the heart of solitude and silence.

The month evoked a fresh and more deeply rooted commitment to ministry, specifically to the parish I was serving. One evening, close to my departure from the monastery, as I sat alone in the darkness of the chapel, I heard myself say, almost out loud, thinking of my return to my work, "Lord, I can't do it," the words carried on the wings of a deep and hearty sigh. The vocational discouragement that had weighed so heavily early in the month seemed to be edging back, freshly unsettling. Though I am not one, normally, to receive answer to prayer in clear and distinct ways, the divine voice seemed unmistakable, with a touch of humor and irony, "Well, glad we've finally settled that!" In the solitude and silence the burdens of ministry, the undue loneliness I had created, the "functional atheism" by which I had labored yielded to a truer, deeper sense of partnership with God—with firm distinction about who was junior partner!

On the personal front, the phrase "work in progress" took on new meaning. A month or so after I got home Betsy made me a little banner of burlap, yarn, and hand-cut felt letters, "Be patient, God isn't finished with me yet." Paul's challenge to "let go of what lies behind, pressing on toward the upward call" touched me in a place deep within. During the following year I had occasion to compare my thirty days on retreat, living as a hermit monk, with three friends who had been through thirty-day detoxification programs. The content of the awesome struggle to be liberated from addiction, theirs and mine, as well as the timetable, had awesome and eerie parallels. I rarely tell this part of the story. Maybe it's time.

I settled into my hermitage and the monastic routine. My cabin, tucked into the edge of the forest out of sight of the others, was roomy if not spacious: an austere single bed, large windows looking out on a small lake, a table for eating, a writing desk, and a cooking corner with a basic supply of pots, pans, cooking utensils, plates, and silverware. A well-worn overstuffed chair was unexpectedly comfortable, and a large wood-burning stove for heat and cooking creaked and hissed continually. Wednesday through Saturday, bells called us to Morning Prayer at seven in the chapel, to pause wherever we might be to say the Angelus Prayers at noon, and to Evening Prayer at five. Mass on Wednesday and Friday evenings and Sunday at eleven was followed by a community meal and robust dialogue around the table, a circle of about a dozen, eight monks and four retreatants. Otherwise we each prepared meals in our own hermitage, carrying supplies from a central pantry. Complete solitude and silence, seventy-two hours without hearing the sound of your own voice, was kept Sunday afternoon through Wednesday morning. Shared work tasks, an hour of spiritual direction every third or fourth day, an occasional walk in the woods or shared meal with another monk, provided the only opportunity for conversation. Some regimen for an extroverted, gregarious, type-A sort of guy!

My life as a monk got off to a fine start, but began a troublesome downhill slide early on. My spiritual director was part of the problem. How could a celibate woman who had lived half her life in a remote monastic order, miles from the real world, even begin to understand me, a man of the world, sophisticated and well read, theologically astute and psychologically insightful? Big surprise! Day three, my first hour of spiritual direction, I shared how much I loved edging a canoe into the lake, paddling northward through a series of lakes, coming ashore at various beachlike areas, delighting in the quiet whoosh of the canoe cutting through the cool water. As we ended, as a sort of afterthought, she gently suggested, "Try not canoeing until we meet next." Day six, a second hour of direction, I said how much I loved curling up in front of the fireplace in the remarkably well-stocked library and immersing myself in mystical contemplative writing, all rather new to me. She offered the same gentle sort of offhand comment as I left: "See what it might be like to avoid the library until we meet again." On day nine—maybe you're getting the picture—I spoke of how alive my journal was becoming, as I wrote dozens of pages each day, recording dreams, reflecting on biblical passages, pondering life and my experiences here at the monastery, awkwardly anticipating her parting comment: "Why not close your journal until we meet again?"

Supper that evening catapulted my slide into a spiral. What I had vaguely noticed at our common meal Wednesday and Friday became vividly clear at Sunday brunch. How to explain it? When I meet new people, I'd just as soon they like me. That they'd come, as soon as possible, to think well of me. Maybe even be impressed by me. So I "leak" information to aid that cause. Sometimes I think of new acquaintances as "cards" I play that can take "relational tricks," if that metaphor works. I'll "leak" an accomplishment or two, and look for an approvingly raised eyebrow, or mention some well-known or highly respected person I happen to know. Speeches I've given, workshops I've led, seminaries where I've taught or lectured typically evoke expressions of affirmation. An article, better yet a book, I've written. That's like "playing an ace." You get the picture. But here's the problem. My cards didn't take any tricks with the monks! There was nothing blatant in their reaction; they were not disregarding, surely not insulting. But none of my cards were winners. They'd nod, not without interest, but clearly they were not impressed. I began to feel awkward, disoriented, rather invisible. I was losing my identity, my authenticity, my very self. It dawned on me that I had confused what I've *done* with who I *am*. It didn't occur to me to call it addiction, but denial is wily.

I went to bed that night on the edge of terror. I was not afraid of the dark, or of being alone in a cabin in the deep woods of Canada, but there I was poised on the verge of primal fear. Peel away a peach, and you come to a seed. Peel away an onion and you come to . . . nothingness. I felt last layers peeling away, hovering on the verge of nothingness. Yikes! It's the tenth night, and I'm signed up for a month. I don't like camp! I lay there plotting a ruse to go home. I'd feign some sort of illness. There, that's it. An old ailment has flared, aggravated by the dank mustiness of the forest floor, and it needs a medication only available in the States. Perfect. I rehearsed a plausible script, and waited for sleep to come. The fear returned, with a vengeance. I resigned to pass a sleepless, restless night. I gave up. Maybe that surrender was the key.

I am not given to mystical experiences. I'm as grounded as they come, an earthy, even earthbound sort of fellow. So what follows falls far outside my range of experience. As I curled my body up in what felt like an instinct of self-protection, I suddenly had a sense of being held. I felt no urge to turn and see if someone was really there, yet I also knew this was other than simply imagination. I *was* being held. My body knew more clearly than my mind, as I surrendered into all-enveloping, reassuring, maternal arms. The arms of Mary, my body decided. As if carried into sleep, I slept as soundly and peacefully as I can remember, before or since. And I awoke in the morning as if awakening for a first time. In many ways I *did* awaken for the first time. There's personal rebirth in the heart of solitude and silence.

A final hour of spiritual direction ended my stay. Sister Pat continued to awe me with her incisiveness, intuition, and timely words of wisdom. She asked me to arrive with a personal covenant, a commitment to a spiritual practice, not broad-brush and general, but with clear contours of a daily, weekly, and monthly regimen. Not so expansive and demanding that follow-through would be impossible, yet not so minimal that follow-through would have no influence. Guided by disciplines I'd practiced with the community—steady and consistent, but not stiff or rigid; ordered, but gentle—I arrived at her hermitage, covenant in hand. She made only a few suggestions, then concluded with a question she discerned I needed to be asked, "How long will you follow your practice before you evaluate?" Sensing immediately that it was a trick question, I intercepted my first response, extending my answer to "six months." There, that'll show her that I'm serious. Her parting words, before a wonderful hug, were, "Try it for five years and then evaluate!" And, by the way, I did.

Jostling back to the airport in the International, same robust sister at the wheel, and on the plane ride back to Philadelphia, I could not get the prophet Elijah out of mind, whom I'd loved since

I was a child. Like it was yesterday, I remembered being in vacation Bible school at age six, piling up tables and chairs, wooden blocks and a trash can or two to make an altar. An old burlap bag, holes cut for his head and arms, pulled down over a children's choir robe, turned my friend Timmy into a convincing Elijah. After similarly robed prophets of Baal concluded their unsuccessful rant to light the altar, Elijah, chest thrust forward, bellowing in as deep a voice as a preschool kid can muster, ordered fire from heaven. Whoosh! Kazaam! Flames of red aluminum foil danced from the altar, pulled upward by thread we had draped over a water pipe along the ceiling. Elijah was my hero.

I didn't learn the rest of the story until years later. Ahab and Jezebel, enraged at their prophets' failure, threatened Elijah with death. What happened to my hero, his defiance and courage? He ran! Forty miles in search of safety, he arrived atop a mountain. God did not chide or chastise him. God did not order him immediately back to the fray. God provided refuge in a cave, angels bringing fresh water and warm biscuits each morning. No rush. Time to replenish. Some R & R. Then, when it was time, a storm crashed against the mountainside. Lightning crackled, wind swirled, thunder roared, rain cascaded down, but God, the narrator says, was not in the drama of the storm. Then God did speak, in a phrase that virtually eludes certain translation, a "still small voice of silence." Elijah did return to this prophetic calling and its work, gifted and filled by solitude, stillness, and silence.

My ruminations about Elijah, about my much-more-than-a-month as a hermit monk, began to morph into a question, and then into the outlines of a plan. No, not yet a plan: a thought, a hunch, a possibility. Could a congregation ground its life and ministry in silence, stillness, and solitude? Could discernment become the operative word in decision making? How would members and leaders respond to the idea of spiritual disciplines, a covenant of spiritual practice? I had read a book titled *Ordinary People as Monks and Mystics* by Marsha Sinetar in the monastery library that intrigued me. Out of nowhere a name came to mind, "monks in the marketplace."

Monks in the Marketplace

I booked the rustic farmhouse at a retreat center in nearby mountains for a full weekend, issued a general invitation to the church community, to "those who would like to experience a weekend as a monk," a time for me to share my experience at the monastery in an experiential way. To my delight and surprise eighteen folks signed up, four of them teens, four others well past seventy, others spread evenly in between. The flow of the weekend was gentle, yet ordered and structured.

Having begun with supper, seated at tables of six, we introduced ourselves over coffee, beginning with those at our table, an easier start for the more introverted. We shared our hopes and expectations for the weekend, and chose a word or phrase to describe how we were feeling as we began. Someone from each table offered a brief summary of the table conversations. We agreed to gather in the meeting room in forty-five minutes, using that time to settle into our rooms and continue to chat, especially with those who were new to us.

Quieted by the crackle and hiss of a roaring fire, I read some verses from Psalm 139, offered a simple prayer, and invited the circle to five minutes of silence. Aware that some would feel more comfortable with some clarity about a plan we might follow, I shared some thoughts about how we might shape our time together. Aware of their curiosity about my monastic experience, I said how much I looked forward to offering some narrative about that month. I indicated that I had arrived with some ideas about how we might experience solitude and silence, as well as how we might structure conversation together. I offered a guideline with which they were familiar, as I usually spoke it one way or another whenever I led groups at the church, that sharing is "an opportunity, not an obligation." They nodded their readiness to begin the process.

Reminding them that at the heart of the biblical narrative are journey stories, I suggested we begin our time together pondering our own journey stories. I had a thought about how we might focus on our spiritual pilgrimage, beginning with a word about where we found ourselves in the present, and that we'd share those reflections with a partner.

The farmhouse is just a few yards from the Appalachian Trail, a trail of 2,175 miles that goes north toward Maine or south toward Georgia, providing virtually every manner of terrain. The trail offered a metaphor. There are steep, arduous ascents, and tedious, demanding descents, right near the farmhouse, I explained—where has your life traversed ascent or descent? The trail may wend through a deep valley floor, dark as dusk at noonday—what "dark valley places" have marked your way? At times the trail is smooth and wide, where your pace can quicken and your pack feels lighter—where has your life journey been easy and undemanding? Quite near the farmhouse, I told them, was a most demanding, even treacherous passage, where unstable rocks slope sharply left to right, where maintaining footing and balancing a pack are risky business—where has your passage seemed unstable and risky? But just beyond that most tiring and unsettling terrain soars Eagle Rock, a breathtaking 360-degree vista to peaks beyond and valleys below—where has your journey been alive with the spectacular, full of awe and wonder?

We sat quietly, each revisiting our life walk, then choosing the terrain that spoke of where we found themselves in the present. The sharing was unhurried, remarkably open and trusting, setting a tone for the rest of our time. The pairs expanded to groups of six, the conversations muted yet animated. A yawn or two suggested gently ending, though several stayed in front of the fireplace after a benediction closed the session.

The first time of silence and solitude, after breakfast and a monastic-style devotion, felt awkward and unfamiliar for this circle of active and busy people. An hour was more than enough. But, at their request, each successive time of quietness was lengthened, increasingly welcomed as gift rather than assignment. We reflected on biblical passages together, walked in pairs like Emmaus Road travelers, found a spot in the meadow to share in smaller groups of four or six, arose at sunrise for Eucharist, and ate some meals in silence. We explored the Buddhist discipline of *mindfulness*, the art of being "present to the present," which we decided was what Paul may have had in mind with *pray continually*.We delighted in mindfully rising and sitting, walking and eating, each movement and motion with awareness, consciousness, fully awake and alive.

Sunday afternoon we reflected on our thirty-six hours together and thought aloud about what might be next. I spread a selection of the Rule of Life of various monastic communities in the center of the circle, ancient orders like Benedictines, Dominicans, and Jesuits, and more modern monastic groups like Little Portion and Nova Nada, each of us choosing one to read carefully. We culled from our reading and shared eight "monastic principles and practices" to which we might make common consent. Four of us agreed to be an editorial team to prepare our own Rule of Life for the name that stuck, Monks in the Marketplace. Then we had a last hour of solitude, during which each of us agreed to write, if only in draft form, a Personal Covenant of Spiritual Practice, to include a daily morning and evening discipline of Bible reading, quietness and prayer; a regimen of spiritual reading, including tapes to play, perhaps in the car; an initial exploration of how to live more simply; and, a commitment to compassionate service to the poor. After each had read the draft of their covenant, the group gathered to pray and lay hands on them.

FAST FORWARD FIVE YEARS

The monks, now twenty-seven in all, set aside three full retreat weekends a year—fall, winter, and spring—the time of silence and solitude lengthening with each gathering. Half-day Saturday or Sunday-afternoon retreats took place in the intervening months. A notebook contained the continually updated Personal Spiritual Covenants so we could pray for and learn from each other's commitment. Each day at seven, morning and evening, we paused, wherever we were, to be mindful of one another, holding each and the group in prayer.

I had returned from that first retreat with some concerns, about how these eighteen people, fresh from an unusual and personally powerful experience, would integrate into the life of the congregation. Mindful that while one can *report* an experience it is more difficult to *share*, how would conversations unfold between the eighteen and those with whom they spoke about the weekend? Might these would-be monks subtly separate from others? How would leadership in the church respond? How would the church's vigorous commitment to outreach and social justice be affected? Three concerns came most clearly into focus.

I had a concern that the group would become quietly elitist, the "truly spiritual folks" in the church, stirring quiet resentment in the congregation. My fear was unwarranted, as it turned out. The notion of disciplined spiritual practice became contagious. Groups of every kind in the church—from committees to ministry teams to the choir—evolved a group spiritual practice as part of their agenda. People constantly approached one of the "monks" seeking guidance and companionship in developing their own spiritual life. Spiritual partnerships formed: sometimes a more seasoned Christian as companion and mentor to one newer to the spiritual walk; longtime friends adding a more intentional spiritual component to their friendship; neighbors meeting for prayer in one another's homes. A circle calling themselves Spiritual Companions began to meet on Tuesday evenings at the church, laypeople rotating leadership, adopting a simple Quakerlike rhythm, opening in silence with quieting music setting a tone and then sharing as the Spirit led: questions, concerns, personal needs, intercessory prayer, words of gratitude typical themes. The circle was always open to newcomers or those who could only come occasionally. Someone assembled a shelf of spiritually focused books in the church library.

I had a concern that the leadership might view this new spiritual focus as a distraction with little to offer the organizational life of the church. That concern was equally unwarranted. A slow, steady, almost invisible transformation seemed at work throughout the church. The official board began to speak more of discernment than merely decision making. People began to come forward to serve, led by a sense of calling and giftedness. Silence and solitude became normative rather than occasional. I remember walking through the sanctuary one Thursday evening wondering where the expected sounds of a choir dutifully practicing had gone. An absolute silence, so rich and beautifully textured that no one seemed ready to end it, lasted for a full fifteen minutes before the director whispered "Amen." One church board member or another would quietly suggest, when a meeting's discussion became intense, when differing opinions edged toward becoming adversarial, or the focus seemed lost and forward momentum faltered, "Why don't we pause, sit quietly together, and pray for individual and collective wisdom." Prayer became the most sought-after common ground, those meditative pauses reminders of whom we served and whose direction we sought. Perhaps the most influential decision, one that began to forge a new paradigm of governance, urged every ministry team, committee, and board to write a mission statement, combining biblical mandate, spiritual discernment, and the work of their team.

I had a concern that the monks would become "merely spiritual folks," quietist and pietistic, withdrawn and passive, one-dimensional in their commitment to silence and solitude. That uneasiness was unwarranted as well. On one of our retreats we each were "assigned" a saint, one of the great mystics of church history, an invisible partner for forty-eight hours, a spiritual companion through our silence and solitude, our biblical exploring and sharing, our meditation and prayer. Meister Eckhart and Juliana of Norwich, Francis of Assisi and Mechtild of Magdeburg, Hildegarde of Bingen and Thomas Aquinas, John of the Cross and Teresa of Avila among them. At Sunday worship we introduced our fellow pilgrim, naming ways in which their stories had interwoven with our own. Over and over a profound paradox was expressed, how these mystics had led us deeper into both communion with God and communion with the human community, especially the poor, isolated, oppressed, and forgotten.

Hildegarde, known as the grandmother of the Rhineland mystics, was a true Renaissance woman: she was a painter and musician, poet and playwright, unrelenting in challenging church corruption, tireless in sheltering the poor and outcast, and she became abbess of a mixed-gender monastery. St. Francis renounced wealth, including his own, stood naked on the cathedral steps leaving all his possessions piled at the door, and then founded a movement of mendicant friars choosing poverty as a visible challenge to the opulence of the church. Mechtild, warned by the church to quiet her constant attack on church corruption, was consistently driven out of town, and several times excommunicated. Meister Eckhart, a passionate preacher and poet, was excommunicated posthumously, likely for his advocacy for women and peasant movements.

MEET JULIE, DELLE, DRAY, AND CAROL

Julie called the week after that retreat asking for a time to chat. Her face signaled an uncharacteristic gravity as she settled into a chair in my office. "Not that I think you would, but I must ask directly that you don't judge me in any way as we talk," she began. I silently nodded. She told me about her wealth, inherited wealth specifically. Her brother and her bankers had firmly counseled that she allow them to manage her assets, make investment decisions, provide distribution of income along guidelines suggested, and designate charitable donations. While that had seemed reasonable and had been, in fact, comforting, she had recently become less comfortable with that arrangement. She paused, looked me in the eye and said in a firm and measured way, "Howard, I am convinced that I have gone as far as I can go with growing and deepening—personally, relationally, and spiritually—until I deal with the reality of my wealth. Will you help me with that?"

The gravity yielded to resolution. She meant what she said. She seemed ready. I mentioned a workshop that, serendipitously, I had just heard about the week before. We called from my office and Julie signed up for an event early the following month with a title that seemed providential, "Women of Inherited Wealth." In the years since, Julie has cofounded a national program offering women assistance and guidance in dealing with money; she has conducted workshops across the country for those wanting to integrate spiritual growth and matters of wealth; she led a series of events at our church titled "Spirituality and Money"; and she has become a generous, conscious, intentional philanthropist. Most important, she broke through her personal impasse and renewed her own spiritual journeying.

Dray, recently retired and struggling quietly with some physical problems, had been a rather shy and quiet newcomer to the church and, by his admission, an unlikely candidate to become a monk. He became an enthusiastic marketplace monk and, paradoxically, as he named it, as the retreats nurtured his *inward* spiritual journeying, an *outward*, mission-focused journey came to life. When he heard the church was hosting Father Roger Desir, an Anglican priest from Haiti who came to the church for periodic rest and renewal from his demanding and exhausting work in Port au Prince, Dray and his wife, Carol, offered their home as a place to stay. From the first cup of tea they shared in the den, a deep bond began to form between these two older, but still vital, men.

Dray joined a mission-group delegation that spent ten days in Haiti the following June and became a vigorous advocate and supporter of Father Desir's Anglican Center. Coincidently, George Schultz, then secretary of state in the Reagan administration, flew to Haiti on the same plane. Carol laughed that George surely went to Petionville, the enclave of the rich and powerful, his only source of briefing about Haitian reality, while they went to Cite Sole, a community Mother Teresa called the "poorest neighborhood on the planet." Who got to know the real Haiti? Dray had decided charity was not enough, but an agenda of social justice was at hand. Dray came to call himself a "contemplative activist."

Delle didn't waste any time. I knew her only as "the woman with the cast" when she signed up for a monk's retreat, and shortly thereafter she registered for a mission trip to Mexico. Delle was trim and attractive. She was bright and articulate, her distinctive voice always impeccably clear. No wonder—she was an actress appearing most often in television ads. She lived with her husband in an upscale neighborhood. She had no idea, she would later confess, where all this was about to take her. "Everything, yes, just about everything, changed. Turned upside down and inside out," as she put it. "I'm not sure I know what I thought about God when I came to church that first Sunday. And I'm not sure my thoughts about God got any clearer, but God's calling in my life became irresistibly clear."

A year later she had amicably separated from her husband and moved to a small apartment. A second trip to Mexico lent greater shape and clarity to her calling, which led her to enroll in seminary. Upon graduation and ordination, she directed a mission center in Mexico for a year, and then accepted a call to work in an indigenous village in Chiapas, the most turbulent region of Mexico. So much for anxiety that the monks would become *merely spiritual!*

Only One Pastor's Story

This is one pastor's story and the chronicle of one church's journey. Another pastor, another congregation, would share a different narrative. An African American pastor warned me of a racial/cultural bias, suggesting that humming a favorite hymn, breaking into robust singing, even drumming, might be his people's pathway to becoming more deeply rooted in the heart of God. A Native American minister reminded me that chanting in his tribe's native language, accompanied by sacred movement, would best accompany his community's quieting of heart and mind. But each agreed that unreflective busyness—the rush that penetrates so much of a faith community's life, our agenda so pressing that we forget to seek the mind and will of God—detours and distracts from faithfulness.

As a pastor and preacher, consultant and teacher, I live in a world of words. I speak thousands of them a week. I speak *about* God in varying settings. I speak *to* God when I pray. But I am less practiced in listening. Jesus was a listener. Henri Nouwen, reflecting on Mark 1:35–39, Jesus arising before dawn and praying alone in a lonely place, reminds us that if Jesus is to follow God's will and not his own, speak God's words and not his own, he must quietly, constantly listen. "Somehow we know," Nouwen writes, "that without silence words lose their meaning, that without listening speaking no longer heals . . . let us look closely at both our life in action and our life in solitude."[4] I must constantly renew my personal commitment and discipline to listening. And how quickly, amid the rush of things, I forget.

I THINK I HEAR A CRICKET

The story of an unlikely friendship and a poignant moment may be a place to end. Adam, a high-powered, upwardly mobile, robust and vigorous New York ad agency executive was considering summer vacation options. Maybe the Hamptons—no, too upscale and contrived. Maybe the Catskills—no, too programmed and familiar. Then, as quickly as the unlikely notion popped into his mind, he grabbed it: a week at a dude ranch in Wyoming. As radically different as any vacation spot he'd visited, he loved it all immediately: the crackle of the campfire each night, as he settled gingerly onto the log bench, protecting aching muscles from the day's trail ride; the taste of sizzling steaks and steaming baked potatoes; the big-sky sunsets and spectacular colors of dawn; solid night's sleep in the rustic bunkhouse.

One afternoon, accompanied by the muted squeak of leather as he pulled the saddle from a muscled palomino, he fell into conversation with a ranch hand, a Native American named Dawson Tall Grass from the nearby reservation. It became an afternoon ritual, this unlikely sharing by persons different in every conceivable way. "Would you come to my house for supper and meet my family?" the ranch hand asked hesitantly. "I'd love to," was the enthusiastic response. This odd-couple friendship deepened enough that the last afternoon's good-bye was poignant. Hearing it himself as odd and awkward, Adam offered the customary departing tagline, "If you're ever in New York, you'd be welcome to visit."

Three months later that familiar weathered voice was on the line, "Adam, I've had some money saved and haven't been sure how to use it. Now I know. I want to come to New York." Arrangements made, Dawson arrived on an evening flight, unpacked and settled into the guest room in Adam's midtown apartment. In the morning they went for a walk before breakfast, chatting as they strolled, Dawson startled by all the movement and noise, having to almost shout to be heard over the din. As they approached an intersection, the Native American touched Adam's arm inviting him to stop. "I think I hear a cricket," he said. Adam laughed, "I don't think we have crickets in New York City. Besides, if we did, you couldn't hear one if you tried." "No, I do, I hear a cricket, and it's ahead of us." They approached the corner, Dawson listening with an attentiveness Adam had never seen. "It's this way," and they crossed an avenue. Pausing for a moment, "It's this way," and they crossed a numbered street. A low granite wall ringed a small park at the corner, with squat, broad cement urns holding evergreens every three or four feet. Dawson approached the third urn, gently parted the leaves at the base of the tree, and there was a cricket!

Utterly amazed, Adam's face said it all. "My ears are no different from yours, Adam. You could learn to hear the cricket too. It's all a matter of what you're listening for."[5]

5

BREATHE ON THE EMBERS

The Gift of Patience

*I*t is late afternoon in a little town just below the summit that offers the first vista of the walls of the great city. Jesus finally arrives at Bethany. Martha, then Mary, chide him for his inexplicable delay. Jesus is moved, the narrator tells us. He weeps. And then orders the stone rolled away. They warn of the stench that will waft from the tomb. "He's been dead four days," the grievers moan. Jesus prays, and then calls into the cave, "Lazarus, come out!" And he does. "Unwrap him," Jesus instructs, "so he can go free."

Some years ago our family built a passive solar home, heated by solar gain and a wood-burning stove. Each night I'd load our Vermont Castings stove, carefully set the damper, and hope the fire would last until dawn. Each morning I'd eagerly clank open the door, hoping glowing coals awaited. When the bed was glowing brightly, I'd simply drop in some sticks of kindling, add a log or two, and head off for the day. When the hearth was gray and cold, I'd have to start from scratch. But most mornings, what appeared at first glance gray and cold revealed at closer look an ember or two still pulsing with life, however tentative and fragile. Breathing new life into the hearth became just that—breathing. Ever so gently at first: too briskly would blow the embers apart, and too cautiously would let them cool and die. Mindful breathing just might coax a sparse scattering of coals into a first tiny and tentative flame, ready for a deftly placed kindling, and only then a log or two.

Some churches have become a cold, gray hearth. Nary a sign of life. Others have stoked and tend a full and robust fire. But in between, I am convinced, there are some congregations, maybe more than we'd guess, awaiting a discerning eye to bend close enough to see the glow of scattered embers, breathing gently to invite those coals to burn a touch brighter, patiently awaiting a first leap of new flame, only then to blow with vigor to fan the spreading fire. *Breathe on the embers, even if the hearth looks dead.*

Scholars suggest there may well be *two* Pentecost stories in Scripture. The more familiar, Acts 2, features high drama, the Spirit roaring as a rushing wind, speaking in foreign tongues and dynamic preaching. The less familiar story unfolds on resurrection Sunday evening, Jesus appearing through locked doors, as the disciples tremble in confusion and fear. Subtle, undramatic, quietly understated, Jesus breathes his peace on them (John 20:21–22). *Breathe on the embers, even if the hearth looks dead.*

I have a particular kind of congregation in mind, and a broad array of specific congregations. They have stories to tell, which I am honored to tell for them. They don't make headlines. You will not find them profiled in a denominational magazine. Reporters don't write features about them in local newspapers. They are unheralded and undramatic. And they are signs of hope.

I want to name names, particular people and specific churches. I am thinking about Jay and Catherine at Trinity Church, a church with a heavy spirit, cautious and wounded, emerging from twenty years of failed pastorates as Jay began his ministry. Knowing them as hesitant about new ideas, close-knit yet distant at the same time, tentative about their future, what a surprise to find a praise band leading the hymns a Sunday I visited, not only an unlikely innovation, but the foursome in the band an unlikely circle. The bulletin announced a liturgical dancer the following Sunday. I eagerly await Trinity's newsletter each month to see what new spiritual growth opportunity, biblical reflection group, or mission team activity has begun. Jay and Catherine called into the cave and new life is being unwrapped.

Terri and Alex come to mind, back-to-back pastors at Honey Brook Church. When I first visited Honey Brook, the congregation had cordoned off two-thirds of the church, hoping that by huddling together in the front pews they would look like more of a crowd. Some older members in moments of candor wondered how long they could stay open. I returned one Sunday a year or two later, a day to honor a longtime faithful leader, and was astounded to find the church so crowded that an usher had to help me find a pew! Three years later I beamed as they cut the ribbon to open a new educational wing. Terri, then Alex, breathed on the embers and the hearth was bright and glowing.

Tony and Katie graduated in the same seminary class, and Tony was hired to serve as youth minister at Westminster Church, one of his denomination's fastest-growing congregations, where he promptly doubled the youth group membership and calendar of activities. A few months later Katie joined the staff as an educator. But a faltering little church just a mile or two away caught their eye, and then their hearts. They convinced Westminster to release them from some of their duties while maintaining full-time salaries so they could work together to see if there was any life left at Dilworthtown Church. A handful remained, proudly announcing themselves as charismatics, dauntless in a belief they had held unwaveringly over twenty years of decline that a time of renewal would come. Tony and Katie, more evangelical than charismatic, tuned to that vision and hope, faint as it might have seemed. They affirmed it, encouraged it, and expanded it. Several families from Westminster agreed to "seed" the church with their presence for a first year. The pump primed slowly, but first spurts and gurgles have become a steady flow.

Susannah, recently ordained, was invited to serve a once-thriving Swedenborgian congregation now worshiping in the farm house at Temenos, their denomination's countryside retreat center, having sold their massive sanctuary in Philadelphia. A wealthy and dominant presence at the beginning of the twentieth century, the congregation had not prospered in the following hundred years.

Susannah inherited a "holding operation," as she called it, a "hang-
ing in there" mentality at best, with little more than survival in
mind, a gathering place for a shrinking circle of faithful but aging
old-timers. But this young pastor had a broader dream—yet not
so broad as to be naive or unrealistic. She saw broader possibilities—combining insistent vision with steady patience. Building
on a commitment to inclusivity, legacy of Emanuel Swedenborg,
she nurtured Temenos as a multifaith gathering place. Susannah
sensed something intuitively contemporary in the teachings of their
founder of three centuries earlier, and soon a scattering of younger
families began to appreciate that message and attend worship. They
soon began, at lay initiative, a small Sunday school. Tapping the
mystical core of their tradition, a Spiritual Seekers group formed
and Dream Sharing Workshops were well attended. Broad smiles
now light the faces of those older members, many in their eighties
and nineties, as they squeeze the folding chairs in tighter rows to ac-
commodate the thoroughly unexpected congregational growth.

Stan, having served ever larger churches across a long pastoral
career, arrived at Wyncote Church at age sixty to preside over what
some at his denominational office viewed as a dying church that
ought to consider closing. Celebrating the fifth anniversary of his
work there, amid totally unexpected growth and vitality, a huge
poster displayed a collage of appreciations from the congregation:
"Your steadiness and good judgment gave us fresh confidence"
. . . "You are above all a pastor who cares for us, which you've
shown in so many thoughtful ways" . . . "You didn't miss a beat
in folding us into your great heart" . . . "You have been a wonderfully humble person, teaching us humility in the process" . . .
"Your greatest leadership trait is your willingness to allow others
to take the lead" . . . "When controversy arose, and we've always
been good at that, you helped us respect each other and keep lines
of communication open."

Owen, an African American pastor, consciously chose a smaller,
struggling congregation after a decade of serving a large and flourishing church. Sensing fatigue and deep discouragement, he offered

a single proposal for the first year. He asked if a dozen laypeople would meet with him weekly for Bible study and prayer. They would have no agenda except to explore the Word of God and pray as the Spirit led. These weekly gatherings were not posed as a strategy, a means to a preconceived end, a church-revitalization tactic. But it became just that. After three months a second circle formed, and after six two more. Church attendance began to swell. Conversations became lighter, more punctuated with laughter. A church supper was planned, spontaneously, by a group sipping coffee after a service. "Didn't the early church spend a lot of time eating together?" someone observed at a supper, which became monthly affairs.

Greg, as gently paced as his southern drawl, healed deep wounds of a congregational fracture that had lingered for twenty years in a rural church in Pennsylvania's Amish country. Catherine, who was invited to serve a church outside a small city whose members reluctantly described their division and conflict as "lethal and un-christian," began by convening a series of luncheon groups with the task to frame a Relationship Covenant, a biblically based yet practical and concrete statement of the qualities of communica-tion and relationship they wanted to learn to embody in their life together. The final version was printed in large type, made avail-able to each member, a framed version hung in each room in the church.

I do not know any of these wonderful stories in their entirety, though I have been graced with significant exposure to each. They are stories too intimate to be shared at greater length. There is pri-vacy I do not want to invade. So I am opting for a literary license about which I want to be clear. I am choosing to introduce a real church, opening with a real incident, to tell a more detailed and complete story of the kind of church of which I have been speak-ing. Vested Suits One and Two, as unlikely as they seem, are real in the humorous tale that gets us started. But Pastor Todd is what I'll call a composite character and the narrative in and around Amagansett Church is a composite narrative. Every element in the story of Todd and the Amagansett Church, adapted only to fit this narrative, occurred in the real-life experience of pastors and congregations I know personally.

MEET TODD AND AMAGANSETT CHURCH

Some years ago, during the months a search committee interviewed candidates to fill their vacant pulpit, I was asked to moderate the official board of a Protestant church in Amagansett, a small town at the eastern end of Long Island. The church was not-so-endearingly dubbed the "Am-against-it Church" by the other pastors in the judicatory. Having proceeded uneventfully through most of the agenda, a clearly younger-than-the-rest board member, leaning forward in his chair and speaking with high energy and enthusiasm, offered an idea. To be fair, this idea was short on clarity and detail, but, for one willing to look more closely, had significant potential. More important, it was proposed by a young person, in short supply in this aging congregation. All eyes turned in unison to Vested Suit Number One, the parish patriarch, who actually said, I kid you not, "Am against it." Nothing more. As if orchestrated by some invisible signal, all eyes turned to Vested Suit Number Two. And yes, doubt me as you might, the same words, "Am against it," without further comment. The proposal was defeated. Within weeks that young man and his family had found another church.

The congregation in Amagansett functioned like a family-size church even though its weekly attendance was well over fifty members.[1] The influence exercised by Vested Suits One and Two make the point. At a monthly board meeting I sat next to the one who was president, watching him place on the table in front of him, close enough for me to see, a set of handwritten minutes. I asked, to make conversation, "Minutes from the last meeting?" "No," he replied in a monotone, "for *tonight's* meeting," including each item of business; each motion duly noted as made, seconded, and passed; and even the new business carefully itemized.

Theories relating to congregational size warn about the predictable and inevitable limitations of influence a pastor can have in a family-size church, defined as up to fifty at Sunday worship. These theories caution, "what Family Size Churches want from their clergy is pastoral care, period."[2] Clergy make pastoral calls, lead worship, and befriend the parent figures—but never disagree with them. And do not yield to any urging, however persuasively or urgently offered and no matter how it might align with your own desire to speak, to challenge their authority. Ironic as it surely is, keep your promising ideas and creative possibilities to yourself. They'll either be promptly rebuffed ("Am against it") or tentatively and reluctantly—more likely resentfully—tried, and then ultimately fail. Folks in the family-size church like things just as they are. Serve your two or three years, then graciously move on.

When I heard that a new pastor was called to the Amagansett Church, and was told by a colleague what a bright, enterprising, and promising young man he was, I was poised to issue appropriate warnings of my own. I chose, instead, to introduce myself with the promise that I would be close by and available, and a commitment to pray daily for him, the congregation, and his new ministry. From time to time we'd meet for lunch.

Todd *was* bright and enterprising—words well chosen—as well as young and enthusiastic, but he was also sensitive and patient, perhaps wiser than his years. He would surely need a substantial measure of tolerance, readying for his first encounter with "Am against it" Vested Suits One and Two. Someone warned him about those who'd likely challenge him on each and every front, which he chose to hear as invitation to make some pastoral calls. Alert and insightful, he discerned almost immediately some steps to take that might be promising, but he decided to put them on "hold" for a season. He visited in people's homes and, since almost everyone worked in the village, dropped by where parishioners worked. Genuinely curious about the church's history, he set up some tables in the church's spacious narthex and invited folks to bring memorabilia that told the church's story across the decades. Starting slowly, a momentum of energy and enthusiasm picked up, as yellowed and faded photos of a generation or two ago appeared. Posters for wartime suppers and invitations to bring coat hangers to provide metal to support the war effort found a place on the table. An octogenarian brought church newsletters dating from her Sunday school days. Everyone smiled as they carefully leafed through their first pictorial directory on the occasion of a church anniversary. The pastor invited parishioners in groups of ten or twelve for coffee and conversation after church. In a quiet, engaging, genuinely interested way, he'd ask, "Tell us when you first came to this church. Who was there to greet you? Who do you remember with fondness and gratitude? Who was in the choir, taught Sunday school, served as ushers? How has this church guided you, supported you, taught you, touched you? What challenges did this church rise to over the years? What are its proudest moments? How did the church reach out to our community?"

Some older women complained, with thinly veiled judgment and annoyance, that the younger women showed little interest in joining the Women's Guild. Todd asked to be invited to the next meeting and made an ingenious suggestion. "Do you remember the founding story of your group?" he asked. Looks of nostalgia crept across their faces as they began to tell, in increasingly animated ways, each adding details others were forgetting, the story of their first gatherings back when these gray-haired women were the mothers of toddlers. As each added a piece of the story, smiles broadened on their faces. "Remember, Sara, you called me, and I called you, Lillian, and we all got together at my house for coffee while our babies napped in coaches in the living room. That was our first meeting," Mary reported. "And we each agreed to invite one other woman," added Lillian, "and soon we were a dozen." "We began to meet at the church and took turns babysitting," Eileen reminisced.

Careful not to interrupt, only when the story was fully, wonderfully told, Todd artfully suggested, "Maybe there's an option to trying to get the young women to join your group. Maybe you could help them birth their own group, just like you birthed yours. You could be their midwives. Maybe you could help them begin a 'founding story' that they can retell years from now." Quizzical looks gave way to nods which became an increasingly energetic conversation about just how they might do that. Two weeks later, responding to handwritten invitations, the older and younger women met. Two months later the church bulletin carried dates and times for *two* women's groups. Todd gently blew on the sparks, barely glowing embers flickering into fresh flame, soon to become, it turned out, a hearty fire.

Not every effort bore fruit. Sometimes when you blow into a hearth you get soot on your face! Searching for a way to connect to the youth of the community, who seemed sullen and distant, he began to dress in jeans and boots and brightly colored shirts. A delegate from that older women's group brought the word, none too gently, about "appropriate dress for our minister." And stopping for a beer where he noticed laborers congregated after work got the rumor mill going immediately. Todd's wife caught first word of the buzz around the grapevine. Someone just happened to share with her that there were still living members of a now-defunct Women's Christian Temperance Union.

One autumn Wednesday afternoon, the trees brilliant with the yellows and reds of late October, Todd couldn't resist going for a brisk walk. No particular itinerary in mind, providence, he would later decide, took him by Wendell's house, Vested Suit Number One. The old former fisherman, his cheeks lined by years of facing into brisk, biting winter winds on the water, looked up with a warmer welcome than Todd expected, motioned him into the yard. Leaves crunched beneath his feet as he approached. He noticed, as he got closer, that the little old dory on which Wendell was feverishly working, nestled upside down on old sawhorses, was, to put it kindly, a long way from seaworthiness. "Pretty nasty, huh?" Wendell smiled, something warmer about him on his own turf, his words and the smile setting Todd at ease. "I found her in the weeds down near the inlet," he explained. "Probably broke free from her mooring in a storm. Owner likely just let her go. I mean, look at her. Hardly worth the trouble to haul her home." Then in words more tender than Todd would ever have expected, Wendell told how that old boat somehow beckoned to him, sort of invited him, to drag her through the weeds to his yard and restore her to her former beauty.

"You've probably noticed. It's become more of a job than I expected," he explained. "I'd remove that faded coat of brown and return the wood to its original grain, which I had reason to guess was rather fine," he explained as his initial plan. "But I'd barely brushed on some paint remover and put my scraper to work across the hull, when the first chips of brown paint jumped from the surface, and there, underneath, was a faded coat of blue. Oh well, a bit more work than anticipated. The brown is mostly gone, you still see a spot or two under the gunnels, and I was making headway on the blue, when a coat of green peeked through! Oh my. Yes, a streak of white, a logical first coat for a dory, followed, but then, finally, a first glimpse of natural grain. Now the work is more tedious."

Neither one proposed it, so it wasn't really a decision, but just about every Wednesday afternoon Todd found himself wandering back to Wendell's yard, where the old man methodically continued his work. A second month into their meetings, Wendell shouted with delight as Todd approached, "I gotta surprise for you," and he waved his pastor toward the barn. "It got too cold to work outside, so I set up in here. Besides, it was too dusty to finish her out there." With the delight of planning a surprise party, with a sense of fanfare and ceremony, Wendell pulled the chain on an old fluorescent ceiling fixture and there she was, reflecting the light in shimmering elegance—the old dory, fully, beautifully restored. Only Wendell's face shone brighter than that freshly varnished hull.

"I put on some water for tea. Wanna join me?" Wendell asked, and they made their way through a back door into the kitchen. Todd pulled back an old oak chair and soon a steaming mug of tea sat on the old and stained oilcloth table covering. A weathered picture frame peeking out from the shadows of a corner cabinet caught the pastor's eye. A woman appearing to be in her forties peered through the smudged glass. "Likely Wendell's wife, who'd died twenty years ago," Todd thought to himself, about whom he rarely speaks, he'd been told. "That's Emily," he heard the old man softly say, making Todd uneasy. He had hoped his glance had gone unnoticed. Before Todd could mutter an apology, as if Wendell had long awaited this moment, he leaned back in his chair, hooked his thumbs under his suspenders, and talked for fifteen minutes, encouraged only by subtle nods and an occasional whispered "uh-huh." Emily was no longer a stranger to Todd.

Wednesday afternoon tea became a weekly ritual, the odd couple chatting with easy rapport and growing trust. They reminisced one day about how that old dory had brought them together. A question, even Todd found curious as it popped into his mind, announced it wanted to be asked, so he asked it—"I wonder what the natural grain of Amagansett Church looks like?"—and then just as quickly he wished he'd not. "Wendell's probably never read a verse of poetry and probably couldn't spell metaphor," he chided himself. Wendell's crisp and insightful response interrupted his self-consciousness: "Bet we'd have to peel off a lot of paint to find out!"

To everyone's surprise, Wendell, most recently known mostly as Vested Suit Number One, originator of "Am against It," became Todd's advocate. A teenager who played the guitar agreed to lead a praise song to replace the middle hymn—unheard of, unthinkable, except Wendell had nodded affirmatively when the idea came to the church board. Someone dared to propose a dance for the youth in the church hall, and Wendell seconded the motion. Vested Suit Number Two caught the spirit, wore an open-collared shirt to the next meeting, and ventured his first smile in anyone's memory. The local print shop submitted a lively design for a church brochure, and multicolored posters to place in the windows of willing shop-keepers in the village. The vote was unanimous.

Not everything went so smoothly. Todd was no stranger to wiping that soot from his face! A college student, a newcomer, was majoring in dance. Surely he'd need no official vote to invite her to perform a liturgical dance one Sunday. Wrong! A chorus of scowls sent the message. One Sunday, hoping to create a more casual mood, Todd left his robe on its hanger, placed a stool between the front pews, where he sat, his feet propped on its rung and preached. An older woman's asking if perhaps his robe needed pressing, which she'd be glad to do, clearly spoke for more than just herself.

Not every new idea flourished. The circle of chairs appeared inviting, in the shade of an enormous tree in a meadow behind the church, the setting for an informal outdoor service designed for the summer population. Only a handful came and the service disbanded after a third disappointing Sunday. A workshop for single parents was offered to respond to an obvious community need, but only two participants arrived. Volunteer tutors offered after-school help to struggling high school students, but not a single student came by those Thursday afternoons.

Everyone noticed when a newcomer arrived at worship, because it happened so seldom. Suddenly there was a lot to notice. A young couple with two kids arrived, and a single mother with teens. It had never occurred to church members to invite neighbors to worship, and no one paid much attention if a moving van arrived down the street. That changed.

The sweet aroma of arriving casseroles had not wafted through the church kitchen in a decade, but regular covered-dish suppers drew more folks each month. That hadn't been Todd's idea, but grew out of a conversation among those cleaning up in the kitchen after a coffee hour. They appointed themselves a committee and planned the first gathering. A middle-school teacher, an infrequent worshiper, became a regular and offered to start a Sunday evening youth group. There weren't enough children yet for graded classes, but a retired teacher, an "everybody's grandmother" type, found curriculum for a mixed-age class and recruited some mothers to assist. Lay leaders were starting to catch the spirit, informal teams linking with board committees to recruit helpers, start programs, and plan activities. Todd had a chance to sit back and watch.

Todd saw the glow, faint as it may have been; embers nestled, almost invisible, under a coat of grayness in that congregational hearth. He breathed ever so gently at first. A too-hearty puff would have blown them apart. Someone brought some kindling. It took a while before a first log could catch. But, with patience and persistence in delicate balance, a hearty fire dances brightly with fresh logs nearby when it's time. If he had not bridled his creativity and harnessed his enthusiasm, the resistance and resentment would have overwhelmed him. It is tedious work, peeling off layers of paint, more than you'd guess as you began, careful not to cut too deeply, awaiting, and then gently coaxing forth natural grain. Easier, of course, just to throw on another coat of paint. Todd's first glimpse at Amagansett Church might have seemed, for all the world, like looking into a cave with disturbing tomblike qualities. But he called into that cave in a way that new life emerged, awaiting gentle, life-renewing unwrapping.

OKAY, HOW?

Todd's story, as I have told it, can seem romanticized and simplistic. As he lived it, it was anything but. Basically confident, positive, and resilient, he was no stranger to feeling disappointed and disheartened. More than once he'd updated his resume with moving on in mind. Fresh in his memory were those times when he nearly "lost it" in frustration and fatigue. He had a towel at hand to throw in at any time. Members of the church were similarly challenged. At a celebration of Todd's fifth anniversary as pastor, they reminisced over lunch about those years, some confessing that they had thought of leaving too. Too many new ideas, too quickly, a circle of longtime members admitted. Newer members chimed in that they wondered at times if the old-timers would never change. They'd almost given up, they acknowledged, when all went so slowly. This work is not easy and the outcome is never assured. It takes a steadiness of pace and staying power.

Remember when Jesus said to that inquiring lawyer, "You are so close to the kingdom of heaven." I've often wondered, in the end, did he close the gap . . . or was "so close" as close as he got? Remember the compassion with which Jesus watched that young rich man as he walked away, unwilling to relinquish his wealth, unable or unready to accept invitation to the very life he came seeking. Does some unrecorded story chronicle his return, the passage of time forging readiness in him, as it had with Nicodemus? I see congregations stir fresh vision, generate new excitement, reorganize for mission and ministry, seeming "so close" to renewal and revitalization, only to snap back, "so close" being as close as they get. I must admit to some uneasiness when I remember someone who recently observed: even Jesus gave up on the church of his day. There was such logic to launching his ministry in a synagogue among the folks who had long awaited his arrival. No need to reinvent that wheel. Early in his ministry, Jesus appears to abandon the synagogue to take his mission and movement to the marketplace, the streets, hillsides outside of town, on the road. People who argue that the church is dead are persuasive. And some churches are! But it takes a knowing, discerning, penetrating look by pastors and laity together to perceive those barely glowing embers, to believe a fine grain lies beneath layers of paint.

Similar metaphors have laced their ways through these congregational narratives—uncovering that which is hidden, patiently coaxing forth what can only emerge over time—metaphors that wend their way through scriptural narratives as well. What lies beneath, within, at the center? The Bible tells and retells this story line.

"Peter," the rock, seems a hardly apt or discerning new name for mercurial, unsteady Simon, but Jesus patiently coaxes forth the rocklikeness lying dormant within (John 1:42). It took all-night wrestling, after twelve years on the run, for devious, deceptive Jacob to emerge as Israel (Gen. 32:22–32). Only after murdering an Egyptian guard in a fit of rage, years of hiding out on the plains of Midian, and rapid backpedaling as the voice spoke in the burning bush, could Moses finally surrender to the awesome call of leading God's people to freedom (Exod. 2:11–15, 3:1–22). Jeremiah celebrates God's desire to write the covenant on hearts (Jer. 31:31–34), Paul appeals to the "inner selves" of the Ephesians (Eph. 3:16 GNT), and Jesus seeks a home in our hearts (John 14:23). Biblical journey stories seem always longer than logic or reason would argue. A two-week walk became a forty-year wilderness trek. Already suspiciously old, it took a quarter-century for

Abram to become Abraham. Closer observation reveals that Saul, after the drama of Damascus, did not commence immediate and fruitful preaching, finally emerging as Paul only after a decade plus has passed.

There may be individuals within these apparently lifeless churches in whom a sense of possibility lingers, who await gentle, hopeful encouragement. They need steady pastoral leadership, preaching tuned to idioms and realities of their everyday life, patient and attentive pastoral care. They may be ready to thrive on intuitive and empathetic listening, subtle artfulness and exquisite timing, high regard and gentle affection.

Visitors to the Duke University campus speak of its sensitive and welcoming architecture, magnificent chapel, its rolling hills and gracious gardens, but always time their visit to hear the carillon, as the singing of these precise and elegantly crafted bells cascades through the campus. Forged in Holland, they were a gift of a wealthy alumnus, who stood by as the installation neared completion, anxiously awaiting a first thrilling performance. A single bell sounded, and then another, and then others in perfectly timed sequence. What can only be fairly described as raucous, cacophonous noise echoed forth. The donor cringed with discomfort and upset. They had sung so beautifully when they had claimed his heart in Holland. What had happened? Swiftly turning toward the technician supervising the installation, his gaze fixed, even accusing, he was comforted by his soft and knowing look in return, even before he explained. "The bells need to be tuned," he said reassuringly, "to this altitude, to this climate, to the temperatures and humidity of this terrain." The tuning process demanded precision, artistry, and focused expertise, a sensitive ear and manual dexterity, taking several days.

Jesus "tuned" the gospel message to the specific "terrain" of a given day's teaching and preaching, the everyday life of those in that locale; the uniqueness of each person he encountered, each one's unique biography, unique gifts and needs, and individual level of readiness and receptivity. I am struck by the rich multiplicity that characterized his teaching; newness and boundless creativity the norm, a given metaphor, story, or simile rarely repeated. The essential message must not be compromised, of course, but his framing of it is wondrously innovative and constantly changing. Noting homes under construction, he makes a point with a simple tale of wise and foolish locations for a sturdy, durable house. Farms as far as the eye can see, he deftly crafts stories with an agricultural motif—seeds and their sower, a tree and its fruit, workers in a vineyard, an unfruitful fig tree, a lost sheep, a bountiful harvest and bigger barns, a treasure buried in a field. Wandering among men pulling their boats onto the beach and hauling nets ashore, nautical themes seem apt—full and empty nets, searching for a priceless pearl, fishers of men. Seeing housewives in the marketplace, Jesus told tales as humble as a woman's everyday routine—a lost dowry coin, the working of yeast, young girls and their wedding lamps. Seeing well-dressed, likely wealthy citizens, his stories become challenging and confronting—compassion for the hungry, homeless, and imprisoned; a greedy farmer, heedless wedding guests, the other Lazarus.

SPOTTING CHURCHES WITH EMBERS

Analysis, paralysis. How does information become transformation? Where does the rubber of the theoretical meet the road of implementation? How do we identify these churches and equip clergy and laity to do this work? I have two proposals, each of which I've had opportunity to field test: one in search of a process to identify the kind of churches of which I am speaking; the other to find and equip pastors like Todd and lay leaders with whom they work in partnership—those ready, or who can become ready, to give this kind of quietly redemptive leadership.

Working with a Lutheran bishop, I have developed a Congregational Assessment Process—a simple, short-term, financially reasonable intervention plan for churches. It is vitally important at the outset that congregations being offered this option are not only clear about what it offers, and how it offers it, but exhibit a minimal level of felt commitment. I have worked with too many churches where the urging of a judicatory official, the hopes of a pastor, and a consensus among the church board were not met with adequate readiness by the membership. Remember that Jesus, with one possible exception, did not heal at his own initiative but watched for signals of readiness in those who approached him. He instructed his disciples to share the good news where they were welcome, but move on from where they were not. Even Jesus, unwelcome in a particular town, "could do no powerful work there."

The typical assessment process involves the following ingredients and phases, though you will notice that commitment to the whole process awaits a right and ready moment. The pastor and official board agree initially to only a *first* step, understanding that it may become the *only* step: an initial visit to include an hour-and-a-half consultation with the pastor and a two-hour consultation with the official board, including the pastor. The goals of the interview with the pastor include establishing a basic rapport and trust between the pastor and myself, welcoming a glimpse of the church from the pastor's perspective: its history, present circumstances, and vision for its future; its strengths and weaknesses and most pressing issues; the basic morale or spirit, what seems both hopeful and discouraging; and the pastor's goals for the church. I hope to get a feel for the pastor's readiness, personally and professionally, to lead the congregation into its future.

I begin the session with the official board scripture reading and prayer, important first words in terms of how I do my work. I introduce myself, usually sharing my call to ministry, now decades ago, and offering a thumbnail sketch of my ministry to date, with emphasis on my consulting work of the last fifteen years. I ask them to introduce themselves, sharing their names, how long they have attended the church, and what they appreciate and celebrate about the congregation. I invite them to share words and phrases that characterize the highest and best about the church, adding, if they'd like, ways in which the church has touched them personally. I watch for not only what they say, but how easily and comfortably these appreciations are expressed, or not. Do answers flow or is there searching for words, awkward pauses and silences? What is their tone of voice? Often this sharing becomes quite personal and touching, widows or widowers sharing the quality of caring when their spouses died, how casseroles showed up when someone was incapacitated for a time, or those who visited or wrote when someone was in the hospital.

Mindful of an agreed end time, I move to a second phase. With conscious intention to frame all input in the positive, I may ask next: What do you wish were different at the church? What qualities would you love to be able to add to what you appreciate about the church? What worries you about the church just now? I often end that sharing with a touch of humor: "Suppose I was en route to your house for dinner, got lost, and called you on my cell phone. What's your first question?" "Where are you?" is the obvious response. "Suppose I am embarrassingly lost," I continue, "so I pick a less embarrassing location and tell you I am there?" Point made. You cannot get to where you're going if you do not know where you are. Church leaders must mount the integrity and courage to see as clearly as they can, with neither positive nor negative spin, without rose-colored or dark glasses, where the church is in the present—balancing strengths and weaknesses, matters of hope and discouragement, good news and less-than-good news as they are able to discern it.

This is often a good time to refill coffee cups and take a break. When they return I invite them to a mini-discernment process, often citing Acts 16 and Paul's experience at Troas, because I see ironic humor in it. Paul, true to character, wants to act decisively, plotting the next leg of their missionary journeying. Deciding to head east, the way was blocked; rethinking, they headed north, same outcome. Whatever the problem—the bridge was out, the camel drivers were on strike, the ship was cancelled—they discerned their foiled plans as the Spirit at work. Then a Macedonian from the west beckoned in a dream. Eugene Peterson's *The Message* delightfully translates a key verse, "The dream gave Paul his map" (Acts 16:10).[3] "How might your dream provide your church's map forward? What future do you sense God is calling you to?" I find a phrase I have borrowed from the United Methodist Annual Conference of New Jersey provocative, "What is the *next* church God is calling *this* church to become?" I take notes, capturing the content of their vision, but listening for their tone as they speak, the spirit that permeates their words, nostalgia wrapped as vision, reality and possibility mingling with the fanciful, even whimsical. The oft-quoted phrase is unsettling, "where there is no vision, the people perish" (Prov. 29:18 KJV)—not struggle, limp along, risk becoming lost . . . but *perish!*

"It's time for a reality check," I announce. With that collective vision in mind, being as honest as you are able, what do you have *going for you*—what are the resources, attitudes, assets, and strengths that create momentum in the direction of your vision? And, this question that invites the most thoroughgoing candor, what is *working against you?* Numbers, finances, too few committed people, and demographics are most frequently named.

A final question seems the most important, "And where are *you*, each of you personally, in all of this?" The responses range broadly from high energy, renewed enthusiasm, fresh hopefulness, and a contagious excitement, to confessions of discouragement, acknowledgment of long-standing fatigue, and a forthright admission of hopelessness.

"Where do we go from here?" is the question I hope they'll ask. I propose that they find a Sunday in the not-too-distant future when I will preach at their morning worship and lead an after-church luncheon workshop, usually an hour and a half, in which the very same format I have used that evening will be offered to the membership. The assessment process would conclude with my writing an Assessment Report: Observations and Recommendations. The matter of fee must be addressed directly. I ask them not to decide that evening, but to reconvene within a week to make that decision.

If they decide to venture a next step, I suggest several formats intended to engage the largest number of church members in a sequence similar to that the officers experienced: an after-church luncheon workshop or two or a series of cottage meetings at members' homes are frequently chosen options. The process gains more substantial ownership by the laity when I train facilitators, working in pairs, to lead the gatherings. The input collated from worksheets that each event participant completes during the meetings, together with notes taken by the facilitators, provide the data needed to begin to frame a vision statement, project congregational goals, and develop a plan to carry the momentum forward.

WHERE ARE THE LEADERS TO BREATHE ON THE EMBERS?

What kind of pastoral or lay leadership is called for in this gentle, patient, and encouraging ministry? The process of identifying and equipping pastors for this work is less given to a clearly outlined process. Often young pastors, first-time pastors—like Todd, Tony, Katie, Susannah, and Terri—seem the likeliest candidates. Salary packages are often minimal, housing marginal, and these churches may be in small towns or rural settings, or city neighborhoods that are in decline. Church size research, however, warns that first-call pastors may be the more vulnerable in these usually family-size congregations.[4] With denominational budgets shrinking, workshop and retreat gatherings for young pastors have virtually dried up. Some judicatories have successfully linked first time pastors with nearby seasoned colleagues, but mentors must be carefully chosen.

Stan and Owen, having served larger churches, consciously chose to end their pastoral careers at smaller churches, accepting a lower salary and living more modestly. Stan, as you recall, arrived with a gentle mandate to help Wyncote Church ease toward its closing, only to find that his relaxed, affirming, and steady presence stirred new life to every one's delight and surprise. As he began, Owen found it difficult to find even a dozen people willing to meet with him for a year of biblical reflection, sharing, and prayer. But that first group spawned other groups across that twelve months and became a basis for parish renewal.

Explicitly or implicitly, qualities for effective leadership have already been profiled in the stories shared. I have communicated directly with clergy and lay leaders in the congregations named in this essay, inviting their reflection in written form or via personal conversations, and have convened an informal focus group of such folks. As I collated my notes, a common emphasis became clear. Their conclusions support author and consultant Steven Covey's thesis—that the bedrock quality that undergirds any organization's health and effectiveness is *trust*, and that the twin ingredients that yield trust are *character* and *competence*.[5] What follows is my editing of their wisdom.

Be quick to listen and slow to speak. Listening, my survey group concurred, was both a set of the heart and an interactional skill. Listening demands genuine interest in other persons, their thoughts and feelings, their joys and struggles, their hopes and anxieties. Some laity said you can "just tell" whether someone is really listening or not, and expressed resistance to those who merely "talked a good game" on the communication front, who'd mastered cliches, the catch phrases of communication manuals.

Be approachable and accessible. They are not synonyms. Approachability is a *character trait*, people sensing when someone is safe and trustworthy, those who are genuinely gracious and receptive. Accessibility is a *discipline*, artful management of calendar and clock. Church leaders are busy, but when they are good stewards of time, able to establish priorities, they are able to be available.

Be a leadership partner. Laypeople do not want pastors to withhold their creative ideas, the fruits of their training and experience, but want them to work *with* them in partnership, seeking their creativity and suggestions too. Unlike many young pastors, who roar in brimming but unbridled energy, often imposing rather than suggesting, armed with the latest and best of congregational revitalization technology, Todd patiently evoked increasingly assertive lay initiative and involvement.

Blend the old and the new. An older member at Honey Brook Church confessed to having mixed feelings about the sudden arrival of young families with new ideas, delighting in the many new faces, but adding she felt a little "pushed off the table." Terri, quick to think on her feet, said, "Then we'll build a larger table." Patient leaders replace either/or thinking with both/and thinking, blending rather than displacing. Todd coached those older women to help midwife a new younger women's group rather than coax them into the existing group.

Be failure friendly. Todd, blowing on the embers, sometimes ended up with soot on his face. Not every new idea takes flight. Some even crash and burn. "Nothing ventured, nothing gained" is a wise slogan. Innovation becomes more unhesitant when success is not the measure of faithfulness.

Love us. People in declining churches lose their self-esteem, feel forgotten by God, and find it easy to blame themselves. They become disheartened and discouraged. They need appreciation and affirmation just for who they are. For years I have had mixed feelings about my name, *Howard.* Each time as a child, when I began at a new school, I tried, always unsuccessfully, to try out a new name. My name evokes unfortunate associations—Howard the Duck, Howard Cosell, Howard Stern. It took a Spanish-speaking priest in a tiny Mexican parish who had a fascination with names and their meaning to help me reclaim my name with joy: *Howard* means *Protector of Hearts.*

What does your experience teach you about this kind of steady, resilient leadership that blends patience and persistence? What do you draw from the stories I have told that speak to the formation of leaders? I am convinced that more than a few churches at risk of being written off, that are seen as dead or dying, still have a hearth faintly aglow with embers ready to be breathed into flame. And I am encouraged, because Todd isn't the only Todd I know.

6

Be Prepared for Good News Resignations

The Gift of Empowering

N ormally, I am not the family gardener. But one fall a few years ago I got psyched. I drew an outline of our home and a drawn-to-scale map of our flower beds. A bulb catalogue at hand, I evolved an absurdly elaborate plan—not only plotting exact locations for each bulb, but projecting a scheme to place each one with both sequence and color coordination in mind. *House and Garden* magazine, here I come!

The carefully planned shopping trip would be the following Saturday. I gathered two dozen green, cardboard, quart-size berry containers, fitting them snugly into cut-down liquor cartons, and grabbed a handful of Popsicle sticks and a marker to make little labels. Working deliberately at our local nursery, I placed each handful of bulbs, located by variety and color, in the berry cartons, each with its identifying Popsicle stick.

I secured the cartons in the trunk of my car and headed home. As I turned into our street, a basketball tumbled over the curb, with a youngster in hot pursuit. Instinctively I swerved and hit the brake. "The bulbs!" I heard myself moan. I parked, popped the trunk, and there they were, scattered everywhere. Every berry container was empty.

The planting was to begin immediately. What to do? I considered holding each unidentifiable bulb in turn, instructing it emphatically, "Listen up! You're to be a red tulip, a purple iris, a blue crocus, or a bright yellow daffodil!" I had no choice—start digging. By the end of the weekend each bed had its share of bulbs in place.

Springtime turned out to be a delightful adventure. Each morning, coffee cup in hand, we'd circle the house to see what bulbs had popped up where. Spontaneity, serendipity, surprise reigned. In many ways the randomness was more wonderful than any arrangement my initial compulsive plan could have yielded. The secret was encoded in the heart of each bulb. Their God-given essence burst forth into a wondrous array of shape and color.

People—"planted" in good soil, watered and tended, growing at their natural time and pace—release their in-born, God-given essence. Wonders of shape and color begin to grace the congregational landscape. When I lead a workshop for congregational leaders and name them as "people with full plates," vigorous nods confirm that observation. Then I ask them how all that "stuff"—all the tasks, the committees they belong to, the meetings to attend—got onto their plate. While they're reflecting, I write eight letters on newsprint: A—A—V—R and C—G—P—P. Their answers generally fall into four categories: I was *assigned*, I got *appointed*, I *volunteered,* or I was *recruited* (A—A—V—R). I suggest an alternative: How is God *calling* you just now (your *vocation,* to speak theologically)? What *gifts* for serving (*discernment,* to speak biblically) do you feel led to tap and manifest at this time? What *purpose* is God guiding you to? Where is your *passion*? (C—G—P—P). The former seems logical and orderly, more manageable and controlled, as an organizational strategy. Map the gardens (identify the leadership slots); then tell the bulbs what species and color to be (neatly arrange leaders in those slots). Discerning one's call and giftedness, becoming conscious of purpose and passion, may prove unpredictable, disorderly, and difficult to manage and control. Wonderful!

Be forewarned, this approach may upset your organizational applecart, not unlike those bulbs ricocheting around my car trunk. You may find yourself facing what I call "good-news resignations." As people begin to name their calling and gifts, clarifying their purpose and releasing their passion, they feel compelled to serve at the church in fuller alignment with that discernment. They may choose to resign from a committee or ministry team and join another. That's not so awkward, unless they chair a committee or moderate a board; in that case, their departure may create organizational disruption, a "bad-news" resignation, it might seem at first. When discernment and faithfulness replace appointment, assignment, volunteering, and recruitment as a basic organizational strategy, any short-term chaos or inconvenience yields, my experience suggests, deeper and more durable commitment, as well as more effective and joyful service. Two stories from a church I know make the point.

Mike had served for over a decade as the property committee chair of his church. A superb manager, able in maintenance skills, he kept the property in tip-top shape. But when time came for his monthly report, he placed his portfolio on the boardroom table, announcing, "I've come with a 'good-news resignation,' to use Howard's words." "But you do such a great job, Mike," came a chorus of responses. He confessed that he had never, until recently, given much thought to what he was being *led* to do as a leader and how to be a good steward of his time and energy. Mike explained that he had helped his wife with some driving chores for the Cambodian family the church was sponsoring, and "they quickly claimed my heart. For the first time ever, I know how God wants to use me. I'll help groom a successor, but I want to devote myself to this new, passionate calling."

The following month—same church, same board—it came time for Janine to give her report for the stewardship committee. "I come with another 'good-news resignation,' she began." Intercepting an onslaught of resistance, she continued, "When that seminary professor preached a Sunday or so back, we got to talking about organizing a Wednesday night Lay Academy. It would be more than an advanced Sunday school—in-depth, seminary-quality reading assignments, the whole deal. I want to put all my time and energy into it." The resistance commenced in earnest. Janine raised her hand and said something that silenced them all, "If you try to talk me out of this, you will be colluding with unfaithfulness."

Her resignation, and Mike's, created organizational inconvenience. Two longtime dedicated leaders, steady and reliable, who would be difficult to replace, took seriously an invitation no one had ever offered. The leadership tasks they had performed dutifully had lost focus and meaning for Mike and Janine. Within a month, redirecting his management skills, Mike had convened a mission team that reached out to a network of Cambodian families who had settled in the area. And the following month a colorful brochure profiled that Lay Academy, complete with faculty biographies, course outlines, and reading assignments.

The "Mike and Janine story" made its rounds through the congregation and started something of a good-news resignation epidemic. Happily, the pastor and board chair quieted an initial inclination to resist and helped the church learn to navigate a season of leadership flux, and even to welcome the changes that this renewed commitment to faithfulness engendered. A rich and thriving spectrum of new ministries evolved, a heightened level of energy and vitality in the church was palpable and, as one board member put it, "it all just seems right."

How might such stories become more frequent and familiar, rather than the exception in congregations? What I will suggest is not a one-size-fits-all, surefire, step-by-step proposal. It is less a matter of strategy and tactic than of obedience and faithfulness. Consider it only if it aligns with your faith and theology of church. That said, a four-pronged approach has proved effective in my experience. First, ground this gift-based and passion-driven approach in Scripture. Develop a Bible study curriculum, preach a series of sermons, and write newsletter articles that highlight biblical narratives in which servants of God come to know themselves as called and equipped, claimed by a purpose and animated by passion.

Second, partner a new members' orientation process and a membership renewal program that offer gift-discernment tools and processes. Mainstream this commitment to gift- and passion-based serving. Discernment is subtle, an art to nurture and cultivate, a prayerful and spiritually grounded practice.

Third, revisit the nominations process. Typically, church board members serve three-year terms, with one-third of members rotating off in a given year, each leaving on the table a leadership portfolio in a particular area of ministry. A nominating committee generally creates a slate of candidates who have demonstrated spiritual vitality and a readiness to serve, but generally without regard to those three in-place leadership slots. Thus a new board member confronts a limited choice of committees to chair, or, just as likely, a particular one already assigned. Some churches have found it helpful to groom candidates from within the ministry teams where a chairperson is rotating off, people whose sense of giftedness and passion is already tested. Other churches have encouraged self-nomination, reversing the sequence—a person approaches the nominating committee, rather than being approached. This shift to discernment-based leading and serving is unlikely in the context of many nominating procedures.

Finally, encourage the formation of what I call *adhocracy*. Often growing churches have a decreasing number of standing committees with fewer called meetings, but a proliferating number of informal circles of people creating educational programs, developing mission teams, informally providing pastoral care, planning a picnic, starting an after-school program, gathering to encourage and support each other, or quietly starting a ministry. As the number of these informal groupings grows, develop linkages, a workable coordination process. New couples, walking into the sanctuary for the first time, are unlikely to whisper to each other as they search for a pew, "I'll bet, if we play it right, we can be on a committee in a week or two!"

Mike and Janine illustrate what can happen when the organizational infrastructure becomes more faithful and flexible. But the real excitement and creativity burst forth when this emphasis on call and gift, purpose and passion infects the membership.

Hearts Claimed, Hearts Broken Open

A cascade of stories tumbles into my mind: Congregations where educational offerings bubbled up from members encouraged and empowered to create their own courses and classes, as the church staff and education committee offer encouragement and direction.

Churches where far-reaching mission ministries emerged as people of common calling found each other and gathered around shared vision to pray and plan and implement their lay-led project.[1]

Tim never did get around to telling his mom he had become a Presbyterian, knowing she'd launch into endless Hail Marys and insist that her forebears were turning over in their graves. His wife, Susie, a lifelong evangelical, was thrilled they'd found a church where they could worship together. They were each invited to become deacons. It seemed only fair, they reasoned, to take a turn at serving, though they never did get clear just what this role was all about. Tim agreed to be an usher, and Susie arranged the altar flowers. Slowly at first, almost imperceptibly, but then clearly and rather disturbingly, their initial enthusiasm ebbed. Their sense of spiritual vitality peaked, and the desire to serve that had prompted their agreement to serve as deacons faded. But a conversation Tim had had with his pastor some time ago stuck in his mind—something about listening for God's leading about how he might make love manifest in the world; something about discerning his life's mission, his unique sense of purpose, that which would claim his heart.

An invitation in the monthly newsletter caught Susie's eye, a gathering after church the following Sunday for anyone who might consider a family mission trip to Mexico. Madeleine was nine, and surely Olivia was too young at six, but they carried their coffee cups to the assigned location, and the rest was history. Four families, including seven kids, ages six to fourteen, flew to Cuernavaca, Mexico, for an eight-day immersion experience. They made "papooses"—spicy potato pancakes—and heard an awesome story of resilience and faithfulness in the midst of death-dealing adversity in the home of a Salvadoran refugee family. Moises and Gloria, tears drenching their cheeks, spoke of the deaths of parents and siblings and fellow villagers, gunned down by paramilitary groups in their country's civil war. They watched Elena, a dark-skinned indigenous Guatemalan woman creating cloth of darkly brilliant oranges and purples, employing an ancient art called waist-weaving, as her husband Macario told a similar tale from his native country.

During a three-day home stay, they slept on mats on the floor as chickens wandered in and out. They bathed in makeshift stalls, ladling unheated water over their shivering bodies. They braved shallow latrines, using comic-book pages as toilet paper. They thumbed through dictionaries and communicated with a combination of mime and halting "Spanglish." They spent a morning at an elementary school, where they found any hint of a language barrier disappearing instantly, as the kids played raucously in the cement schoolyard, then took turns imitating the movements and sounds of animals, shouting out guesses in English and Spanish.

But it was the visit to La Estación, an immense squatters' settlement in the heart of this fairly prosperous city, that claimed their hearts, and then broke them open. In streets teeming with children, the youngest would rush forward with a welcoming handshake or, more often, a robust hug, some with orange hair that crackled at a touch, a sign of malnutrition. They walked the community's narrow streets, dust swirling in the summer heat. Tightly packed along the walkways were shacks made of anything or everything you could stack, wire, tape, or (if one was lucky) nail together—bedsprings, vegetable crates, splintered plywood, pieces of cement block. Scraps of corrugated, oil-soaked cardboard sheets nailed through soda-cap washers formed makeshift roofs, trapping the sweltering summer heat and offering a partial shield against torrential rains.

Doña Magdalena beckoned the group into her home, as her oldest son pulled flimsy chairs into a tight circle so the group could sit. Difficult to distinguish the inside of the house from outside, three mattresses were stacked together in the shadows of a far corner, concrete blocks held shelving and a scattering of canned foods, and a gas range sat against an outside wall. Our Lady of Guadalupe peered out from a smudged frame. Magdalena's four- and six-year-old daughters were selling chewing gum at a nearby intersection, where her seven-year-old son washed windshields. They were the household's primary breadwinners, she explained. A curl of thin rope, one end tied to the leg of the bed, caught Tim's eye and his curiosity, so he asked about it. Magdalena hesitated, her head and eyes bent downward. "I sometimes have a few hours of ironing at a home a half-hour's walk from here. There's no one to take care of my three-year-old, Marcos, so I tie him to the bed frame." At that point, something broke that wouldn't mend in Tim and Susie and the others around the circle, all now engulfed in awkward silence. Even as they said their good-byes and bent to exit, a commitment was forming in their minds.

Mi Universo Pequeño, a small, struggling preschool run by two sturdy and dedicated Catholic sisters, was the next stop, a short walk from Magdalena's. "Why isn't Marcos among the three-year-olds?" Susie asked. At fifty students the school was at capacity, Sister Juana explained. The visitors' commitment started to take shape.

That was August 2001. Fast-forward seven years. Enrollment in the preschool has tripled to 150. Two rooms piled with debris have been cleared and painted, as have all the classrooms. Once sparsely used shelves now brim with books and supplies. An overgrown lot has become a playground, with outdoor boys' and girls' restrooms. Last year a separate effort raised $25,000 for construction of a two-classroom, two-bathroom addition. Three new teachers have joined the staff.

In 2004 an adjacent abandoned building across a former railroad bed was restored and became a nutrition and family life center. Second-hand commercial-grade kitchen equipment installed by volunteers allows rotating teams of mothers to prepare a breakfast hearty enough to provide those 150 children with a full day's nutritional needs. A social worker was hired to work with individual families and to organize workshops with themes that include preparing for employment, parenting, planning a healthy diet on a minimal budget, and building self-esteem.

Tim and Susie had been home less than a week after that initial August visit when they began to invite family and friends to share this calling with them. The first year they meet a $12,000 commitment, an amount that grew in the next calendar year to $25,000. Watching a video of the dedication of the new classroom building, Tim remembered his pastor's words that had stuck in his mind, and now he understood.

The good news is that the pastor's words were remembered and Tim and Susie serendipitously heard their call and found their passion. Their less-than-fruitful tenure as deacons might have pointed in another direction, toward diminishing interest and participation at the church, a pattern all too familiar in congregations.

A colleague and friend, curious and troubled by a pattern he came to view as common, if not epidemic, in churches across the country, conducted exit interviews, an extensive survey of people completing their terms on church boards. He asked them to indicate on a simple one-to-ten scale their basic level of satisfaction in serving. Then, using an open-ended question format, he asked that they name both what was satisfying and what was disappointing in that leadership tenure. He was startled to find well over 50 percent of respondents expressed overall dissatisfaction, with 20 percent expressing substantial disappointment. He further noted that the dissatisfactions fell into oft-repeated categories: "I wasn't clear at the beginning, in the middle, or at end just what I was supposed to be doing." Expecting that serving on a church board would be somehow different, "I couldn't see much of a difference, really, between working on the church board and working in some other organization, even going to work," was a common complaint. Meetings were described as dull, long, lifeless, and without discernible spiritual grounding. But the most commonly expressed concern was the most troubling: "I was invited to serve because I was perceived as someone deepening spiritually, and I looked forward to a term of service as a way toward even greater spiritual growth, but to tell the truth, the trajectory of my spiritual growth flattened, hit a plateau, detoured, and even diminished."[2]

NOTHING WORKS? CREATE YOUR OWN!

Adhocracy works closer to home. Most churches employ what I call the "producer/consumer method" of adult-education programming. A few people—trusting wish or whim more than data collecting or simply "asking the customer," as the marketing world

calls it—plan programs they decide church members will surely
want, or should want. No one asked for an all-church covered-dish
supper, but a few people decide it's a great idea, put announcements
in the newsletter and Sunday bulletin, and complain when only
half the tables are filled. "We ought to have an inspirational speaker
to bring us all together," some members eagerly agree, promptly
consulting a speaker's bureau, printing tickets, lining the social
hall with enough folding chairs to seat a hundred, and complain-
ing vehemently when only twenty-five straggle in. Churches with
a burgeoning calendar of enthusiastically attended adult learning
and sharing opportunities are listening to what people are aware
they want and need—to grow spiritually, to deepen relationships,
to learn from their faith tradition, to serve those in need who claim
their heart.

Rich, after years in a large church, wondered what a smaller
congregation would be like. Its sanctuary seemed hardly larger
than a spacious living room compared to the gothic cathedral-like
one he'd come from. At first glance, he found its program offerings
disappointing, almost meager by comparison. He had to admit,
however, that for a small church, the schedule of events for the
coming week in the Sunday bulletin was long, and the newsletter
bulged with opportunities. But he had loved the huge buffet of
lectures, classes, and forums on every imaginable theme at that
bigger church each day and evening of the week. Maybe he'd made
too hasty a decision. He gave it six months, dropping in on a group
or two he'd circled from the program calendar.

Rich made an appointment to visit the pastor and voiced his
second thoughts about coming to the church. "I don't mean to
criticize," he said, "but I don't see an adult program that quite
speaks to me." Without a hint of defensiveness the pastor replied,
"Got any ideas about what might work for you?" A response came
more quickly than even Rich expected, "I'd like to be part of a men's
group." Then he remembered that he'd recognized some men from
the church on the station platform as he awaited his morning commuter train. "I wonder if they'd be interested in arriving an hour
earlier and having a light breakfast and Bible study at the diner

across the street." At coffee hour the following Sunday the pastor helped Rich meet the guys from the station, encouraging him to offer his invitation, which, to Rich's delight, they accepted.

After a month, the men found themselves pushing two tables together in a spot toward the back of the diner the owner had set aside. Each took a turn leading the discussion, which became increasingly comfortable and lively. Each week more of the men felt comfortable with praying aloud. One morning a men's retreat was suggested, and two months later fifteen men converged after rush-hour traffic on a Friday afternoon at a Catholic retreat house not far from the church. A monthly men's group grew out of the retreat, and when their circle became as large as felt comfortable, they helped a second group form. A Habitat for Humanity volunteer in the group offered to swing by the church each Saturday morning en route to the job site for the week, part of his personal mission commitment. As often as not, his eight-passenger van was full.

METHOD IN THE MADNESS (OR NOT ENTIRELY COINCIDENTAL)

Mike, Janine, Rich, Tim, and Susie are real people whose stories are rooted in real, though different, faith communities. One of those churches deserves a more "up close and personal" look. Glenbrook Church "built it, but they did not come," though the story is more subtle than that. For eighty years the congregation gathered in a small clapboard building in a village made up of six or eight large estates with elegant manor houses, a small village center ringed by lanes with small-single story cottages, a narrow street with tightly bunched row houses, and a development of modest, post–World War II brick homes. The little church included a sanctuary seating eighty, two or three small classrooms, and an attached home for a pastor.

When an expressway opened, linking the center city with a growing number of suburban communities, an exit positioned Glenbrook to develop as a prime, high-end bedroom community.

It was the first exit across the city line, making for an easy commute to the center city. Glenbrook's rolling hills and stands of mature trees lent unusual privacy to its spacious homes and kept summer temperatures several degrees below that of the urban center. Winding lanes and a network of cul-de-sacs with elegant homes immaculately landscaped sprang up on large tracts of open land, and the village population soared. A majority of the new homeowners found the larger and more prestigious churches a short drive away more comfortable, but a few were drawn to the "country church" nestled in a now more bustling but still quaint and quiet village. The little wooden church began to burst at the seams.

After an enthusiastic and generous response to a building fund drive, the congregation relocated to a fieldstone complex on a wooded lot in a residential neighborhood. The next decade saw attendance flatten, then decline. Low-grade controversy expanded into at times nasty conflict, with nostalgia voiced for the "good old days" in the now demolished former church.

A more promising decade lay ahead. Attendance slowly increased, drawing a remarkably diverse spectrum of people—faithful old-timers, residents of the elegant new homes who weathered the difficult decade, and an array of others, many driving a significant distance. "We'd need a large map to put pushpins for all the locations of our membership," someone noted. In a casual moment the pastor was heard to say, "I stand at the pulpit, look out across the congregation, and say to myself, 'How ever did this group of such disparate and unlikely people make their way to this out-of-the-way church on a Sunday morning?'"

Given their off-the-beaten-track location, everyone knew the church would grow only by invitation. One Sunday, as worshipers crowded into coffee hour, they arrived to find the silhouette of a winter tree, branches exposed, painted onto a floor-to-ceiling piece of butcher paper. People were asked to position themselves on a branch by writing their name on a Post-it Note and placing it just farther out on a branch from the name of whoever invited them, with someone they had invited securing their note just further out that same branch. It took some negotiating, jostling, and laughing as they jockeyed to properly locate their names. Finally finished, they stepped back to see the finished product, their flapping sticky notes creating an autumnal tree, a concrete and visible celebration of the gifts of inviting, welcoming, and hospitality they had offered each other.

Church growth, despite the promises of church-growth strategies, is generally halting and uneven, as it was at Glenbrook Church. An active leader who'd caught the unusual spirit that seemed to have captivated the church observed, "We love new ideas—though most fail, you know. If a major-league baseball player gets three hits every ten times at bat, he's a hero. But that means he walks back to the dugout more often than he gets on base. So, we know we've got to venture new ideas and then be failure-friendly."

It may be more exception than rule, that the serendipitous, the unplanned, what "just happens" is often more fruitful than the carefully orchestrated and methodically planned. A woman in Glenbrook Church, accompanying a delegation from another church, participated in a three-day event sponsored by Church of the Savior in Washington, D.C., the first day and a half at a retreat farm outside the city, followed by time spent visiting ministries in the city that had been created out of the life of that church's seven worshiping communities. When she returned, her enthusiasm was so contagious she hardly had to speak a word of encouragement. Two months later a delegation of four others experienced the same event, followed by several other groups.

A new approach to congregational development was not created instantly, but one was evolving. Certain basic principles became increasingly visible, more in their embodiment than in spoken or written words. "Discernment," an unfamiliar word or concept to date, began to be heard in conversations and in committee meetings. At a church board meeting one May, this new approach took a next step toward greater clarity and institutionalizing. Indeed, a board member, a senior management executive, made a comment toward the beginning of that meeting that gave the ensuing exploration momentum. "We often treat 'institutionalizing' as something negative," she explained, "but I would suggest that, if what is happening here at Glenbrook Church is to have durability, longevity, and real impact, we must take on the responsibility, with wisdom and sensitivity, to do just that, institutionalize it."

Mercifully, that meeting produced no grand plan. "Grand plan" was not what that board member had in mind. Convinced that congregation-wide commitment to spiritual deepening would not exceed their own, and that the quality of community among members would not rise above their own, the board members committed to begin and end the following church year with a spiritual retreat. And they decided to begin each month's meeting with a time of biblical reflection, personal sharing, and prayer *not led by the pastor.*

Listening quietly—as they decided to invite the membership to begin to serve as they felt called, with recruiting and seeking volunteers a secondary strategy, an idea borrowed from Church of the Savior—the pastor suggested that each board member place his or her current leadership/management portfolio on the large boardroom table. Then he invited them to push back their chairs from that table for a prayerful interlude. The pastor would later confess that he was anxious as he offered a final direction, more an option than an obligation, that each member pick up from the table the portfolio that most aligned with her present sense of personal discernment, his own awareness of how he was being called.

Predictable hesitation, uncertainty, and then a halting but quietly decisive response ensued. Some reached for the portfolio they had previously placed on the table, and others chose a different one. Sometimes two people reached for the same portfolio and moved to sit together, placing the portfolio between them. Some portfolios were left unchosen. "I've created an organizational nightmare," the pastor thought to himself, relieved when a longtime board member commented, "Now we're starting to walk the talk."

They made one more decision that evening, of both policy and procedure. Looking to Jesus's broad and inclusive welcome to all as a rationale, becoming a member of the church had been as easy as simply wanting to. Literally. One Sunday, as a small group of newcomers was coming forward to be welcomed into official membership, a man stood up and asked impulsively, "Can I join too?" The pastor, evoking affirming nods from board members whose eyes he could catch, said "Sure." Aware of the influence of this biblical rationale, and knowing the current practice was the pastor's preference, a board member rose to question that policy, clearly apologetic as he began to speak. He expressed concern at what appeared to be a trend, that though it was rewarding to see the membership growing, new members were uneven in their follow-through, especially in becoming part of the work of the church. Two others voiced immediate support. One of them summarized the issue succinctly: "Instead of constantly saying, 'Now that you've joined the church maybe you'd like to get involved,' I'd like to hear us saying, 'Now that you've gotten involved, maybe you'd like the join.'" A new policy was not finalized at that meeting, but within months a new-member orientation program was initiated that required a curriculum and activities that spanned six to eight months. Fewer people joined, but the quality of commitment clearly deepened.

A physician on the board would later comment that the church had changed its basic view of church growth from a numeric to a *pediatric* one. As a pediatrician, he knew that monitoring signs of healthy growth was more holistic, and that height and weight were only two indicators among many. A manager at a neighborhood nursery caught the spirit, arguing they had chosen a *horticultural* metaphor—with a solid root system, timely pruning, disciplined feeding, and judicious watering as essentials.

There is no magic potion for congregational vitalization, and the many books and programs available are only as helpful as patience and determination, openness to trial and error, readiness to taste celebration and disappointment are mustered. The library at Glenbrook Church had a shelf or two of resources for congregational leaders. Both pastor and laity, over time, attended a number of workshops on themes related to nurturing healthy church life. One was titled *We Build the Road as We Go* by Roy Morrison, an apt caption for the way a congregation's future unfolds. As one congregational consultant stated it, "Plan as we will, in reality, we only see to the next bend in the road."

The pastor of Glenbrook Church used the "bully pulpit" art-fully and enthusiastically, a favorite theme of his being that "in church there are no grandstands and no spectators, only players." The church is not an "ecclesiastical supermarket," he'd repeat, where member-customers fill their shopping carts. It's not a market at all, but a co-op. It's not a catered meal, but a perpetual covered-dish supper. He loved metaphors. He was never more emphatic on this theme than when he talked about worship and preaching. Even Frank Sinatra could not play the same house for more than a week, he'd point out, reminding them he stood in that pulpit forty-six weeks a year. But he got most passionate talking about the *process* of preaching. He'd say it in the prayer before the sermon, always some form of a reminder that no truth can be written or spoken unless the Spirit guide it, nor can a word of truth be read or heard, taken to heart and life, and become healing and transformational unless the Spirit guide it. A sermon is not a performance but a dialogue, even if only one voice is sounding.

Typically, especially if the small sanctuary was full, a row of folding chairs sat across a back wall, often occupied by half a dozen of the church's more raucous if lovable young men. The pastor, as fitting irony would have it, had made one of those impassioned pleas about the sermon not being a performance. As he approached that last pew during the recessional, each of the six, simultaneously, held up a shirt cardboard, each boldly lettered with magic marker: "8.6"; "7.9"; "9.2"—as if they were ranking a diving competition. Point made!

EVEN EXCEPTIONS PROVE A RULE

Maybe Glenbrook Church, Mike, Janine, Rich, Tim, and Susie are anomalies, exceptions to the rule, and would only be frustrat-ing to imitate. Or maybe not. I am convinced that within each person is a homing device, that there is more than poetic truth in the phrase *our heart knows the way*, that destiny is hardwired within us. It begins with discernment, manifesting a clarity that emerges from within. An inner sense of calling and giftedness awakens, a defining purpose comes into focus, an animating passion arises. My sister is a nutritionist who helps people choose a diet that promotes optimum physical health. My son's brother-in-law is a personal trainer who helps people follow a regimen of exercise that will tone and strengthen their body. My wife is a psychotherapist who helps people nurture their personal and relational lives. I am a pastor who helps people develop a spiritual practice that may deepen their communion with God. But none of us can do what we do *for* anyone so much as *with* them. Ultimately, each individual must chose to be physically, relationally, and spiritually healthy, and then make choices aligned with that decision, seeking companions and guides along the way.

This longing to become more than we are, to stretch and expand, to fulfill a destiny, to accomplish a mission, to discern and pursue a purpose, is encoded within us. It is encouraged more than taught. It is awakened. I am convinced that churches that embody that belief attract people who've been awaiting, maybe more deeply than they realize, that gracious invitation. I have been thrilled to watch and to be a partner with congregations that exude that kind of spiritual hospitality.

If the impulse for spiritual exploration is inborn and natural, the deep desire to reach toward the holy and touch the sacred, so is the impulse to make love visible and concrete in and through each of us. If we bear the image of God, then we are loving-kindness at our center. Scarred as we may be by hurt and pain, sturdy as our defenses may be within and without, wounded by betrayal and abandonment, understandably cautious and wary, beneath it all, I believe, is a longing to reach out in purposeful, passionate, and loving ways. What better place to heal wounds and soften defenses, venture and risk, find companionship and encouragement than a faith community.

All of this is programmatic as well as poetic. The call is not to some synthetic or contrived belief in the human spirit, a stratagem to employ, an experiment to test, but a bedrock trust in the creation, the creature, and the creator. The pages you have just read are, I am convinced, a testimony to a conviction, the manifestation of a personal and corporate creed, fruits of a spirit. Mother Teresa said that we are called to faithfulness, not success.

THE COURAGE TO PULL THE PLUG

The Gift of Letting Go

*D*o you have a living will? The words seemed to pop out of my mouth, surprising, even confusing me, as much as they did the small circle gathered around the table. An older woman, outgoing and extroverted by nature, offered an answer to ease the awkwardness: "Yes, I do, and so does my husband." Others nodded that they had made similar arrangements. I gathered my composure enough to pursue this promising direction. "If someone asked you," I continued, "just what is a 'living will,' how would you answer?"

The first response was succinct and clear. "It authorizes my family and medical professionals not to employ extraordinary means to keep me alive, if I have passed beyond a point of significant quality of life."

"It means I am giving my permission to disconnect life-support systems if my capacity to support life myself has ceased," someone else added.

"It tells them to pull the plug!" chortled the oldest among us, with a cheerful smile.

"Thank you for being so open," I offered, making eye contact with each in turn. "What I asked was rather personal, I realize. I appreciate your candor and your trust of each other. Now consider the question in a different way. *Do you have a living will for your church?*" No one spoke at first, and glances around the table conveyed a mix of confusion and restlessness. "What do you mean?" asked Ben, a longtime member, likely speaking for the others. I paused, hoping they might wrestle a bit more with the question, wondering if the silence was more symptomatic of uneasy clarity than true confusion. "I know exactly what he means!" Josh, the youngest of the group by two decades, blurted out. "He wonders if our church is on life support."

"I hate to say it, but maybe it is time to pull the plug, or at least consider it," added Sarah, the starkness of her words surprising her and unsettling the others. Reluctance even to consider this possibility was etched on their faces. Words of resistance seemed poised to be spoken. One or two glanced toward Ben, then Sarah, with thinly disguised irritation.

An uncomfortable silence descended. Feet shuffled audibly. Eyes shifted downward. Dan, the president of the board, who had been sitting quietly, sighed, then sighed again. The second, a deep, almost prayerful sort of sigh, seemed to ease the tension. All eyes looked toward Dan for comfort, reassurance, and wisdom. He was, after all, their leader. They clearly respected his long years of faithful service. Surely he would shift the momentum. Dan sighed again and slowly turned to me. "Howard," he said, "I don't like your question. I hate your question. But thank you for asking it. It's a question I think we must ask. I don't know the answer. We may not know the answer for some time. We have lots of thinking and sharing and praying to do. But I am ready to ask that question. I hope we all are."

A LITTLE CONTEXT

I had been invited by the pastor of Hope Lutheran Church to start a conversation among the church's board members about its future. Hope Church had stood nobly for nearly one hundred years on this corner of what was once a thriving small city outside Philadelphia. Not long ago, or so it seemed to longtime members, worshipers nearly filled the massive sanctuary at each of two services, the choir loft at capacity, reflecting what was widely recognized as an outstanding music program. Once children had streamed to Sunday school classes in a sprawling two-story complex of brightly painted classrooms, and adults of all ages had attended a broad offering of education classes. Rambunctious teens had crammed into the youth lounge. Newsletters from the 1950s and 1960s overflowed with notices about events, programs, and ministries every day of the week. Generous congregational giving provided a large church staff, amply supporting that rich program life and an exemplary commitment to mission work near and far. In a community with churches on almost every corner, Hope Lutheran Church was the most active and prosperous.

Each of those "churches on every corner" has sadly similar stories to tell about the past three decades—steady, unbroken decline on every front: membership, attendance, program life, and financial support. Hope Church, whose story so closely paralleled the others, had a reprieve in that a church-related agency had rented a large portion of its space for the past ten years, generating income that had balanced the books each year, though barely. That money created an impression of self-sufficiency, but the lease was about to expire, and the tenant had announced plans to relocate. Everything was edging toward crisis. Then church leaders told me sheepishly about the endowment. For years their portfolio's income had covered increasing shortfalls in the annual budget. Hesitantly, modestly at first, five years ago they had begun spending down principal at a greater percentage each year. Slightly over one million dollars remained.

Pastor Cynthia, having spoken frankly with the bishop, hoped I might be able, in ways she could not, to coax forth candor and courage, a bold reality-conscious conversation about the church's future. As is my custom, after introducing myself in a way that I hoped would generate a level of comfort and trust, I invited the board members to introduce themselves, naming something from the church's life and ministry, past or present, that they appreciated or were proud of, including ways in which the church has ministered to them, and then share as well something of their vision for the church's future. The sharing was delightfully personal and heartfelt. Eyes glistened as many shared powerful ways in which their lives had been touched, how "at home" and "with family" they felt whenever they arrived at Hope, and how they had appreciated specific people across those years. Hope Church clearly remained at the very center of how they lived their lives.

I found myself needing to remind several of them to share, as well, something of their hope for the future. They groped for words, wondering aloud why things weren't "like they used to be." They longed for full pews, the happy sounds of children's voices, the energy of youth returning, but their voices, heavy with weariness, strained for optimism and conviction.

BACK TO THE MEETING

For the rest of that first meeting with Hope Church, the board members shared their vision, with some promising developments reported. A few newcomers had joined the choir. A group of mothers had initiated a midweek children's and youth tutoring program. Local teens welcomed the invitation to use the gym on Wednesday afternoons. But the group was quick to interrupt any false optimism by posing the difficult questions about the congregation's viability, given the region's shifting demographics. After three decades of a dramatically increasing African American population, there was a current influx of Latino families. Candor and courage ascended, even as appropriate discouragement arose. A growing consensus was most telling: that they were tired, that "the faithful core" was tired too—deep tired, long-term tired, bone tired. An odd sense of relief seemed to be the gift of their shared admission. Hardly knowing them, I felt proud of them. I decided to close our time together by telling them the story of a parish I had served a dozen years before, people about whom I had fond and deeply appreciative feelings, whose story might illuminate their own.

HOW TYPICAL IS HOPE CHURCH?

Even this first glimpse into the life of Hope Church, a narrative of one evening's meeting, may stir discomfort and discouragement. All this talk about "living wills" and congregational decline and financial crisis may seem depressing. How typical is Hope Church? Is it the exception or the rule?

Pause for a moment and consider the following mini-questionnaire, putting a checkmark by each statement that applies to your congregation.

____ Our membership and attendance have been declining for a decade or more.

____ Our membership and attendance have been in decline for forty years or more.

____ We have only occasional visitors at worship, and few stay or join the church.

____ Our average age is steadily rising.

____ We find it increasingly difficult to recruit a critical mass of workers to carry out the basic ministry of the church; our cadre of leaders and willing workers is shrinking.

____ Our annual congregational giving no longer supports our current expense budget.

____ We depend on endowment income to supplement our annual budget.

____ We have begun to spend down our endowment principal.

____ We have had an awkward or contentious relationship with some recent pastors.

____ Our pastors have served shorter and shorter tenures over the last twelve to fifteen years.

____ We are burdened with a larger church plant than we need, with large maintenance costs and deferred maintenance needs.

____ Conflict and controversy have become more prevalent among us. Some of us have gotten upset and left the church.

____ We have tried several strategies for church renewal but, after early excitement, they seem to have failed.

____ Speaking realistically, there seems little likelihood things will significantly change.

____ We love our church and are proud of its history, but we have become discouraged.

The odds are, if you are a church member, I am talking about your church. A conservative estimate suggests that this profile embraces at least 75 percent of so-called mainline denominational congregations across America. A colleague who attended a national meeting of our denomination told me that 95 percent of Presbyterian churches were in decline; only 5 percent were holding their own or growing. A line graph tracking attendance, membership, and financial receipts in American Protestantism since 1964 shows a steady and unbroken downward slide.[1] Faithfulness is not merely a matter of numbers, but these numbers seem symptomatic of a troublesome malaise and a trend that shows no signs of bottoming out.

St. Mark's Church

The congregational story with which I ended the meeting at Hope Church, the parish I had served a decade earlier, was about St. Mark's Episcopal Church. When I think Episcopalian, I think stone, formality, gothic architecture, stained-glass windows, and walled courtyards. St. Mark's Church, located amid tightly crowded row houses along narrow streets, was a charming oasis featuring modest brick buildings, garden-lined walkways, and whitewashed fencing. As long as anyone could remember, the town of Upper Darby had been a community of successful blue-collar workers, skilled journeymen in various trades, government employees and schoolteachers, people of modest but solid income. Well-known anchor stores and high-quality shops, spread over four square blocks in the town center, formed a thriving shopping district that has gone through several incarnations and continues to draw customers from a significant distance. After its founding at the end of the Civil War, St. Mark's thrived for nearly a century. Decline began gradually through the sixties, becoming precipitous over the last fifteen years. My friend David, serving as the parish's interim pastor, suggested that I lead a board retreat, and a Sunday afternoon date was set.

Participants completed a pre-retreat questionnaire, naming their hopes and expectations, which seemed sweeping and ambitious for so small a congregation, a board of eight and a membership of sixty-five. Most expressed hope for renewed energy, a brighter future, and a new era of church growth, but I sensed something forced and hesitant even in their written words. One or two used the questionnaire to confess their discouragement.

We met in the rectory living room. David opened our time with a simple liturgy. They agreed to save introductions until after an opening exercise I proposed. I gave each person two nametags—one his or her own, the other an unfamiliar and in most cases unfamiliar-sounding name. Most needed help just to pronounce them. Each person also received a three-by-five card that "introduced" the unfamiliar person, who was to be role-played for the next hour. Though they had fictitious names, they represented the racial and ethnic identities of the people who lived in the area immediately surrounding the church, few of whom attended St. Mark's.

I asked participants to walk alone a block or two, out of sight of the church, and then slowly approach the church, wearing that second name tag, as if they were that person. I invited them to be aware of their impressions of the church as it came into view. What did the church seem to "say" as they approached it? I asked them to pause again as they crossed the street and entered the church property, noting any impressions. What "message" did they get from the building and grounds? I asked them to be particularly mindful as they walked up the front steps and entered the vestibule and then the sanctuary, noticing what thoughts ran through their minds and what feelings they experienced. Finally, I asked them to sit for a few moments in a pew, as that person with the odd-sounding name. At some point all had returned, sitting in different places around the church. I rang a bell to call us back to the living room, where I asked them to remain in character for a few more minutes, sharing their experiences. Though this sort of exercise was unfamiliar, they shared with remarkable insight and sensitivity. It gave them fresh perspective, a deeper understanding of this multiracial, multiethnic population, even though, in reality, they knew little about these neighbors. The experience was disconcerting as well, and I admired their courage as they shared. Each removed that second name tag, replaced it with his or her own, and took a coffee break to step back out of role.

"Howard, how can we reach out and welcome these folks we have just talked about?" a younger leader asked. My invitation to brainstorm answers to that question gained little traction. "Maybe the diocese can offer us some guidance," a middle-aged woman suggested. "There must be other churches like ours in changing neighborhoods." Then Edith, who'd been baptized at St. Mark's eighty-three years before, uncharacteristically quiet to this point, began to speak, and a respectful hush fell. "I wonder if our work at this corner is coming to an end," she said in a solemn yet resolute way. "Don't talk that way, Edith" was the first, hasty response. "You, of anyone, Edith," a man nearly her age added. "No, listen to me," she continued. "Hear me out. The bishop's going to come for the keys sometime. Sooner or later. Maybe not this year or next, but it's only a matter of time." She sat up as straight as her bent back would allow, her eyes bright. "Let's take the keys to the bishop!"

I sat there rather stunned myself, wondering how to adapt my plan for the rest of the day, now clearly out of alignment, as Edith's words struck a chord, propelling the group in an unexpected direction that slowly gained momentum. Silence proved the best strategy. Their sharing was an honor to behold. Each spoke in an assured and measured way, each listened with breathtaking attentiveness. The matter of their endowment, a bank balance that had shrunk to $100,000, was raised. It was enough, one argued, that with prudent budgeting, they could survive for at least a while. "I don't want to just survive," Edith insisted. "And it's just not very good use of that money," another quickly added, each head around the circle nodding agreement. Finally, surprised and saddened, yet empowered and ennobled, midstream in a "visioning" retreat designed to reignite the fire and inspire a revitalized future, the board of this church called itself to order. The members prayed for wisdom, discernment, and courage, and voted decisively and unanimously to dissolve the church and to invite the congregation to concur with their decision. Six months later, the Sunday after Easter, with robust singing and hearty remembering, flowing tears and deep joy, they held their last worship service in that sanctuary.

Elisabeth Kübler-Ross's *five stages of dying*—never, of course, experienced in such neat and orderly ways—provides a lens for understanding the intervening six months.[2] My friend David's leadership and moderating skills were put to the test. The first congregational meeting was a raucous and unruly affair. A groundswell of solidarity immediately coalesced, with people insisting that this decision was simply and clearly inappropriate and unnecessary, that the church's ministry, though in admitted decline, was still vital and healthy, that the board had acted impulsively and prematurely. Referring to hastily penciled notes, a longtime member curtly reported that the bank balance, though not immense, guaranteed they could "keep going" for another eight to ten years by his calculation. Another veteran member, blanching at the sound of "keep going," wondered aloud if that was good stewardship, even if the math was accurate. Kübler-Ross calls this stage *denial*.

If reasoned argument is the soft-sell form of denial, anger lurks nearby. "My great-grandmother, my grandmother, and my mother sat in this pew, and I sit in this pew. My parents were married in St. Mark's, I was married in St. Mark's, and I want my kids to be married in St. Mark's," fumed a middle-aged woman. "I've sat in every Sunday-school classroom and taught in each to boot," stormed another, claiming permission for raised voices and clenched fists, "and you're gonna take that away from me?" The *anger* stage. David and the board, wise enough to respond with quiet understanding, in nonconfrontational ways, provided the needed nonanxious presence, defusing if not resolving the dynamics at play. The senior warden reminded those gathered that this meeting was intended solely for discussion, with no decision to be made. It ended awkwardly.

Much telephoning went on in the next weeks, as members anticipated a second meeting at which the motion to close the church would be offered. Everyone had a carefully crafted plan for easing the financial stress and silencing this talk of closing the church.

They could rent space in the church to community organizations, postpone maintenance projects, recruit volunteers to cut the grass and shovel the snow, and worship during the winter in the parish house to save fuel costs. Kübler-Ross calls this stage *bargaining.*

Evidence of passing through step four, *depression,* was evident in members' slow-motion gait, slumped postures, and muted and muffled words at that second meeting. Stoic and resolute at best, warding off feelings of failure and defeat, facing an inevitability that seemed more imposed than chosen, they voted by a substantial margin to close the church. As adjournment time neared, Edith, acknowledging that it was she who had set this process in motion, rose to speak. Her voice resonant with a mixture of grief and celebration, her countenance mingling deep sadness and profound joy, she insisted they were not "throwing in the towel" or "giving up" and congratulated her fellow members for their faithfulness and stewardship. "We are more than just a handful of worshipers, and our church property is in good repair. And yes, we have a bank balance on which to draw. We could survive. But simply surviving is not what God calls us to," she concluded. Then inviting them to stand tall, she looked down to an open pew Bible she held in her hand, and read, "We have fought the good fight, we have finished the race, we have kept the faith. From now on there is reserved for us the crown of righteousness, which the Lord, the righteous judge, will give to us on that day, and not only to us, but also to all who have longed for his appearance" (2 Timothy 4:7–8, adapted).

Denial and bargaining, anger and depression seemed ready to yield to the final stage of dying or grieving, *acceptance.* An older voice cracking with both age and emotion got it started, and the group began to sing the Doxology.

All was not smooth sailing. Staying the last months' course meant navigating some difficult waters. A young man's funeral broke free a scab, and fresh anger erupted. Freshly honed bailout plans reemerged. Singing a sentimental hymn or reading a favorite psalm stirred aches of sadness and depression. But clarity and that abiding sense of faithfulness and stewardship held. At their final worship service the members sang with abandon, David preached with fervor, and they wept as they received communion, knees pressed into those tattered needlepoint cushions, their hands unconsciously caressing that weathered oak rail for the last time. A spirit of festivity overflowed at the meal that followed. And, yes, they took the keys to the bishop the following week.

There is a postscript that deserves to be told. The church was sold to an ethnic minority congregation that is thriving at that corner. The proceeds from the sale, together with the unspent funds, supported several congregations in the diocese in a redevelopment process. And whenever people from St. Mark's return as worship visitors with that new congregation, they are welcomed as honored guests, as patriarchs and matriarchs of a vital Christian presence of the past. And, as they went their way into differing congregations, they named themselves as "St. Mark's in diaspora," would-be missionaries carrying the spirit of St. Mark's with them, including Olive at age ninety-five.

A Shoe That May Fit

I've been itching for years to tell publicly this story of St. Mark's Church. Sometimes, when I've told it privately, someone has dared to ask if I am the "Dr. Kevorkian of congregational consulting." Risking hyperbole, I say without hesitation that no congregation has claimed my admiration, my hearty applause, my deep respect quite like St. Mark's Episcopal Church. If I were to choose, among many churches I have worked with over twenty years, the one I most wish could become an inspiration and challenge to "faithfulness and stewardship," it would be this one. I am convinced that this story of St. Mark's, if widely shared, has the potential to touch a wide range of congregations in profoundly transformational ways, as much as any congregation I have known or read about.

Questions unite, answers divide, someone wisely said. Rainer Maria Rilke in *Letters to a Young Poet* urged that young poet to more robustly and patiently love the questions. But questions can be disturbing and unsettling, probing and provocative as well.

How many churches, if a spirit of "faithfulness and high steward-ship" blew in like a fresh wind, would choose with nobility what St. Mark's chose? How many bishops, if graced with gifts of cour-age and persuasiveness, would lovingly but unwaveringly "ask for the keys" of churches whose only signs of life are the life-support systems? Where are the Ediths, those whose years of service have won them the right to speak, willing to say with authority, "our work here is coming to an end"? Where are the Dans, those ready to craft a "living will" for a church poised at the precipice of vi-ability? What would it take for potential Ediths and Dans reading these words to dare to hear a similar calling?

Focus for a moment on the matter of endowment. How many congregations across America are *living on inheritance*—staying alive through a private, internal welfare system that subsidizes the present membership? What did those generous donors from a generation and more ago originally intend for their bequests? I'm guessing they had vital, outreaching mission and ministry in mind, not underwriting a handful of folk, widely scattered across larger-than-needed sanctuaries, demanding outrageous per-capita assistance to "keep the church going."

I hasten to add that an endowment can become yesterday's generosity for today's revitalized ministry. Just as a building is a legacy of the past, an endowment can inspire creativity, make pos-sible innovative approaches to reach out to new populations in new ways, providing new wineskins for new wine. I wish this were the norm, rather than the rare exception.

It is clearly anecdotal evidence, but just for fun, I randomly chose ten congregational folders from my cabinet of client files, pulling each church's year-end financial report, and conducted a simple research project. Try it with your church's report. Write down, less monies assigned for local or overseas missions and social ministries, the total annual expense budget, dividing that amount by the total number of members, which yields the annual per capita cost to maintain the church. Write down total congre-gational giving, divide by the number of members, yielding the per capita giving. Now subtract total congregational giving from the expense budget, or subtract per capita giving from per capita costs, if costs are greater than giving. Either way, you will likely see a hefty difference, a deficit funded from other sources: rental income, special fund raisers, denominational support—and endowment. Math was never my strong suit, but those figures, by my calculation, name in dollar terms the stipend or grants from the internal welfare system. And, remember, we are talking about an enormous number of congregations.

While I had those files out, I computed the aggregate endowment of those ten randomly selected churches, which totaled a staggering $11,750,000. In each case endowment income was being tapped to meet current expenses, and in seven of the ten, endowment principal was being spent down. The collective total endowment of such churches nationwide—those, I am arguing, that "faithfulness and stewardship" may suggest closing—would be unimaginable, overwhelming, gargantuan—and, may I say it, hugely embarrassing. The numbers are soft and imprecise, but I'd guess there are ten thousand churches in the greater metropolitan area where I live, and that five thousand of them are marginal at best, what I am calling subsidized, internal-welfare-based and endowment-dependent churches. Just play with the logic and math. Five thousand marginal churches, reasonably presumed to have an average endowment of $100,000, could release to the broader work of mission and ministry, in a region in almost desperate need, half a billion dollars.

BACK TO HOPE CHURCH

Originally written for adults, *The Neverending Story* by Michael Ende has become a movie geared for kids, shown regularly on children's channels. The story revolves around Bastian, a shy and self-effacing boy of about nine or ten, who avoids the pain of his usually unsuccessful interaction with peers by losing himself in books. He becomes engrossed in one rather engaging book, *Fantasia,* whose characters utterly captivate him, but becomes terrified when he suddenly realizes that the story cannot proceed without his participation. The protagonist in the story suddenly seems literally reaching out to "pull him in." Using a clever cinematic convention, the fictional story line and Bastian's real life are superimposed and interwoven. Finally Bastian decides with trepidation to jump into the story line, to respond to the fictional characters calling for his help. As he moves back and forth between these two "worlds," his decision diverts a plot line careening toward disaster, and his involvement becomes the key to a positive ending. Having chosen to be the transforming presence in the narrative, he himself is transformed.

This is not unlike the ending to Mark's Gospel. Evidently a growing scholarly consensus concludes that Mark ended his writing at 16:8, as open-ended, perplexing, and tantalizingly incomplete as it reads. Some women walk to the garden at dawn, see that the stone that sealed the tomb has been rolled aside, and enter. A man in a white robe offers comforting and explicit words of both explanation and instruction. The crucified one has been raised. They are to go and tell the disciples that Jesus goes before them into Galilee, where they will see him. They rush from the tomb in amazement and terror, and "they said nothing to anyone, for they were afraid" (Mark 16:8).

That same last page offers half a dozen "other possible endings" of varying length, usually printed in smaller type. Are these attempts to save the Gospel from an awkward, incomplete ending? Do they serve to "tie up its loose ends," to craft a more orderly, less annoying ending? Or is Mark employing a literary convention not unlike Michael Ende, engaging us as "Bastian" to "enter the story" and thus write its ending?[3]

I offer those reflections to segue back to the story line with which we began, that council meeting at Hope Lutheran Church. An unlikely metaphor—a living will for a congregation—had stimulated disarmingly candid conversation; inspired courage to name and face realities the members confessed they'd chosen not to acknowledge, let alone engage; and, painful as it was, led them to ponder the possibility that there was little hope for a vital future.

Looking on from a Bastian perspective, hovering above their unfolding congregational story, watching it veer toward an increasingly negative outcome, these leaders want to act with faithfulness and decisiveness, but they are unsure how to "jump in." Not unlike the women at the tomb, they sense a message coming to clarity but are unsure how to speak it. My last words at that council meeting, before the pastor offered a closing prayer, reminded them that the foundational metaphor of our faith is resurrection, not resuscitation.

If not a "never-ending story," theirs is an unfinished story and, as I write, new chapters are being written. During that first meeting I projected a broad-brush plan for moving forward they might want to consider, profiling a first step in greater detail, and then briefly describing possible steps to follow. They decided to take that first step.

Six weeks later I preached at each of their worship services and then led an hour-and-a-half workshop open to the entire membership. The workshop followed a format akin to the one I had used at the council meeting. The room buzzed with the lively sounds of their sharing what they appreciated and loved about Hope Church, and after representatives from each table shared their lists, someone started what became a rousing singing of a favorite hymn. Momentum was slower to build when I asked them to project elements of their vision for the future, but soon each table glowed with smiling faces and animated speaking.

Reporters from the tables spoke in more muted tones, their energy more restrained and their dreams of the future sounding more like reminiscence from the past, nostalgia punctuated by lament. But a younger contingent, some of them sitting at each of the tables, helped the others name what seemed to be promising possibilities for the future. I wrote words or phrases to caption each vision on a white board. The final table assignment was a more deliberate task: with those vision captions in mind, propose an agenda for four or five ministry teams that could form to initiate movement toward that future. Four suggested themselves from the summaries of the work at their tables: (1) a church growth team,

(2) a building assessment team, (3) a children and youth team, and (4) an "outreach to our community" team. I wrote the name of each team on the top of four large pieces of newsprint.

As our appointed end time approached, I asked each participant to take three brightly colored Post-it Notes from the pads at the center of their table, with this comment and assignment: "Your leadership team serves this church with devotion, steadiness, and hard work. You know that. You appreciate that. But—and I have their permission to tell you this—they are tired. Very tired. For too long they have done too much. They need your help. The vision you have begun to project is *your* vision, and the work to be done is *your* work. Before you leave, use your three stick-on notes. You may have a suggestion for one of those teams, which you could communicate via a note or two. But use at least one note, with your name and phone number, to indicate your readiness to join one of the teams. If your work here today is a ballot, this is your chance to vote." The pastor pronounced a benediction and, as people rose from their chairs, I noticed the council members watching intently, wondering how this process would go.

I watched too, remembering four or five other churches, not unlike Hope, where I had used a similar workshop strategy. A church in a seashore town came to mind, where a beleaguered and overextended leadership team voiced little optimism about my "Post-it plan" as they called it, only to see five newly formed ministry teams spring to life over the next six months. I remembered an inner-city church with virtually no active organizational structure, a board with no working committees, simply working together to get the work done. They assured me that few Post-its would wave from the newsprint sheets. Self-conscious about their pessimism, they became delightfully surprised when six teams of at least six persons each suddenly materialized. They invited me to return to conduct a leadership workshop to train and coach these teams into effectiveness. They went from having no committees to six ministry teams, each one flourishing over the next year, giving creative and markedly effective leadership in the congregation.

The pastor's tap on my shoulder brought me back from my reverie and to an unsettling awareness. Precious few Post-its hung from the newsprint sheets. And a quick glance at those that did found names of the "same old, same old"—those who had already confessed their fatigue, on whose behalf I had made what seemed a fruitless plea.

As I drove home, beginning to ponder the assessment report I had promised to write at this point in our work together, a biblical story came to mind that, frankly, had always confused and perturbed me—until a woman in a Bible study group, a horticulturalist, offered a most helpful piece of information. Jesus, walking from Bethany toward Jerusalem with his disciples, approaches a fig tree in full leaf, looking for a fig to eat, but in a season, the narrator tells us, when fig trees do not bear fruit. How unjust, it seems, that Jesus curses the tree. The next day, the tree now withered and dead, Jesus launches into an extended teaching. I confessed my discomfort with this story to that study group, adding that traditional interpretations just didn't work for me. Hesitant, knowing she was not a biblical scholar, that horticulturalist reported that some trees, fig trees among them, in the process of dying put forth, in their last season, foliage heartier and greener than ever before. No one had to kill the fig tree. But it helps to know that a burst of apparent healthiness can precede demise.

I knew in a moment why that story came to mind. Much of my visit to Hope had been what I'd name in my report as a "series of delightful surprises." The building, significantly larger than they needed, was in remarkably good repair, the sanctuary was freshly painted, and the entranceway, inside and out, was inviting. The worship services were better attended than I had expected, the age range was broad, and more children and youth were present than I had anticipated. A choir of fourteen sang a complicated and demanding anthem flawlessly, accompanied by a talented organist and a fine trumpeter. I watched with delight as people gathered, and found their words and gestures of welcome, to each other and to me, to be warm and genuine. Maybe Hope Church was better off than I thought. The foliage was green and lush.

I have written that report. I congratulated them on all that I found so delightful. But the meager response to the Post-it invitation could not be ignored. I thumbed through the church directory to discover how few members lived remotely close to the church, since many had moved when the community shifted ethnically and racially. The council president confirmed that the average age of the congregation was moving steadily upward and that the scattering of new members failed to replace those who died or finally moved their membership closer to home. An even cursory review of the year-end financial summary revealed a rapidly widening deficit that would demand a more rapid spend-down of the endowment.

At my most recent meeting with the board the members asked a good and timely question. As Dan stated it, "How do we know if or when it is time to 'pull the plug'?" I flipped to a fresh sheet of newsprint on a nearby easel and suggested we brainstorm together a list of possible criteria, knowing the answers they framed would ground them in their discernment more than any I would offer alone. Someone edited what I had written, bulleting each item, and used it as an agenda for a subsequent board meeting, and then distributed it to congregation members for their reflection.

- Can we inspire more people to come forward to expand our ranks of willing workers?
- Can we recruit and equip more leaders?
- Are we willing to develop a plan to reach out to the community to invite and welcome newcomers and, when we have visitors, will we incorporate them into the life and ministry of our church?
- Can we develop a plan for alternative uses of our building, not only to augment income but to provide programs and services relevant to our neighborhood?
- Can we envision ways to use our endowment to work with partner organizations to minister to our community in new and creative ways? Do such partner organizations exist? How do we find them? How might we help them come into existence?
- Are we willing to be flexible in our style of worship and types of program offerings, given the changing ethnic and racial trends in our neighborhood?

- Can we develop a plan, with specific and time-targeted goals, to reverse the trend of decreasing membership, participation and financial support? Do we have the human resources to carry out such a plan?

The Hope Church story ends with an uncertainty not unlike Mark 16:8. It is not my task as a consultant to predict or promote particular outcomes. The process at this moment is open, and my role, if any, is undefined. At the moment, I am faithful to my commitment to pray for Hope Church. This introduces a last Post-it. Whenever I am asked to pray for someone, or for a congregation, I write their name on a Post-it and place it with the others on a page in my journal. Each morning, I lift the notes one at a time, from yesterday's page, placing them on today's page, but pausing with each in turn rather literally "holding" them in prayer. Bo and Betsy . . . the Gross family . . . Bill, his wife and his doctor . . . Don, struggling with alcohol . . . Gene, facing surgery . . . Jason and Carol, whose marriage is in crisis . . . Tim in Iraq . . . John, looking for work . . . my sons, their wives, and our grandchildren . . . *and Hope Lutheran Church.*

8

A Long And Winding Road

The Gift of Hope

I am old enough to cozy into the leisurely pace of retirement, declining invitations to new and arduous journeys, no matter how promising the destination. But there is always that restless sense that God isn't finished with me yet, that I remain a work in progress. Urged on by Paul, no kid at the time himself, I want to let go of what's behind and press on toward tomorrow's upward call.

The last six months have been such a journey for me. Unsure when it commenced, its ultimate destination still uncertain, it has not traversed a particularly orderly or efficient route. But then, I am not author of the story! Some months ago I awoke—in stark, vivid, almost overwhelming ways—to the myriad realities of global degradation, the overwhelming human cost of injustice, convincing and unsettling doomsday scenarios unfolding in every sector. I became aware that others are wrestling with the same issues, as if these awesome realities are assaulting our defenses, as our strategies of denial are faltering, at risk of collapse. I began to realize how frightened and hopeless many people are, and how disabling that fear and despair can become. Close behind my own fear, discouragement was unmasked. Finally, in the midst of the distress, I began to awaken to a calling: to face more and more boldly and unflinchingly into those global realities, to engage unwaveringly with my own fear and hopelessness, that I might become more firmly grounded in courage and hope, a voice and witness for a sweeping mission, dreaming a different future for our planet. I had no idea how wrenching, disturbing, and grueling this journey would become.

WHAT SEEMS THE DEPARTURE POINT

Heat and humidity come early to Biloxi, Mississippi, where Betsy and I had completed a third ten-day stint as reconstruction workers with Katrina victims. Biloxi remains awash in signs of discouragement and despair, emergency services and supplies having dwindled long before even basic needs have been met. The Gulf Coast has edged off the media radar screen and out of public awareness. Church-based teams remain the backbone of the rebuilding effort, tantalizingly slow-going as it is: Presbyterians in blue shirts, Methodists in red, and Lutherans in green. Vans and supply trailers converge at building sites, as eager volunteers get ready for next reconstruction steps on their assigned house. Occasionally a bell rings, beckoning those within earshot to gather for a tree-planting ceremony at a completed house, while the owners stand beaming, posing for a photo op. Betsy and I walked down that street one afternoon, after the crews had left, passing finished homes, those in process, and those still in ruins. I confessed to a jumble of feelings: joy, then sadness; hope, then despair; peace, then agitation. "I guess where we look determines what we see. I guess how we feel depends on where we look," Betsy said quietly. I could feel her words imprinting on my consciousness.

We altered our route home to visit friends in Charleston, South Carolina, and to attend a workshop titled "The Awakening the Dreamer/Changing the Dream Symposium." Arriving early, we looked over the event literature and then found seats among the gathering participants, twenty-five in all. A quote was handwritten on newsprint in the front: *If you are not pessimistic, you are not open to reality. If you are not optimistic, you are not open to your heart.* I had no idea how prophetic those words would become, a caption aptly summarizing the seminar, and a perfect title for my personal journey now gaining momentum. The mission statement of the sponsoring organization was on the screen: *To bring forth an environmentally sustainable, spiritually fulfilling, and socially just presence on this planet as a guiding principle for our time.* I had no idea in that moment how thoroughly and deeply that mission statement would claim me six months in the future.

This finely crafted workshop blended crisply presented data, magnificent video clips by respected authorities in several fields, and perfectly timed opportunity for reflection and discussion in small groups. But at noon that day I might have said otherwise! The day starkly divided into two halves, at least for me. Simply stated, by lunch I felt utterly overwhelmed and exhausted, discouraged and hopeless. The human family is clearly, unarguably in peril: momentums toward unsustainability gaining convulsive velocity, the gap between rich and poor broadening exponentially, mechanisms for global dialogue in collapse, and the authority and power of traditional custodians of spirituality and divine wisdom waning. I sat alone with nowhere to go but up, as they say.

As I swallowed the last of my soda and comforted myself with a chocolate-chip cookie, I would have never guessed how differently I would feel at 4:30, as the day concluded. Signs of hope, however tentative and fragile, were highlighted—promising strategies to confront the planetary crisis, hopeful testimony from scientists and activists, and hints, however subtle, of awakening consciousness. "Exhilarated" would not be too dramatic a word. Energized, full of vision, ready to "change the dream," and hopeful—yes, above all else, hopeful. Like the Wise Men, though the itinerary remained shrouded in mystery, I knew I was departing for home "by another way." I was mercifully unaware that what lay ahead was a long and winding road.

A LONG AND WINDING ROAD

Chris is a kindred spirit. We have a similar restlessness about life. Viewing ourselves as thinking outside the box, we are drawn to

speak and act on matters of peace and social justice, sending each
other articles from radical websites. He had called to ask if we
could meet and chat over a cup of coffee, and we found ourselves
sequestered on my back porch one warm day in early summer,
two months after our Biloxi sojourn. The sense of hopelessness
that prompted his call was evident in the way he slumped into
a wicker chair. Ever so subtly, beneath or beyond my consciousness, I slipped into the role of encourager, source of optimism and
hope, any real personal presence and genuineness slipping away
in the process. Firmly ensconced in "helper mode," I managed a
confident tone, offering a seamless message of optimism and hope.
Chris left, he later confessed, feeling worse than when he arrived.
And in the hours, then days, then weeks that followed I dropped
into my own dark night of fear and hopelessness. *The "morning
half" of the symposium, the despair and hopelessness at lunch, returned
with a vengeance.*

A conversation with my friend George always helps me get
perspective, to renew my grounding and focus, so I called to arrange an emergency lunch. A therapist by trade, blending gentle-
ness and firmness, he encouraged me to "voyage through" rather
than "seek passage around" whatever was up for me, not to settle
for the "pseudo-hopefulness" I had offered Chris. There seemed
no way *to* a place of renewed, sturdier hope, at least for me, than
through this valley. George was right and I was grateful, though
only a touch relieved.

A deluge of dreams erupted: lengthy, images repeating themselves, some scenes dramatic and unsettling. A series of dreams with
assaulting repetition: *remodeling jobs where nothing fits—a random
assortment of plastic tubing and fittings that I cannot configure for a
plumbing installation; odd-sized pieces of drywall like puzzle pieces
that I cannot fathom; electrical wiring with sections each cut just too
short. I awake tossing and turning with frustration.*

Another set: *I cannot solve the riddle, break the code, unscramble
the letters, the failure to do so having dire though vague consequences.*
And still another: *a series of dreams where I am being pursued, hunted*

down, on the run, breathless and frightened. The frustration from the dreams carried into the day. Waking or sleeping, nothing fit.

A blend of sadness, depression, and mounting outrage deepened. I felt overwhelmed, bursting at the seams, poised at some breaking point. I felt uncharacteristically vulnerable, persistently discouraged, and hopeless, all which I hated to admit, especially to myself.

A few days later a "third installment" arrived from The Dream-Maker, two more dreams even more dramatic and emotion-laden than the others. *Betsy and I are cornered outside a building on a seminary campus by men wearing skullcaps who announce themselves as "orthodoxy partners," enforcers of truth, and they have been tracking us down . . . Betsy and I and our son and his wife are nestled securely in an overstuffed couch mesmerized by a broad vista across pounding surf. A WWII era plane rumbles over, flying low, suddenly diving into a fiery crash, a gigantic and lengthy explosion. I brace for a wave of flame to engulf and incinerate us; but it rushes by, hot but not burning.* I awaken from each bolt upright, sweating, and breathing rapidly. Yet I remained convinced that beneath this turbulence and upheaval lay a pathway toward hope, and prayed for stamina to stay this course.

I found clarity and a touch of comfort in a sentence that emerged from somewhere in my unconscious: *hope that cannot look fully and courageously into the face of reality is not worthy to be called hope.* My hope, it instructed me, was neither *large* enough, nor *deep* enough, nor *courageous* enough. Our grandkids collect hermit crabs, literally, by the hundreds at a children's beach at the shore. "Look, Pop-pop," the six-year-old exclaimed, "here's a little crab in a big shell, and a big crab in a little shell." As a hermit crab outgrows its scavenged shell, cautiously, susceptible to predators, it leaves and seeks a larger one. My hope needed to risk getting *larger*.

And grow *deeper*. When the leaves of our nearly century-old jade plant, a legacy from my grandmother, began to lose their sheen and steadily droop, we panicked. We carried it carefully to our local nurseryman. "Its roots are ready to go deeper," he quietly assured us. "You must transplant it to a taller, deeper pot. But do so carefully, as exposing the roots is traumatic to the plant," he instructed. This odd, unlikely sense of kinship with hermit crabs and a jade plant offered encouragement in this traumatic and vulnerable season of my journey.

And become more *courageous*. If Lutheran pastor Dietrich Bonhoeffer distinguished between "cheap grace" and "costly grace," was I being urged toward "costly hope"? Did my hope cower from looking squarely, without denial or defenses, into that face of reality? Biblically, hope seems to reside on the other side of fear, the nativity story brimming with illustrations. "Do not be afraid," the angel assured Zechariah, startled and terrified, "overwhelmed" by fear (Luke 1:12–13). Only as Gabriel quiets her fear can Mary declare, "Let it be with me according to your word" (Luke 1:38). His fear stilled by a dream's angel, Joseph is able to mount such staggering trust (Matt. 1:20, 24). The very glory that overwhelmed them, and the angel of the Lord that terrified them, invited the shepherds beyond their fear to venture into town and the birthing place (Luke 2:9–10). Some version of "be not afraid" appears seventeen times in the New Testament, each a prelude to faithfulness and empowerment. I had good companionship on my awesome voyage.

The Fog Lifts

August arrived and with it a visit to Monhegan Island, an hour out to sea off the coast of Maine, in recent years a sacred space. Its rugged climbs to spectacular views of the sea, its endless forest trails meandering along jungle-like terrain, gently invite a more leisurely pace. I sat one morning, virtually motionless for three hours, perched on an outcropping of granite boulders, awed by the siege of the rising tide, pounding and crashing in breathtaking relentlessness. An almost primal awe clutched my chest as foam and spray leapt around me. Yet I felt unwaveringly safe, those ancient stones beneath me. Something inside was shifting.

The faltering beam of an old and flimsy flashlight probed the darkness, barely illuminating the rough and narrow trail up Horne Hill, as step by carefully placed step I made my way toward Burnt Head, the island's highest elevation, offering the broadest sweep of the sea. I tugged on a hooded sweatshirt as an evening chill set in, settled onto a tattered old chair cushion I'd found in our cottage, and gazed toward the barely discernible horizon. Though I'd lived by the sea for a time and have vacationed along the East Coast every summer of my life, I'd never seen a moonrise. If light can whisper, such was the first bare hint of a brightening in the distance, so faint I wondered if it was my imagination at play. No, a glow, a hint of light, ever so faint. Then, like a low-voltage sunrise, a pinprick in the darkness expanded into a richly subtle orb of yellow-orange, its beams shimmering and dancing across the rippling outgoing tide. And something quieted inside, a calm I had not felt for months.

Weather changes abruptly out to sea and a nor'easter rumbled in just before dawn, the windows in our rustic cottage vibrating, wind whistling under the eaves, pounding rain, then stillness, and then dense fog. Resisting the urge to curl in front of a cozy fire, I donned my raingear and ventured toward the town dock, dripping with moisture as I arrived, turning a crate on edge as a place to sit. I could see nothing. Gradually, slowly and steadily as that rising tide, subtle and silent as that moonrise, the fog began to lift. The winch at the end of the dock peeked into view. Boats in the lagoon tugged at their moorings as a breeze freshened. The sweeping silhouette of the adjacent island loomed into view. Startled by a blast of the horn announcing the arrival of the morning's first ferry, I felt some inner fog lifting. I found myself humming an old pop tune, "I can see clearly now, the rain has gone." "Hope," I whispered to myself, "I think this is about hope."

We boarded that ferry the next morning, headed home. "Land ahoy!" someone should have shouted. Had something shifted in me? Was hope of a more bedrock nature firming beneath my feet?

Was I ready to venture going public with a more genuine message of hope and possibility, a new dream and a fresh vision? It had taken endless wandering down some dead-end streets, rushing off on fruitless tacks, jettisoning erroneous assumptions and months of trial and error to approach this new clarity. It seemed across my weeks in search of hope I needed to learn first what hope was *not*.

WHAT HOPE IS NOT

Hope is not a matter of logic. Someone once said that we do not "think our way to a new way of living, but we live our way to a new way of thinking." Largely unawares, I had been trying to put together a case for hope, a solid and airtight argument, bolstered by convincing evidence. I wanted a blueprint, a handbook, an absolutely reliable plan. Like those houses of cards I used to build on rainy afternoons with my grandmother, my reasoned, cognitive enterprise, just when it seemed on the verge of completion, tumbled down. Hope built on logic proved as sturdy as that house built on sand of which Jesus spoke.

Hope is not a feeling. Hopelessness *is* a feeling, pervasive and debilitating. My mind, maybe yours too, has a tendency to tell me, with its own sigh of resignation, that the problems are too big, that I am too small, and we are too few. Signs of discouragement are, arguably, everywhere; scenarios of a less-than-desirable if not disastrous future come all too vividly and disturbingly to mind. One can track movements toward environmental collapse, global unrest, the threat of lethal weapons in rogue hands. Structures of stability—governments, economic entities, organizations for international dialogue and cooperation, public- and private-sector charitable groups, even religions—appear in disarray, on the verge of collapse. But when people yield to fear, and bend under the weight of hopelessness, these momentums accelerate. Fear and hopelessness may constitute our greatest threat. Yet, paradoxically, hope is *not* a feeling.

Hope is not a place to arrive. There is truth in that familiar phrase, "the journey is the destination," or a passage from T. S. Eliot:

> We shall not cease from exploration
> And the end of all our exploring
> Will be to arrive where we started
> And know the place for the first time.[1]

How I wanted to simply come out some other side of my dark place, as the Shaker hymn sings it, "by turning, turning we come round right," a place to settle down and call home. Paul reminds us constantly that he is a person not only geographically but personally and spiritually "on the move." The Gospels offer us glimpses of Peter's process of formation, celebrating his faithfulness and learning from his failures. Biblical Jews seem more faithful in tents than in temples, as nomads than city dwellers, on the move rather than set and settled. Google Earth may be able to monitor a journey toward hope, but there is no MapQuest to plot a course to a destination named Hope, unless you're headed to Arkansas!

Hope does not ensure outcomes we will see. Deuteronomy reports Moses's last instructions and final speech to the people he led out of slavery, now encamped by the river they will cross to the Promised Land. His stirring words are meant to send those pilgrims forward brimming with hope. But he will ascend a nearby mountain and die. No one who survived the hasty and drama-filled escape from Pharaoh's pursuit, except Joshua and Caleb, lived to cross the Jordan. Fifty thousand deaths and fifty thousand births mark that wilderness sojourn. Jeremiah buys a piece of land in a city poised for destruction, a sign of hope of a future he will not see. Martin Luther King Jr., echoing the words of Moses, thunders a declaration, that he has seen the Promised Land, while his words become suddenly softer, almost whispered, as he senses he may not walk that land himself. Theological giant Reinhold Niebuhr distinguished between *proximate* and *ultimate*. Challenging us to be people of vision and purpose, setting goals and working tirelessly for their accomplishment, he reminded us that these time-targeted goals, these inspired and inspiring aspirations, these high and important strivings are human, thus limited, *proximate* goals. Only God has *ultimate* vision working ultimate outcomes.[2]

Hope does not depend on outcomes at all. The value of hope is intrinsic. It envisions but is not contingent on an outcome. Czech Republic and world leader Václav Havel spoke of hope as he challenged his beleaguered people to dare a new dream, "Hope is a state of mind, not a state of the world. Either we have hope within us, or we don't. It is a dimension of the soul; it is not essentially dependent upon some particular observation of the world . . . (Hope) is not the conviction that something will turn out well, but the certainty that something makes sense, regardless of how it turns out."[3] Life provides continual, sometimes anguished evidence of this.

Hope Is a Choice

Tony Campolo, a well-known author and speaker and a longtime colleague and friend of mine, has spoken thousands of words, but a single sentence, a line from a sermon I'd heard him preach, is etched in my memory: "Frankly, the argument against believing in God or against placing one's trust in Jesus is every bit as persuasive as the argument for it. So, I chose to choose to believe and trust. And that choice has made all the difference." "Choose to choose" can seem awkward and redundant, but it may be a necessary first step in search of a genuine hope. This is not splitting hairs or playing word games. *Choosing to choose* is different from merely choosing. It evokes a sturdy intention, flexes against doubt and resistance, hones resilience, and sends down hearty roots. It has stamina and longevity, poised for a long-distance run. It is resolute and determined. Merely choosing can be unreflective and impulsive, while choosing to choose is reasoned and measured.

A two-word imperative, "choose life," concludes Moses's final speech on the banks of the Jordan (Deut. 30:19). After a long season of divine patience, Elijah announces a time of choosing is at hand: "How long will you go limping with two different opinions?"

Elijah asks. "If the LORD is God, follow him; but if Baal, then follow him" (1 Kings 18:21). "You cannot serve God and money," Jesus proclaims succinctly; a choice must be made. Be hot or cold, but not lukewarm; hear the knock and open the door, the Spirit speaks to the church at Laodicea (Rev. 3:15–16, 20). It is a matter of choice. Choose to choose hope.

HOPE IS CHOOSING WHERE TO LOOK

Betsy's words, as we ended that workday in Biloxi, were prescient: *I guess where we look determines what we see. I guess how we feel depends on where we look.* Nothing frivolous or Pollyannaish here. No recycling of some "power of positive thinking." No rose-colored glasses or naivete. Evidence for hopefulness and despair abounds, and beckons constantly and persuasively. Negativity surrounds us, taunts us, and seduces us relentlessly. Paul counsels us to choose where we set our mind—on that which is true and honorable, just and pure, pleasing and commendable (Phil. 4:8). *Hope begins with where we choose to look.*

Read the morning paper with an eye for the hopeful. The rapes and murders, burglaries and fires that saturate the front pages are worthy of note, if nothing else to pause to pray for both victims and perpetrators. Only a more patient, inquisitive, and discerning eye will notice the story of the newly opened school on the West Bank where Jewish and Palestinian children sit side by side. Buried on page eight is the touching story of a neighborhood party to raise money for medical care for a five-year-old child wounded in the crossfire of a gang shoot-out. A tiny piece at the end of a Sunday paper's magazine section informs us that Bhutan, a Himalayan kingdom that only recently opened its borders, has crafted a five-year development plan that defines, measures, and monitors as first priority its GNH (gross national happiness), then secondarily its GNP (gross national product). *Hope begins with where we choose to look.*

Focus on headlines of hope from the past, attentive to simple heroism, the quiet power of vision and hope, news photos indelible in our memories: the African American five-year-old clinging to her mother's hand as they strode defiantly into an Alabama elementary school in the mid-fifties; that Chinese student racing from the crowd to stand his ground in the face of an army tank in Tiananmen Square; members of a tribe in the Amazon rain forest blocking a mammoth grader poised to overrun their family farms and denude their tribal landscape; a returning seaman embracing his girlfriend in Times Square. *Hope begins with where we choose to look.*

Collect stories of hope. Collecting seems a common human trait: autographs or baseball cards, buttons or figurines, dolls or matchbox cars, stamps or coins. I collect stories of hope—like Thomas Clarkson's story. Can a turning point in history occur on a single day? There had been some form of slavery on every continent for five millennia of human history. On June 17, 1785, Clarkson, a poor divinity student, won a prestigious essay contest traditionally claimed by a Cambridge or Oxford student. His theme was "Is it lawful to make slaves of others against their will?" Moved and troubled himself by his firm denunciation of slavery, he had gathered by sundown that same day a small group willing to think the unthinkable: that society, contrary to prevailing belief, would not collapse without the immoral slave trade. Slavery was finally abolished in Britain four decades later, nearly a century later in the United States.[4]

And there is Wangari Maathai's story. This Kenyan woman, winner of the 2004 Nobel Peace Prize, was enraged by the deforestation of her nation's countryside, devastating the life of the planet and the lives of her people. So she planted a tree, and then some more trees. The women of her village, and then of her entire country, joined her, eventually planting thirty million! Claimed by a vision and by dauntless hope, she would not be stopped. When asked about the source of her passion, she tells an African fable about a hummingbird that, while other animals cowered in fear as a forest fire raged, made trip after trip to the river, filling her beak with water and dropping it on the fire. When the other animals asked her why, she replied, "I am simply doing what I can do!"[5]

Who would have expected the British to leave India nonviolently or apartheid to end without massive bloodshed? Who would have predicted the Berlin wall coming down or the Soviet Union collapsing? Women's suffrage or the 1964 Civil Rights Law? The astounding success of microlending or the emergence of environmental consciousness?

Watch for the hopeful close at hand. Notice people around you who, often in subtle and unpretentious ways, act with sensitivity and loving-kindness, inspired by a hopeful attitude: the conductor on my commuter train whose broad smile and hearty greeting fills the car and its passengers with joy; the greeter at our church who makes every arriving worshiper, newcomer or regular, feel like royalty; the circle of deacons who take love along with the altar flowers to shut-ins after the service; the person who senses when others are in need and knows what to say or do without being intrusive; the couple, concerned about the disposal problem of Styrofoam cups and paper plates, who volunteered to wash china cups and plates after coffee hour. *Hope begins with where we choose to look.*

HOPE IS AN ATTITUDE THAT SHAPES BEHAVIOR

A Cherokee elder, a tribal story goes, sat with his grandchildren around a roaring fire, teaching them about life. "There's a terrible fight between two wolves going on inside me," he began, his eyes glistening, reflecting the flames, the children's eyes widening. "One represents fear, anger, envy, sorrow, and resentment," he went on. "And the other stands for joy, peace, love, hope, and kindness." He paused and the children leaned forward, resting their hands on their palms. One inquisitive youngster asked, "Grandfather, who will win?" The old man looked into each child's eyes before he answered, "The one I feed."[6]

Attitudes inside manifest themselves outside. The third-generation childhood favorite, *The Little Engine That Could,* hinges on a single line, "I think I can, I think I can, I think I can." Attitude influences outcome. Find a dime-sized washer and a piece of thread and I'll prove it. Tie an eight- or ten-inch length of thread to a washer, pull a chair up to the dining-room table, hold the end of the thread between your thumb and forefinger, letting the washer hang motionless. Your eyes fixed on your hand, moving your fingers as imperceptibly as possible, set the washer in motion, left and right, or out and in, as you choose. Then let the washer come to rest. Now shift your attention from your hand to the washer, the task of your fingers to remain still. Begin to *imagine* the washer beginning to move left and right, or out and in, envisioning that movement, but not creating or assisting it. The washer will begin to move, perhaps slowly at first, in an arc that may be subtle and small or, to your amazement, quite vigorous. Finally, imagine, just imagine, the washer slowly coming to rest. And it will.

But it's more than that, more powerful than that, more mysterious than that. As hope changes something inside, cultivating a new way of looking, an attitude influencing our behavior, it becomes contagious, inspiring others, a model motivating imitation and action. Hope transmits an invisible and mysterious energy that not only *inspires* action but is *itself* an action. *Attitudes inside manifest themselves outside.*

Three hundred ninety-three cardiac patients admitted to a coronary care unit were each treated according to protocol, with one additional variable: one group was prayed for (192 patients) and others not (201 patients). The study was conducted according to rigorous research criteria—a "randomized, prospective, double-blind experiment"—and patients, doctors, and nurses were completely unaware of the study; those praying were simply given their patient's name. The results were overwhelming: the prayed-for patients were five times less likely to require antibiotics and three times less likely to develop pulmonary edema; their average stay was two days shorter. The physician who conducted the experiment said the results suggest that *not* to prescribe prayer could be considered malpractice![7] *Attitudes inside manifest themselves outside.*

Teachers, told that students had been tested to determine intellectual potential, were given a list of students expected to excel.

However, the list was actually a *random* list of students with average intelligence and differing potential. At the end of the school year those on the list scored well above the class average, based on a number of testing instruments; the only actual variable was the teacher's attitude transmitted to the students.[8] What would happen if all teachers everywhere were told they had a whole class full of high-potential students? *Attitudes inside manifest themselves outside.*

Princeton and Stanford Universities produced groundbreaking results from a series of fascinating experiments with what some call "non-local" communication, surfacing, rather serendipitously, a most remarkable discovery. Briefly: pairs of "senders" and "receivers," one in California and the other in New Jersey, were issued computer-generated geometric shapes that they were to *send* telepathically across the country, noting the date and time of the sending. At the same time, when they felt they were *receiving* the shape being sent by their partner, they were to draw it, again noting date and time. Computer evaluation of the shapes "sent" and "received" determined more than random similarity in just over half of the exchanges. But even more remarkably, in more than one-third of the "successful" transmissions, the shape was received one to three days before it was sent![9]

Moses invited an unruly, rambunctious band of pilgrims, when discouragement or dissension mounted, to close their eyes and picture in their mind's eye what their human eyes would not see directly for decades, a "land flowing with milk and honey." The vision stirred hope and they pressed on. Abraham, expecting a shorter journey between promise and fulfillment, began to lose heart and stamina, when God led him outside his tent on a starry night. Could he count them, God asked, with the promise that his descendants would outnumber the stars? Vision inspired hope, and Abraham journeyed on. In his last appearance to his disciples Jesus cast up a vision, that they carry the mission to the ends of the earth, and that ragtag bunch got it started. Here we sit halfway around a globe of a magnitude beyond their wildest dream, because they were claimed by a wild dream, an outlandish vision, and an arguably impossible hope.

HOPE IS A MOVEMENT
APPROACHING CRITICAL MASS

I agree with environmentalist and author Paul Hawken (whose recent book *Blessed Unrest* has profoundly influenced me, a book I frequently and fervently recommend) and a remarkable coalescence of native and indigenous peoples—the Hopi Indians of North America, the Achuar and Shuar peoples of Ecuador and Peru, the Maya of Central America, the Nauhuatl of Mexico, just to name a few—that there is a movement arising and gaining momentum that is without precedent in human history, a movement grounded in hope. Joanna Macy calls it The Great Turning. I believe that we are graced with the opportunity and challenge to live the most significant and meaningful lives ever lived, because we are faced with history's most extraordinary threats to life on earth. A movement unnoticed by most, including those within it, a convergence of groups so loosely knit that they are largely unaware of their affiliation. Neither created nor planned, it is emerging, morphing, coalescing naturally. It is spontaneous, a movement whose time has come. A movement without a name, not even approaching "ism" status, it eludes being manipulated or marketed. It is a movement without visible spokespersons, charismatic leaders, dominant figures, so it avoids becoming cultish and personality-centered. Those drawn into this movement do not shy from harsh realities, but refuse to surrender to discouragement and hopelessness.

Is a hope-based movement under way? Is it gaining momentum? Is it nearing critical mass, a "tipping point"? Is a "good news epidemic," as I've come to call it, spreading among us? When I was young, maybe six or seven, someone told me that it is impossible to fold a piece of paper, any piece of paper, in half ten times. Years later I still find myself, often unconsciously, folding a paper napkin in a restaurant booth, or a piece of plastic wrap on our kitchen counter, to test that prediction one more time. If the plastic wrap were the size of a football field, it would surely fold ten times. Imagine a standard eight-and-a-half-by-eleven sheet of paper that you have successfully folded in half ten times. How thick would the stack be? A thousand twenty-four pages, over two reams of paper, seven inches thick. Now suppose you double that stack, then double it again, a total of fifty times. How tall would that stack be? A refrigerator? The peak of your roof? The top of the Empire State Building? Wrong. The stack would reach to the moon! And, doubled again, extend back to earth. The stack, like the hope-based movement I am describing, grows exponentially, not incrementally, like widening circles around where a fish jumped in the pond.

Suppose I have a virus, contagious today but not symptomatic until tomorrow. And further suppose I infect one other person today. My virus will spread, but soon dissipate, no threat of epidemic. But suppose I infect two other persons today, and they in turn four others tomorrow. By folding-paper math, 1,200 people will be symptomatic in ten days, a rapidly spreading epidemic needing immediate medical intervention. So what is a "good news epidemic"? Suppose I become infected with vision and hope, and infect two others, who in turn spread it at the same rate. We just might have a movement rolling! Maybe what Jesus had in mind, and the disciples carried out. The movement grows logarithmically, not merely steadily?[10]

HOPE IS TRUSTING GOD

My pastor Victor demonstrates this trust poignantly, grounding this cornerstone quality of hope in a personal and powerful way. He could not contain his excitement one Sunday morning, just six weeks from becoming a grandfather. Caroline, his daughter, called at midnight to say that complications prompted an immediate cesarean section. Victor and his wife, Jane, departed immediately for a three-hour drive to Washington. Ellie McKay arrived, hale and hearty, though just four pounds, nine ounces, and Victor headed home. He was looking forward to an early bedtime after a totally sleepless night, but a late-afternoon call brought news of an unexpected and life-threatening medical crisis for Caroline, which set him back on the road.

The following Sunday he shared his wrenching experience of speeding through the darkness, blinking back tears, praying aloud in the emptiness, wrestling like Jacob and his midnight angel, wondering, he said, if his faith was strong enough, resilient enough to see him through. His eyes glistened with tears, his voice cracking and fading and for lengthy moments falling into silence. "I prayed, of course, for healing, that Caroline pass through this dangerous time, that she survive this crisis. I prayed for the doctors and nurses and the elaborate technology at their command," he said, just before the longest silence. "But could I fully entrust her to God," he said slowly and softly, "no matter what?" Tears now cascaded down his cheeks. "Could I entrust her even into death, even as I dreaded the thought?" Caroline's dangerously high blood pressure normalized and her platelet count, the most threatening complication with fear of postsurgical bleeding, rose to acceptable, then normal levels. In fact, she had returned home awaiting the baby's release in a few days.

But my friend Bill's story must be told as well. Director of a Christian counseling center, a pioneer in prayer-based psychotherapy, and a speaker and workshop leader across the country, Bill saw the concern in his physician's eyes as he sat on the edge of his hospital bed holding in his hand results of medical tests. "You have multiple myeloma," he said with a steady, gentle voice. "What does that mean? And tell us the truth, doctor," his wife Jeanne insisted bravely. "If it follows its usual and predictable course, you have about eighteen months," he responded forthrightly. "You'll feel rather healthy and be mostly symptom-free until the last month or two," he added.

As a nationally known and widely loved figure, thousands of people began to pray for his healing. Masses were said, healing vigils convened, and prayer meetings where Bill had visited as a teacher held prayer marathons. Noted Christian healers came to his home from across the country, laying on hands, anointing him with oil, praying boldly for his perfect and complete return to health. Toward the end of the eighteenth month, having lapsed into an ever-deepening coma, Bill died.

The clearest permission and encouragement to pray like Victor and Jane, and like Bill and Jeanne, is Jesus in the garden. He did not hesitate to pray for his own desired outcome, fervently and forthrightly, "Let this cup pass from me," let me escape this garden, flee this city, return to the countryside to continue my ministry of teaching and healing. Then, and only then, "Not my will, but yours be done."

What is it about stories from our childhood that become so indelible, a gift that keeps on giving? Maybe it's like the books kids want to hear over and over again. Though my grandchildren find it impossible to believe, I managed to survive the first six years of my life without television. And those early programs, locally generated, were hardly production masterpieces. Every Saturday morning I found a certain program utterly mesmerizing. And it was so very simple. A woman—Miss Johnson as I recall—stood before a newsprint easel, a bundle of crayons stuffed in a coffee can on a table to the side, a circle of children at her feet. A child would volunteer, take a black crayon in hand, and just scribble on the pad. Then Miss Johnson would work with the crayons in a deft and artful way, turning the scribble into a picture. One Saturday a particularly enthusiastic boy scribbled and scribbled, nearly covering the sheet with crisscrossed lines. Whatever would Miss Johnson do with this one? It took time, and she worked patiently; but slowly, steadily, magically the scribble receded, and then disappeared, as a picture, perfect and complete, emerged.

Sometimes my desire to remain hopeful, my advocacy for the poor and marginalized, my witness for peace and justice can seem like so much scribble. But God turns it into clarity and meaning—

my *proximate* perspective, to return to Reinhold Niebuhr, transformed into *ultimate* meaning. We plant and water and tend . . .
God harvests. I'd guess I am not alone in having Romans 8:28
posted on my refrigerator, "We know that all things work together
for good for those who love God, who are called according to
God's purpose." I find it hard to trust at times, though I seek always to choose to trust that it is *God* who works it all together for
good—not "most," not "some," but "all" things—and my work is
to love God and seek to be called to divine purposes.

Elizabeth Sahtouris is an evolutionary biologist whose work I
find captivating. Who would expect to find a seminal and foundational metaphor for hope embedded in biological research? It is
about the process of metamorphosis of a caterpillar into a butterfly.
A caterpillar, at a certain point in its development, suddenly becomes a voracious and gluttonous eater, able to eat three hundred
times its own weigh in successive days. Finally, overwhelmed by its
gluttony, it falls into a deep sleep, its bloated skin hardening into
a chrysalis. Within the carcass, by a yet unknown process, what
biologists call "imaginal disks" begin to appear in the body of the
caterpillar, which its immune system begins to attack. But these
disks get stronger and begin to connect with each other, maturing
into full-fledged cells, fending off the assault of the immune system,
though they remain a distinct minority. The body of the caterpillar begins to putrefy, melting into a "nutritive soup," out of which
these imaginal cells, as genetic directors of the transformational
process, create the miracle of the butterfly.[11]

Imagine you and I are "imaginal cells," finding each other, linking and connecting, instinctively driven by hope and possibility,
to participate in a miracle of transformation on our planet. That's
the choice I have chosen to make.

9

WANTED: PROPHETS

The Gift of Outrage

For three hundred years the voice of prophecy had been silent in the land until John appeared, brusque and outlandish, one "crying in the wilderness." How odd that they came to him in droves, even as he addressed them as a brood of vipers, announcing an axe poised to cut them down at the roots. Even hard truth catches some inner, discerning ear. They were baptized by the hundreds, Jesus among them.

The voice of prophecy may not be totally silent in our time, but where is it being sounded with vigor and volume, with relentlessness and outrage? Then again, who would choose the role? Look what happened to John! And that's nothing new. Moses, feeling overwhelmed and frustrated, pleaded for relief or death (Num. 11:15). Jeremiah, constantly wracked with sadness and anguish, lamented God's call and his own consent (Jer. 20:7–18). Who wants to run the risk? Nathan told his king a gentle tale with an awesome edge, that his successful plan to possess the woman of his choice was called murder (2 Sam. 12:1–15, 31–33). Hosea endured a disastrous marriage as a public appeal to a wayward people. Amos and Micah spoke with faithfulness and then ran for their lives. Who wants to go there?

Imagine a modern-day Amos, an outsider from another state, maybe another country, roaring his battered pickup to a screeching halt and bounding into a worship service in progress. "Stop the singing. Now. Stop! Close your hymnbooks and sit down. Shut down the organ. I can't stand your noisy songs. Put your offering envelope back in your purse; put those clenched bills back in your wallet. That's not what God's after. The Lord wants justice flowing like that stream that runs through your property, righteousness like the river into which it flows" (adapted from Amos 5:21–24). Surely some modern-day Amaziah will bellow, "That's enough, prophet! Go back to where you came from and do your preaching there. Let them pay for it!" (Amos 7:12).

In a time of escalating fear and hopelessness, will we nurture a new generation of prophets? Will they be unafraid to stand against the empty promises and illusions of security offered by an ethos of domination and power? Who will arise to trust boldly in God's promises of fullness and grace and reconciling love?

WANTED: PROPHETS

We are seeking women and men who are spiritually grounded, rooted in Scripture, steady faith-journeyers who keep a disciplined devotional practice, to rise to an urgent and awesome task:

1. *Confronting denial.* Mounting the courage to dismantle outer defense systems against the hard and harsh realities of a planet in peril, a human family at risk, and inner defense systems against the heartbreak, anguish, and outrage that lie within,

2. *Reclaiming the prophetic voice.* Facing reality and mobilizing outrage, sounding the prophetic voice, naming and challenging relentlessly the unfaithfulness and injustice of individuals, social structures, governments, and the religious establishments.

3. *Speaking and acting for change.* Grounded in hope, the power of repentance of a God who "makes all things new," constantly "doing a new thing," to announce a new day, point toward a new direction, and give leadership to a movement.

If you feel claimed by this call, report immediately to a site of your choosing, perhaps a church, and begin the work.

1. Confronting Denial: Beginning with Me

It's 2:45 in the morning. What am I doing at my computer? This is not the first time. Betsy is right—I ought to be careful what I read or watch before I go to bed. This time it was *Sicko*, Michael Moore's documentary on health care. I turned off the television and read a few pages of a slow-moving novel, hoping it would tire me. It seemed to be working. I blinked my way through to the end of a chapter, enjoyed a hearty yawn, and turned out the light.

The edge of sleep was as close as I got. My mind and body colluded, my body twitching and twisting with thoughts and feelings churning faster than I could name them. Scenes from the film flickered and darted, everyday Americans victim, the film insisted, of a broken health-care system. What *was* I feeling? Sad, yes, deeply sad. Touched, yes, touched. But mostly, steadily drowning out the others, I was angry. My stomach knotted, my leg and shoulder muscles tightened in unison, and my chest seemed poised to explode. I was very angry!

Lying in the dark, annoyingly sleepless, can offer a unique opportunity to gain perspective. What's going on? This is not unfamiliar. No, not just prior sleepless nights prompted by provocative reading or viewing at bedtime, but more familiar than that. Mission trips to Haiti, Mexico, India, and Nicaragua flashed to mind, firsthand exposure not only to daunting human struggle but to the gnawing sense that people like me, and countries like mine, are part of the story.

A thought came to mind, initially comforting and reassuring, but then, just as suddenly, jolting, disturbing, and embarrassing—*Be patient, Howard, you'll feel more relaxed by morning, all this will be out of your system by bedtime tomorrow night.* That thought morphed into one pithy, gnawing phrase after another, their indicting power laserlike in their simplicity: *you'll get over it . . . this upset will pass . . . your anger will subside . . . it'll all wear off.* So that's how it works! Damned, that's how it works! Some harsh, unjust reality careens through my defenses; some awesomely painful situation, everyday life for millions of people, explodes front and center into my awareness; some unarguable injustice, littered with my nation's fingerprints, splashes onto my radar screen. And that blend of sadness, upset, embarrassment, and outrage bursts through every clever tactic of denial. But if I remain calm, if I bide my time, take a deep breath or two, I can turn it all into a problem to be solved, a direct encounter with hard truth to be deftly avoided with the artfulness and grace of a toreador.

Denial, I have come to realize, ally though it poses to be, is costly at every level. Distorted vision, muted hearing, and psychic numbing may protect us from facing harsh realities, hearing anguished cries, and feeling our own outrage and despair. But in the process it dims our delight in springtime flowers and red-orange sunsets, mutes songbirds and symphonies, limits our resilience and creativity, and saps our passion and exuberance.

The Blind Eye and Deaf Ear of Denial

The Bible draws its analogies from everyday life, and Jesus's stories were rooted in the familiar, so this summer scenario from my neighborhood offers a simple, everyday metaphor. The boat launch at the river that defines the eastern boundary of my community is in constant use on a summer Saturday. Motorboats head north, sailboats and canoes south. A large and thundering waterfall, totally inaudible where you edge your canoe into the water, lies just two miles downstream. The warning system is clear: a sign with large letters issues the caution in detail at the launch site and clearly visible reminders dot the river's edge. Enjoy a mile's paddle, the exhilaration of accelerating currents, and then the challenge of turning at that mile marker and heartily paddling back upstream. But do not pass that last dominantly placed marker. Each year a canoe or two crashes down the falls, an adventure no one survives. Did they fail to read the sign, forget to watch for reminders, or consciously risk the waters past the final sign? The morning paper's coverage of a canoeist's death often includes an interview with a fisherman who tried in vain, arms flailing, to shout a final warning from the shore.

The nation blithely paddles downstream, the first warnings of the prophet summarily dismissed. Denial, we've named it. Leading economic indicators are firm, political power stable and strong, the military prepared and well armed, the erosion of basic values visible only to the prophet. Sound familiar? Paddle on. Political process falters, the economy misses a beat or two, and a powerful neighbor threatens attack. The cost of unfaithfulness is now more obvious, yet the prophet's warning remains unheeded. It's not too late, he declares—yet. They paddle on. The roar at the edge of the falls drowns out a last fervent warning call from the bank. Now it is too late!

Denial draws a crowd! Those ready to collude with denial surround us, ready to collaborate in strategies to look the other way, find other explanations, even create alternative realities. Our call to be prophetic is constantly interrupted, distracted and diffused, when denial prevails. Denial, innocent as it seems, is lethal. This isn't easy!

2. Reclaiming the Prophetic Voice: Qualities of a Prophet

Biblical prophets, and those who would dare to assume that mantle today, must be persons of inner strength, rooted in faithfulness and prayer, tolerant of loneliness, able to withstand vigorous opposition, even rejection. They must see with penetrating vision, discerning the subtle, the barely visible. They are no strangers to grief and deep sadness. Willing to be impolite, inappropriate and outrageous, if occasion warrants. Two qualities seem consistent and foundational: compassion and outrage. *Compassion*, theologian Marcus Borg reminds us, is deeply visceral, arising from the gut, literally "womb-like." More than merely a feeling, compassion is a way of being, a gut connection with others and life, a hearty, multi-textured, and earthy word.[1] And *outrage*, which seems to have slipped into ecclesiastical exile, a blend of deep anger, unapologetic ferocity, and unfettered indignation. The prophets felt deeply, feelings typically expressed in animated ways: angry but not hostile, their outrage never hateful; compassionate but not condescending, their empathy never pitying. The prophet's voice sounded loudly, thundering at times, but never harsh or strident. Their posture was firmly grounded, but never pugnacious or entrenched. This call is awesome and unsettling, the costs unpredictable, and costs there will surely be.

A prophet has no crystal ball, is not a prognosticator by trade. Though prophets may have precognitive gifts, their role is less complicated than that. They proclaim a basic formula: Hear God's commandments and follow them; be obedient and faithful; know the sacred texts and heed the word of the prophets. Well-being, individually and as a nation, will follow. Moses speaks last words to the Hebrews as they await the Jordan crossing, "Choose life. Love the Lord your God, obey him, and be faithful to him" (Deut. 30:19–20 GNT). Amos's words are familiar, "Let justice roll down like waters, and righteousness like an ever-rolling stream" (Amos 5:24). Micah seems more detailed, "He has told you, O mortal, what is good; and what does the LORD require of you but to do justice, and to love kindness, and to walk humbly with your God" (Micah 6:8). Obedience and faithfulness yield peace, prosperity, and well-being. Ignoring God's commandments—coerced by the lure of power and privilege, trading military prowess for trusting divine protection, wooed by the way of the world—can only lead to decline and destruction.

It is important to note, as we ponder this invitation to assume the prophet's mantle, to distinguish two kinds of biblical prophets. There are the *bombastic prophets,* who speak from *outside* the political and religious establishment, who sweep in from hometowns far away, their message sharp and explosive, uncompromising and unrelenting. Amos and Micah come to mind. Then there are the *pastoral prophets,* who speak the prophetic word from *within* the political and religious establishment, along the streets and lanes of familiar neighborhoods, in the town square and marketplace of their hometown. They buy provisions in local shops, carry water from the nearby stream, and share the common life of the community. Nathan, Jeremiah, and Ezekiel offer illustration. The bombastic prophetic voice must be sounded, but becoming a steady, sensitive, unhesitant pastoral prophet may be the more pressing challenge. In either case, ministers of congregations, and lay leaders who sense a call to speak and act in the tradition of the prophets, must add a hat to the many they wear. They called it the "four P's" when I was in seminary: priest, pastor, preacher, and prophet. Are "prophets' hats" gathering dust in the back of the closet, infrequently—if ever—worn?

Formation of a Prophet

For those who hear and heed a call to a more intentional and vigorous prophetic ministry, the work of preparation will demand steady initiative, bold creativity, and hard work; because, as an hour or two of website exploration proved, there's not a lot of help out there. I examined the curricula of five seminaries across five denominations, finding survey courses on the Old Testament prophets, but no course offerings specifically focused on contemporary prophetic ministry. An array of majors was offered—in biblical studies, pastoral ministry, preaching, liturgy, systematic theology, church history, or administration, for example—but none in prophetic ministry. I investigated doctor of ministry offerings at a half-dozen seminaries, in a time when the trend in these postgraduate programs is toward greater specialization and thematic focus, with similar results. I tried various web-based strategies to compile a listing of continuing education offerings by a variety of sponsoring groups, and not a single seminar or event appeared designed to equip those called to prophetic ministry. Has the theological education enterprise colluded in subtle silencing and covert discouragement of any prophetic resurgence?

A review of recent book offerings was more promising, though variations on "prophetic ministry" as a search phrase pulled up mostly resources for renewing the voice of prophecy in charismatic-oriented contexts, a survey of prophetic resources relating to Islam, Judaism, and Mormonism, and options related to esoteric sites such as the work of Edgar Cayce. For me it has been the writing of seasoned veterans like Ron Sider, Jim Wallis, and Walter Wink; Marcus Borg and Ched Myers; Elaine Pagels and Dorothy Day who have been my most influential mentors and guides, together with liberation theologians like Jon Sobrino and Leonardo Boff, Rigobertu Menchu and Elsa Tamez, with contribution from secular prophets like Noam Chomsky, Riane Eisler, and Howard Zinn.

So add "lonely" and "resourceful" to the list of qualities demanded of a fresh cadre of prophets. You will likely discover, as I have, that becoming a prophet demands being a continual learner, a work in progress, someone who "work[s] out [his] own salvation" (Phil. 2:12). It will mean *un*learning as much as it means learning, jettisoning untruth and updating partial truth. I was raised in a household and church with a singular focus on individual salvation. Social context, it argued, was merely the stage on which the salvation drama played out. Race, ethnicity, and nationality, though acknowledged, were incidental. Anyone's workplace or neighborhood, socioeconomic status or affiliations were no more than scenery or backdrop. Political dynamics and global economics, national policies or international relations, structures of education or health care, availability of food or housing were not unimportant, but largely irrelevant to the centrality of the salvation story.

Why did Jesus overturn the money changers' tables? For years I had a ready if untested reply: they had stepped over the line; they had brought the flurry of the marketplace into the precinct for prayer; they were buying and selling where people were to be praying. And I liked that interpretation: comfortable and familiar, dramatic and dynamic, but unthreatening. I am now convinced by scholarship that argues that it was not *where* the money changers had set up shop, but the *kind* of business they were doing—unethical and exploitative, a coalition of the rich and powerful, and an unholy alliance of economic and religious players that outraged Jesus. Was he symbolically "turning over" a system, not just the tables of a few offenders?

Have professional exegetes and preachers colluded to sanitize and domesticate the prophetic thrust of Jesus's teachings? As I heard one rather audacious preacher put it: What if the message of Jesus is not so much a *spiritual teaching with political and social implications* as a *political and social teaching with spiritual implications?*

Prophets Ask Difficult Questions

Prophets are prone, even driven, to ask irreverent, awkward, even offensive questions. They wonder if people of power, privilege, and wealth—especially from the United States—may constitute a substantial and troublesome threat to the survival and sanity of the planet. Peace advocate and social critic John Perkins, whom I regard as a "secular prophet," suggests that what he calls the *corporatocracy*, the collective and often colluding action of multinational corporations, has intruded on the sovereignty of particularly Third World nations with little concern for their environment or people. These corporations have been, he argues, the front line of oppression by our nation, followed where necessary by "dirty tricks," the jackals, and then, if all else fails, the dispatching of our troops.[2] What if a handful of people, none elected, who could sit together around a small table, virtually run the world? I wonder if linguist and historian Noam Chomsky, another "secular prophet" who has profoundly influenced my perspective, is right, that Americans can tolerate the idea that some decisions and policies of our nation over the years *inadvertently* caused harm, were *unintentionally* unjust, that *mistakes* were made, but cannot tolerate the idea that such decisions and policies were *premeditated,* knowingly, consciously, intentionally harmful.[3] I have come to believe this proposition to be true. Not to know might excuse silence. But to know and remain silent seems less and less an option. An increasingly intolerable silence for me.

Might it be an older story than that? Historian Howard Zinn, still another must-read "secular prophet," argues that the founding fathers—however worthy of respect for their courage to break from empire, even when they were beneficiaries of that

empire—simply proceeded to form and frame a *new* empire, with
no more than cosmetic interest in democracy, in "liberty and justice for all." What if this country's founding fathers, as vigorous
as their debate seemed, deftly concurred and colluded on matters
of the highest self-interest, writing founding documents carefully
crafted to protect the privilege and prerogative of the elite few
at the expense of the masses? What if successive elites, across the
generations, successfully received and passed on that leadership
mantle and mandate, dividing constituencies in the populace that
might find common cause, artfully manipulating government and
the governed, producing timely provocations to justify harsh and
crushing retribution, be it against domestic or foreign populations?[4]
That thesis is becoming harder and harder to refute—indeed, more
and more persuasive and convincing.

It may be, I fear, an even older story. How else to name it than
genocide, the "ban," the Hebrews' utter destruction of the Canaan-
ites, guided by what they heard as instructions from their God?
Writer and social activist Riane Eisler argues in *The Chalice and the
Blade* that the Norse sweeping southward, and the Hebrews northward, having learned to alloy metals to craft an arsenal for warfare,
shattered the ancient "partnership paradigm" of the prehistoric human family, replacing it with a "dominator paradigm."[5] What if the
history of the church, the expanding spread of Christianity from its
humble roots, especially after the "conversion" of Constantine, is
one of increasing oppression, the power of the state melding with
the power of the church to form a lethal force for amassing wealth
and controlling peoples, the message and movement of Jesus lost
in the process?

I write these paragraphs with sadness. Maybe I should fashion
new excuses not to tell the truth, my truth, the truth as I see and
feel it. Yet, can I live with myself if I remain silent and inactive
in face of the overwhelming burden of what I now believe to be
significantly true? And, as a Christian, one seeking to be faithful
to that message and movement of Jesus and the prophets, what
choice do I have? I want to discern what to speak, where to speak
it, and what action to take. While these paragraphs may be trouble-

some to read, my deepest desire is to articulate, follow, and inspire a positive, proactive, faith-based, forward-looking message and movement, grounded in hope. A realist who asks hard questions, I remain exuberantly hopeful. Such, unavoidably, is the role of the prophets!

3. Speaking and Acting for Change: The Prophet Confronts the Nation

Years ago a wise mentor challenged me, as a would-be prophet, to be a *critical lover* or, if you prefer, *loving critic*—of my country, my church, someone I love, or even myself. To be merely *critical* risks becoming cynical and sarcastic, brusque and harping, solely negative. To be only *loving* risks becoming undiscerning and unchallenging, bland and lethargic, solely positive. This surely becomes most delicate and demanding when the target of a prophetic word is a nation and its government. Only a critical lover can be a prophetic patriot, striking that delicate balance between pledging allegiance to a flag and a Lord, affirming that of our history that is noble and heroic, and challenging that which is duplicitous and destructive. There are those to the right who only love our country, its history, its role in the world, its leaders, its exercise of power, "love it or leave it" at the extreme. It stands in need of no prophetic word, and may challenge the patriotism of those who dare to speak one. There are those to the left who see nothing good about our country, which they characterize as universally and thoroughly wrong, premeditated and unrepentant in its destructiveness, a scourge on the planet. One who dares speak as a prophet to the nation may find themselves lonely and isolated.

So here we are, we who dare to heed the prophet's call. As merely a concept, it sounds fine. In generalities it might seem reasonable. Jesus the prophet got in trouble by being specific. But compassion blended with outrage mandates speaking and acting.

As I write these words, the Iraq war has cost this nation $538,069,945,907 ($4,681 per household);[6] en route, conservative estimates predict, to well over a trillion dollars.[7]

Allocated for housing, that would provide 4,279,715 new units nationally, 254,272 in my home state. Designated for children's health care, it could fund health insurance for 7,852,612 kids. New elementary school teachers: 10,777,823.[8]

Over four thousand U.S. soldiers have died, with over 30,000 wounded,[9] and over 750 amputees,[10] the veterans' health care services strained beyond capacity. No fewer than 75,000 Iraqi civilians have died.[11]

Is anyone outraged? Where is the voice of the prophet?

Forty-seven million Americans have no health insurance, many of them children, and 18,000 people will die this year for only that reason.[12]

We are the only industrialized nation without some form of universal health-care coverage.[13]

Watch a group of black and white expectant mothers at a playground or in a market: a black woman is twice as likely to lose her baby;[14] her child will live a life seven years shorter than the child of a white mother,[15] and be three times more likely to live under the poverty line.[16]

Is anyone outraged? Where is the voice of the prophet?

In the United States the top 1 percent own 38 percent of the wealth; the top 10 percent own 71 percent; the bottom 40 percent, only one-fifth of 1 percent.[17]

Globally, the top 2 percent own 50 percent of the world's wealth, the top 10 percent own 85 percent, the bottom half less than 1 percent.[18] The aggregate assets of the three wealthiest individuals in the world exceed the GNP of the lowest 48 countries.[19]

The United States has the third largest inequality of wealth distribution in the world, our largest since 1928, behind only Russia and Mexico.[20]

Is anyone outraged? Where is the voice of the prophet?

Two and a half billion people in the world live on less than two dollars a day. Half the global population struggles to survive.[21]

Thirty-six million people in the United States are "food insecure"[22] and thirty-seven million live below the poverty line. One out of six children in America is poor.[23]

Federal food subsidies have been reduced by 50 percent, and twenty-five states have reduced child care funding in the last two years. Over the last five years food-stamp programs and health-care subsidies have steadily decreased, while the number of children in poverty has increased.[24]

Is anyone outraged? Where is the voice of the prophet?

Fifty percent of the planet's species may be extinct by the end of this century, including African lions and elephants, polar bears, turtles, and whales.[25]

There is a "dead zone" at the mouth of the Mississippi the size of Massachusetts.[26] There is a swirling mass of floating, non-biodegradable debris in the North Atlantic the size of Texas.[27]

We breathe 30 percent more carbon dioxide than our grandparents did.[28]

We have deforested; drained aquifers; polluted rivers, streams, and oceans; created soil erosion at a cumulative 90 percent rate in the last fifty years.[29] It would take "five earths" to sustain the present global population if the seven billion consumed and produced waste as we in the United States do.[30]

Is anyone outraged? Where is the voice of the prophet?

Writing and reading these paragraphs may leave us both depleted and discouraged, resistant and resentful. Denial reappears, offering refuge. It *is* overwhelming. Last Sunday, as I turned into our church's parking lot, I wondered why my head was turning steadily, awkwardly, only to the left. I'd done the same last week, I realized, and the week before. My curiosity unmasked a tactic of denial at play. I simply did not want to look again at the "Save Darfur, Not on Our Watch" sign posted near the driveway across the street. There simply was no more room in my heart for human pain, particularly a tragedy of such immense proportions. I was at risk of overload, psychic burnout. I cannot ask more of myself than I am able to give. I accepted denial's offer.

The Prophet Confronts the Church

If balancing *critic* and *lover* is delicate and difficult when speaking prophetically to the nation, it is more so when the prophetic word takes aim at the church. Not unlike the way Jesus provoked the outcome at Nazareth, it's when one dares speak truth in concrete and specific terms that resistance, even animosity, arises. I am about to run that risk! And since prophets were primarily speakers, their most pointed words to the church might be to preachers. The first of the following vignettes is, I am convinced, tragically typical; the second, sadly, clearly the exception.

The Prophet Addresses Preachers

Betsy and I found ourselves slipping into a pew for a Sunday service at a rapidly growing church in its crisp, attractive, and newly completed campus. The sermon text was Jeremiah 18, that incident at the potter's house, and I immediately found myself firmly positioned in its crosshairs, its warning to the nation uncompromising. I thought of Jeremiah's withering assault on wealth and power, his broadsides against accumulation and acquisition, his accusations of disregard for the poor, of rigging the judicial system, of economic exploitation clearly backdrop and context for this pivotal text for the day.

Walking from our car we had passed a number of BMWs and high-end SUVs, Lincolns, Cadillacs, and a Porsche or two, mingling with Chevies, Fords, and Volkswagens. As we sang a hymn before the sermon, I scanned the congregation. Brooks Brothers suits, Laura Ashley blazers, enough Ralph Lauren polo ponies to field a team. This was clearly an upwardly mobile congregation. I quieted my musings and turned my attention to the pulpit. Would this preacher help that passage keep me in its sights? Or would he shrink back? After all, Jeremiah fared poorly with this message. An earlier glance at the bulletin, which listed "Have Thine Own Way, Lord" as the last hymn, its most familiar line, "Thou art the Potter, I am the clay," gave me a clue.

An opening story from the pastor's fraternity days offered the first opportunity to edge away from the text's wary gaze, and a couple of vignettes about people in his life who had yielded themselves to the Potter's shaping hands turned down any lingering heat from that no-longer-lethal text. I thumbed back to the text to confirm that the "clay" is the "nation," not the individual. The tone of the sermon became poignant and soothing, inviting the listeners to surrender to the loving-kindness and tender care of God. I turned back to the text. Maybe I had misread it. No, there it was—the clay is the nation. I think Jeremiah would not have been pleased.

Agitation got the best of me, so I mailed a note to the pastor, a friend and colleague. "You're a better exegete than that," I wrote, choosing to be direct. I was in that kind of mood. "I think you knew, as you crafted your sermon, the basic thrust of that text—Jeremiah was addressing the nation and its unfaithfulness." Maybe I was a little brusque. He replied without defensiveness that he did not want to distract the spiritual growth of new Christians in the church. He reported finding Jeremiah's critique of the nation complex, difficult to relate to today's world. Jeremiah was living in a theocracy and we live in a nation committed to separation of church and state. Finally, he did not want to raise issues of possible political divisiveness, knowing his membership represented a broad political spectrum. My agitation barely eased.

A few Sundays later we visited another church, a rather eclectic congregation, we'd been told, given its suburban location. We'd heard that it was a progressive church. We were curious. The first thing that caught my eye was the sermon title: *Big Macs, Unblemished Bananas, and Dead Babies.* And wouldn't you know it, the biblical text was from Jeremiah, words of doom to "the one who builds his house by injustice . . . a mansion with spacious rooms. . . [who] panels it with cedar . . . . You violently oppress your people" (Jer. 22:13–17 GNT). How would this pastor interpret the passage? Having noticed that the sanctuary had no pulpit, we were not surprised to find him standing between the front pews to start his sermon. He explained that the preacher's task begins with the homilist's basic tools: biblical commentaries, theological treatises, and the like, the goal being the fullest and most accurate understanding of the text in its original setting. That task continues with the more difficult but pivotal search for illumination and guidance, application and implication of the text for today. I thought I saw

a subtle smile wrinkle his face as he reported an interpretative co-
nundrum around the morning's passage. The scholarly consensus
was divided, offering two quite different interpretations at a pivotal
point. He suggested an odd solution—that the congregation vote.
This was surely unorthodox biblical scholarship. He commenced
to tell the narrative twice.

All interpreters agree about the *setting,* he explained—Jeremiah
standing at the foot of a street lined with utterly magnificent
homes, built with the finest and most costly materials, ostentatious
by anyone's standards. Nor was there textual argument about the
content of what the prophet had said. The difference arose about
what he *meant.* He profiled a first option: Assume there are eleven
houses on that street. Jeremiah is saying, this option argues, that
some of the houses, say two or three, were built by unscrupulous,
dishonest people. The focus of this interpretation is on individual
sinfulness. Then a second possibility, decidedly different: Jeremiah,
standing at the foot of that street, argues that the very *existence of
these houses* is the sin! The distribution of land outlined in the book
of Numbers was fair and equitable, by tribe and tribal family. Provi-
sion for periodic redistribution, to adjust for accumulation or loss
of land across a generation or two, was detailed in Leviticus and
Deuteronomy, most especially during the Sabbath Year and Jubilee
Year. Archeologists conclude that this strategy had worked for two
hundred years, but began slowly, then precipitously, to change in
the next two hundred years, into the lifetime of Jeremiah.

There was awkward silence. They were asked to consider their
choice, though no actual vote was taken. I already admired the
courage of this pastor, where more than a handful in the pews had
driven from homes not unlike those in the biblical story, and, at
the same time, given the diversity of this congregation, others had
departed from lower-priced and more modest homes.

The transitions in the sermon were too numerous to track, but
the ending related to that odd title, bringing the New Testament
text into play, Matthew 2:16–18. Assuring the listeners that he accused no one of killing babies, he wondered aloud if they found his
sermon title perplexing, even uncomfortable. Herod's slaughter of

the children was premeditated, tactical, and immediate. Fearful of a pretender to his power, he took direct action. Then, in a curious turn, the pastor, after confessing he was a Big Mac lover, profiled the continuing practice of large hacienda owners in El Salvador who co-opt subsistence farms from the very poor for cattle grazing for export beef. He reminded them that their church supported a missionary in that country. Admitting a lifelong aversion to bruised bananas, he said he had recently learned that it takes three times the acreage to produce unblemished bananas, the only kind acceptable for cash-crop export—thus more land the poor had used as family gardens was confiscated. He spoke slowly as he finished, suggesting that there may be a connection between our demand for beef and unblemished bananas . . . and dead babies.

I worship in a variety of sanctuaries and hear many preachers across the months. My goal is to worship, to listen for God's word, and to find divine guidance in all parts of the service, but I struggle to still my critic's ear. One person's anecdotal experiences fall short of a research project, hardly warranting definitive conclusions, but having shared notes with others like me who worship in many churches, I suspect that the cautious and timid treatment of challenging texts, like that of the first preacher, is closer to rule than exception, and that the bold and courageous words of the second, sadly, more the exception.

The Prophet Speaks about Stewardship

There is a difference between *stated* beliefs, *announced* values and principles, *named* priorities—and *operational* beliefs and values, principles and priorities. Nothing reveals more clearly those operational beliefs, actual values and principles, the real priorities—of an individual, family, organization or congregation—than the way they steward their resources, especially how they spend their money. If there is not a prophet in the house, unfaithfulness may grow unchecked.

On a consulting trip to a suburban community in the Boston area, a region I know well, I stopped to visit a church where a seminary classmate is on the clergy staff. It was a charming revo-

lutionary-era church nestled on a rolling hillside just out of view
of nearby elegant homes. After a robust hug and some personal
catching up and reminiscing about seminary days, I asked how his
work was going. He had joined the clergy team a decade before
toward the end of a quarter-century of congregational struggle—a
series of pastors with whom little partnership formed; constant tension, never erupting into open conflict but always distracting and
debilitating; uneven attendance and financial shortfalls. But most
damaging was the lethargy, the ennui, the lifelessness. All that had
changed in the last decade, he said with a smile. A young, spiritually grounded and engaging senior pastor had led the congregation
through ten years of growth on every front. New members' classes
filled the church parlor, several each year, and attendance had soared
as the congregation added a third, then a fourth Sunday service.
The newly constructed sanctuary, towering above an otherwise
modest complex, had caught my eye as I arrived.

My friend introduced me to the senior pastor, who in turn
invited me to tour the new sanctuary. My search for a plausible
excuse failed, and we walked briskly down an outside walkway, since
the full effect demanded entry through the front doors, he said.
Standing inside the entrance door, an immense and soaring tower
claimed first attention, vaulting upward, its base a full thirty feet
square. A huge mahogany plant stand with a cascading arrangement of silk flowers was centered beneath its tapering height. I
felt an odd sensation, subtle at first, stirring in my stomach. It felt
like nausea. We turned through the archway into the sanctuary,
striking in its austerity, engaging in its simplicity, overwhelming
in its elegance. Beveled-glass chandeliers hung in stately alignment
above cherrywood pews. The pipes of the new organ, funded by a
specially planned companion fund, sparkled in the afternoon sun.
A twenty-four-hour climate-control system ensured a temperature
never below sixty-seven and humidity at a constant level to protect
the organ. That nauseous feeling became more distinct, as my
shoulders tightened and a bit of a headache started to throb.

What was I to do? I was surrounded by the work of an archi-
tectural genius, I supposed, constructed with the finest materials

in every detail. My host surely expected an "ooh" or an "ah" at the least, some affirming comment about design and construction. I had no desire to be ungracious, certainly not dismissive or critical. But there was my nausea, tight shoulders, and now pounding headache. I am sure he noticed that my nods were unenthusiastic and my comments sparse, at best. *Was no one outraged? Where was the voice of a prophet?!*

How did such a good-news story, a decade of fruitful ministry, lose its way? Why didn't deepening spiritual vitality translate into more conscious stewardship? Did anyone chronicle the decision-making process? Wasn't there anyone to think out loud about alternative possibilities for that ten million dollars? Then again, could the church have raised that extraordinary amount for anything other than brick and mortar? The previous sanctuary was small, plain, clearly dated, "a little shoddy, to tell the truth," a lay leader who accompanied our tour had commented. That said: *A sanctuary may be the planet's most inefficient, cost-ineffective piece of real estate.*

My thoughts raced as I drove away, a rush of prophetically inspired possibilities coming to mind. I knew the surrounding neighborhoods fairly well, the cluster of communities that formed this high-end suburban region. Though health care remains unsettled, hardly exemplary in many ways, nearby hospitals began collaborating recently in some promising ways. One has a birthing suite, and another specializes in heart and lung disease. One has a state-of-the-art orthopedic wing, and another has a thriving family-practice team. If one purchases a particular multimillion-dollar testing machine, another secures testing equipment in another area of specialty. A fleet of ambulances transports patients among hospitals, depending on testing or medical care needs. Financial considerations drive this arrangement, of course. If hospitals can do it, why not churches?

The region's most truly old and elegant church came to mind, its gothic-style sanctuary seating twelve hundred, its traditional architecture accommodating differing denominational tastes. Suppose leaders of that church announced to churches throughout the area that their sanctuary could become the funeral and wedding site for everyone. Now my mind was racing, full of outrageously innovative ideas, I told myself. A slowly declining church near a shopping area had rows of classrooms perfect for an after-school tutoring program and a large, if seldom-used gym. A congregation with a lovely racial and ethnic mix in an old neighborhood of modest row houses could host ecumenical and multicultural gatherings. A Roman Catholic church had a number of large, comfortable, lounge-type rooms perfect for seminars, workshops, and events that would draw larger crowds. And finally a United Methodist Church came to mind that had an unusually large hall ideal for dances, receptions, parties, or other festive events. Why build for every need at every church location? Financial considerations might drive the arrangement—why not? *A prophet in the house, with unapologetic outrage, might have raised some questions and stirred this kind of creative thinking.*

In delightful contrast, Rosedale Unitarian Church, a liberal church experiencing rapid growth, built an adequate but modest complex to replace its building that burned to the ground fifteen years ago. Raising more money than the actual construction costs, members made a principled and disciplined commitment to use the surplus to fund a variety of mission projects. In fact, as part of the process, they sponsored a congregation-wide survey that yielded a Statement of Basic Values and Principles. More recently, as their fiftieth anniversary approached, initial plans to expand their building and make some renovations were quickly vetoed by a groundswell of members, appealing to that statement. Minor building improvements and some deferred maintenance seemed prudent, but the anniversary fund will augment and expand their already ambitious outreach ministry, balancing charitable projects and a commitment to peace and social justice.

The buildings at Harvest Community Church are quaint and charming, but appeared inadequate to contain the rapid growth in membership and program when suburban sprawl extended to the church's previously rural location. The newer members from upscale homes could have easily subscribed a substantial building expansion, but an alternative if unlikely dream prevailed. The congregation did brighten the building's rather dark and dreary interior with lighter, more buoyant colors and creatively reconfigured the space, but as I write, members are deciding whether to build residential housing space either for migrant families or unwed mothers, to use a portion of their acreage for community gardening, and to develop worship opportunities across a seven-day calendar, using their present limited sanctuary and exploring alternative worship sites.

The Prophet Calls for Civil Discourse

A workshop participant at a church with a history of tension and discord laughed at herself as she said it: "I wish we could do everything with graciousness and goodwill like they did in the Bible." The Old Testament narratives are rife with dissension and rebellion, competition and conflict. The positioning and rivalries among the disciples dismayed Jesus. And virtually no one signed aboard for a second missionary junket with Paul. It doesn't take reading between the lines to see how deep the conflict was between Peter and Paul, though Acts 15 narrates its resolution. Biblical characters, failing to close the gap between differences, bridged them. The issue is not *whether* there will be broad and ardently held differences of opinion, but *how* those differences will be expressed. In a time when civility is in collapse, when public discourse is riddled with innuendo or outright assault, the church can model an alternative. Sometimes it does. Too often it does not.

This sad tale unfolds in a downtown church in a major East Coast city. It is not pretty. And it is not unfamiliar. I find it *infuriating*, a word consciously chosen over *frustrating* or *annoying*, either of which would be gentler and kinder but would constitute, in reality, a lie. A denominational judicatory is holding its monthly meeting, three hundred delegates in all, clergy and laity, a six-hour agenda at hand. Although the chatter accompanying coffee and pastries seems innocent and amiable, smaller circles of kindred spirits tighten, whispering tactics anticipating the engagements of the day. The "issue that will not go away" is on everyone's mind. Should this denomination ordain clergy and lay leaders who are openly gay or lesbian? At day's end, with everyone weary and bloodied, the issue looms larger and more potent than ever, and ardent adversaries are more wounded and divided than when they began. Given an opportunity to speak and listen with open minds and hearts, even as they speak their truth with vigor and persuasiveness, they collapse into a cacophony of name-calling and assault.

Imagine they had called the Salvation Army in advance of that Tuesday meeting, offering three hundred people to be deployed around the city for six hours. Eighteen hundred person hours! Imagine the senior citizens they might have visited, the kids they might have read to, the meals for the homeless they might have prepared! They might have attended to homes that needed to be weatherized for the approaching winds of winter, the parks that need to be raked and swept, the patients in a public mental hospital who would benefit from a visit. It was no one's conscious choice, but choose they surely did—to do pitched battle in a musty old sanctuary, in take-no-prisoners combat, impossible as in most wars to declare victors or vanquished, or, join the other army's campaign to respond to human need. *Was anyone outraged? Where was the voice of a prophet?!*

There is little about which I am prouder, as I look back over my twenty-three-year pastorate at Gladwyne Presbyterian Church, than the members' ability to face and engage one another even in the face of sharp and potentially destructive differences of opinion on even the most divisive of issues. The congregation marshaled a sensitivity and courage in fully integrating the prophetic mandate with a gentle and loving pastoral ministry. Though in many cases my political leanings were rather transparent, I made a commitment not to advocate partisan positions from the pulpit—a decision that was not received with universal appreciation. People who were gay and lesbian were angered that I would not unequivocally advocate for their position, as were those who found homosexuality unacceptable. Pro-life and pro-choice folk complained, at times vehemently. I maintained the right to speak my biases vigorously and persuasively, but only when my preaching robe was off.

Three particular strategies employed across those years are worthy of sharing. In the midst of some national debate, the content of which I forget, a member felt prompted to place a large table in the back of the church, complete with a sign that read *Faith and Social Concern,* inviting people to place reprints of articles that articulated their point of view on any pressing issue. Soon the table overflowed with reprints advocating opinions on various issues, local, statewide, national, and international. Worshipers were urged to select broadly to become informed about differing points of view. Few left church without a stop at that table.

A second strategy emerged during a season of run-up to war—it could have been the debate over aid to the Contras, the decision to invade Afghanistan, the first Iraq War, or the second—when the mission committee was leading worship one Sunday. After fifteen minutes of typical liturgy, worshipers were dismissed to one of two rooms prepared for their arrival. In one waited a representative from the Quaker Annual Meeting of Philadelphia to speak against the contemplated war; in the other a general from the War College to advocate for the war. The instruction was to choose the speaker and point of view *opposite* to the one you held and, once there, to speak only to ask questions for clarification. Your task was to become as fully, deeply understanding of that viewpoint as you were able. We returned to the sanctuary for a closing liturgy that urged open-mindedness and prayer for discernment and wisdom for all key decision-makers.

Third, I remember how familiar it became to see petitions on various issues circulating in the coffee hour, sometimes several petitions, often on differing or even opposite sides of a given issue. On one particular Sunday members learned that two rallies were scheduled at adjacent locations in Washington, D.C., the following Saturday—a pro-life rally and a pro-choice rally, and each group had arranged charter buses to carry participants. Sign-up lists for each rally appeared at coffee hour. This would surely test the limits of our tolerance. I watched, a twinge of anxiety stirring, as women, approached by others clipboards in hand, promptly signed up. That was easy enough. But I also watched a woman approached, then another, a conversation ensuing that left the sheet unsigned, clearly pro-life and pro-choice women chatting. I'm no stranger to strained, coarse, and hostile exchanges between adversaries on this difficult and delicate issue, and so my anxiety spiked. Such exchanges typically end, at best, in cool and dismissive silence. My anxiety dissipated and my eyes teared watching these women of divergent and strongly held views smile warmly, some embracing. I wished the world were watching.

After lengthy and patient discussion, consensus was reached on a basic principle—the affirmation of a fourfold process for relating our faith to social issues.

First, become broadly informed on issues at hand, open to as many points of view as integrity and conscience allow. *Second*, study Scripture and pray, bringing neutrality and openness to that exploration. *Third*, as study, biblical research, and prayer yield sufficient clarity, articulate your position, boldly and humbly. *Fourth*, advocate for that point of view unapologetically, speaking and listening with equal care. That principle had manifested among those women in a truly remarkable way.

The Prophet Assails Trivia

The prophetic voice has rarely spoken with such stark frustration as to the angel of the church at Laodicea: "I know your works; you are neither cold nor hot. . . . So, because you are lukewarm, and neither cold nor hot, I am about to spit you out of my mouth" (Rev. 3:15–16). Sadly, "lukewarm" is in every ecclesiastical quarter.

Each year congregations in my denomination submit their official board minute books, including the annual financial report, to the judicatory office for review. A team of volunteers conducts the review, with each member of the team reading submissions from eight or ten churches. No one wants the job, so everyone looks the other way when the committee is being recruited. But it seemed fair that I take a turn. The task is to take home that stack of congregational minutes and financial reports for "reading, review, and comment" as the instructions word it, according to "guidelines for congregational record-keeping." Bolstered by a freshly brewed cup of strong coffee, I folded open the first book, and a thought came to mind. A biographer once wrote that two data sources that most assisted his work were diaries and financial summaries; he insisted that nothing gave clearer insight into the values and principles by which a person really lived. It suddenly occurred to me that board minutes are a church's diary, including financial summaries. They are the clearest window into the operational values and principles, the implicit purpose and mission, the truest statement about the life of a church. Tedious as the task would be, I was about to get the inside view of what each church is all about.

I do not want to overstate the case or cherry-pick my references. There were churches with vision and vitality, creativity and imagination, spirited worship and diverse programs. In some congregations membership and attendance were on the increase, leadership teams were broadening, and member participation was contagious. Some churches were thriving and growing. No, let me be honest: "few" is more accurate than "some." A colleague, returning from a meeting of my denomination's National Assembly, reported to me that ninety-five percent of congregations in my denomination across the United States are in decline. I found little to argue with that grim statistic. Why are financial reports and property issues always at the top of the agenda, when energy is freshest? And why do they take so long and evoke such angst or controversy? Survival anxiety seeped through the pages of most months' minutes. Why do so few people, so often the same people, do most of the talking and make the majority of the motions? Why are new ideas met with such resistance? Why do meetings seem to accomplish so little and run so late?

I return again and again to thumb through my worn and faded copy of C. S. Lewis's classic *The Screwtape Letters,* delightful correspondence between a seasoned, senior devil, Screwtape, and his protégé, a devil-in-training named Wormwood. Screwtape's words of encouragement are dotted with strategic suggestions about how to waylay anyone at risk of "going over to the Enemy." A master at escalating trivia, Screwtape helps Wormwood see a tactical opening in a church, heaven forbid, on the edge of thriving, to foment a debate whether to use "mass," "Eucharist" or "holy communion" to describe the "Lord's Supper."[31] Ingenious at turning subtle differences into fracturing divisiveness, he teaches Wormwood to encourage people toward extremes: "All extremes except devotion to the Enemy are to be encouraged."[32] Write your own. "The Episcopalians have been neutralized, investing so much of their energy into high- and low-church dissension, with the always ready and handy homosexuality issue thrown in," I can hear Screwtape say. "Good work, Wormwood, encouraging doctrinal purity. The Presbyterians are subdividing at a furious rate." But the one that formed in my mind, as I my eyes began to glaze over reading those minute books, was "Wormwood, we've done it. We helped them raise trivia to an art form. Irrelevance reigns. You've gotten them busy with so many things that they've completely lost sight of the mission and movement of the Enemy." *Isn't anyone outraged? Where is the voice of a prophet?!*

Heed or Hit Bottom?
How did, how does, how will the prophetic story end? Odds are, in the short term at least, not well! Amos was the first to warn the northern kingdom, unmasking the unevenness of a national prosperity limited to the wealthy, the emptiness of religious piety, and an illusion of national security. Hosea followed close behind, using his own disastrous marriage as a living metaphor to sound alarm. Failing to take heed, Samaria fell in 721 BCE. In prophecies spoken nearly two centuries before the fall of Jerusalem in the southern kingdom, Isaiah insisted that the greater threat to the nation was disobedience and unfaithfulness, not Assyria. Micah, his contemporary, more bombastic in his assault on the oppression of the poor, the corruption of national leaders and the deception of false prophets, offered an early warning system to Judah. Jeremiah predicted the unthinkable, bought a field, and prepared to accompany his people into exile. Jerusalem fell in 586 BCE. The history of this stubborn and unheeding people cascades toward rock bottom.

In the long term, avoidably but tragically long term, the story ends with the promise fulfilled. The prophetic writings exude the vision and expectation of ultimate renewal and restoration, none more touching that a verse from Hosea, "How can I give you up, Israel? How can I abandon you. . . . My heart will not let me do it! My love for you is too strong" (Hosea 11:8 GNT).

There are exceptions worthy of note. David, confronted by the courage of Nathan and a clever parable, wept in guilt-ridden anguish and lived to bear the consequences of his sin: forbidden to build the temple and witness to the deaths of two sons. But David, heeding and repenting, was forgiven and continued a fruitful and faithful reign. The Book of Deuteronomy, unearthed at a construction site near the temple, inspired Josiah's reform in 621 BCE.

Visit an Alcoholics Anonymous meeting, and you'll hear poignant, often anguished tales of hitting rock bottom, the story line of most in recovery. My friend Jason is an exception to the rule. Realizing the paralyzing destructiveness of his drinking, heeding the confrontation of a loving friend, he chose, shy of rock bottom, to stop drinking, and recently celebrated his fifth anniversary of sobriety at a nearby AA gathering.

I chronicle the story of Honey Brook Church in another essay. After two troubled pastoral tenures, infected with chronic negativity, attendance and morale in free fall, the church was host to a visiting minister who preached a prophetic sermon. "Implausible as it sounds," he began, "when I arrived at your church this morning I found two Sunday papers on the front step." Their curiosity piqued, worshipers leaned forward. "Odd as it sounds, each carried the same date, the second Sunday in May, exactly ten years from now. The papers were identical, except for the features sections, which were different, though each carried a front-page story about Honey Brook Church," he went on. Intrigued, this sometimes restless congregation sat utterly still. "Each included a full-width photograph. In one you are crowded together on the front lawn for a ribbon-cutting ceremony, the newly constructed education wing visible in the background. In the other a handful of you look

on as your pastor hands the keys to the pastor of the congregation
that had purchased the building, having outgrown its prior site."

After church the coffee hour was abuzz with animated conversation. Some members were annoyed, even offended, at a sermon
that seemed to them insulting and demeaning, surely not encouraging and hopeful. A few resented the preacher describing a clearly
impossible dream. Others appreciated the preacher's directness. In
the midst of it all some spark was ignited, a fire lit, fresh energy
generated, for some just to "prove that preacher wrong." It would
appear in retrospect to have been a wake-up call. The church board
moved up the date of its next meeting to discuss the new ideas that
seemed to be popping up everywhere. Circles of laypeople, forming
spontaneously, initiated a variety of new activities. Some women
planted a brightly colored garden to enhance the sanctuary's curb
appeal; another group, working in pairs, with a church bulletin
and a basket of goodies in hand, spent Sunday afternoons visiting
the newly built homes in a nearby subdivision; some young adults
made plans to resurrect a long-defunct youth group. Progress was
only faintly visible after a month or two, but a year later there was
clear evidence that something had changed.

It may seem an unbelievable ending, but ten years later, to the
season if not to the exact date, that visiting preacher's face was in
a photograph of the ribbon cutting for the new education wing!

Where is the church, where are the churches, headed? Heeding,
or hitting bottom? Unless the grip of denial is broken and the voice
of the prophet vigorously sounded, unless we reclaim the calling
to anguish and outrage, unless we act with bold prophetic vision,
there is nothing to heed.

10

Get off the Sidewalk and Join the Parade

The Gift of Partnership

hen I think of the state of the world, an image of an ill-fated parade comes to mind. Imagine you are part of this parade. Toddlers are perched on their fathers' shoulders, helium balloons dancing from strings tied to their wrists. Teenagers in baggy jeans and oversized T-shirts, their faces painted the colors of their high-school teams, whirl and dance and high-five along the sidewalks. The thunder of bass drums sounds a cadence. Newcomers pour in from doorways and side streets, and the crowd swells.

The parade route, you assume, has been carefully mapped. Barricades block the side streets to point the way, and a police motorcycle brigade leads the line of march. Echoes of a brass band reverberate, and the tone is exuberant. People lean from open windows, and children wave flags along the curb. Everyone loves a parade!

You stand on your toes, and then jump up and down, to catch a glimpse ahead. The parade is headed toward a gaping chasm from a massive excavation in the middle of the street. You see huge cranes twisting and straining, their buckets dropping rocks and earth into waiting dump trucks. The bucket of a crane falls deep into the opening before it hauls up its next load. "We'll turn at the next intersection," you comfort yourself. The throng surges straight ahead. "The grand marshal has surely noticed," you mutter silently, but he is too busy waving this way and that. "The motorcycle brigade will halt the march," you assure yourself. But they

185

are too engaged in their precision maneuvers and absorbed by the acclaim of the crowd.

You cry out a warning, but your voice is muffled by the mounting din, and your gestures go unnoticed. You dig in your heels, but momentum carries you and the throng, uninterrupted, straight ahead. Those who hear you only scoff. You cannot even slow the pace. You try to wedge your way out, first to the left, then to the right, but you are locked in. The march moves inexorably forward.[1]

I am not an alarmist by nature. Among the stories read to me as a child, *The Boy Who Cried Wolf* took on inexplicable indelibility. I have always hesitated to exaggerate, avoiding words like catastrophe or crisis, apocalyptic or cataclysmic. But I would not want one who spots a lurking predator to remain silent. If potential disaster lies ahead, will someone please speak up? Do yell "Fire!" if there is smoke in the theater. Don't understate the truly catastrophic. The human parade marches blithely and blindly toward an abyss.

Our planet is, I am convinced, in peril. The human family is in jeopardy. There are differing momentums—distinct yet interrelated, accelerating, exacerbated by fear and hopelessness—toward a surely unappealing, arguably disastrous future. Who will lead us in a fresh direction? Where are the visionaries with dreams of a new future? Who and where are the resources for transformation? The Bible, especially Jesus and the prophets, brims with a *message and movement* vital and urgent for our time. But where are the churches? Where are the bearers of that message and movement? I write to challenge the churches to awaken to that call. But I write also as one increasingly joining with "people of God" outside the church and increasingly stewarding my time and energy with "secular prophets" whom I perceive to be speaking God's word and doing God's work in the wake of the church's abdication.

EVEN JESUS BAILED OUT

Jesus *began* his life firmly within Jewish law and custom, circumcised at one week, purified in the temple on the eighth day, making the sojourn to Jerusalem with his parents at twelve, likely for his bar mitzvah. Educated in Jewish schools, he observed the high holidays. John's Gospel suggests that he journeyed to Jerusalem for Passover each year of his public ministry. And he would *end* his life in the embrace of Jewish tradition, observing a seder as his last meal, dutifully buried before sunset on the Sabbath, with women arriving at the tomb on Sunday to prepare his body for final burial according to Jewish custom. He remained fully and completely Jewish, continually interpreting himself and his actions in light of Old Testament prophecy and, both subtly and overtly, revealing himself as the Messiah, the Anointed One, or, his apparently favorite designation, Son of Man.

Jesus's ministry tells a different story. Who am I to read Jesus's mind? Yet it must have surely seemed logical, an obviously sensible strategy. Why reinvent the wheel? The Jews, a vast population spread in diaspora across the known world, yet still concentrated in and around Jerusalem, had been awaiting his arrival for six hundred years. A theology of expectancy was in place. Here was a religious institution with branch offices in every city, town, and rural village, a network of thousands of synagogues in place. There was a vast cadre of Pharisees and Sadducees, priests and scribes, a highly trained religious hierarchy, custodians of tradition for a faithfully waiting people. What could be more perfect: an expectant people, houses of worship, leadership and theology, eagerly awaiting the Messiah? Everything was all set.

I carefully reread the Gospels through this particular lens— tracking Jesus's ministry and his visits to synagogues, the ways he employed the in-place institution, leadership, and people. It is difficult to name a specific number of synagogue visits in Jesus's three-year itinerary, uncertain where different Gospels write of the same or different occasions, but somewhere between eight and twelve seems a reasonable guess. But the more intriguing question is this: "How did those visits go?" The earliest visits are reported in a general and generic manner and may represent many visits in different parts of Galilee, offering no narrative of particular occasions but suggesting a basic missionary strategy. Town to town, synagogue to synagogue—teaching, preaching, and healing, the people astonished and amazed, the crowds steadily growing—was

proving a successful plan (Matt. 4:23–25), though his pitying the
people as worried and helpless, like sheep without a shepherd, a
paucity of workers to gather the harvest, hinted that trouble lay
ahead (Matt. 9:35–39).

The "synagogue-based strategy" came upon serious trouble
when he debuted in his hometown, a familiar narrative. He read
a prophetic text, declared himself its fulfillment, and the locals
were impressed. The mood shifted as he predicted his approaching rejection, and got distinctly sour, then murderous, when he
cited hated enemies as special recipients of God's graciousness and
healing. Only the power of his person allowed him to walk away
from their execution plot (Luke 4:16–30).

There appears to be only one more truly fruitful synagogue
experience, where Jesus healed a man with an evil spirit, the
people responding with amazement at his authority and power,
his reputation spreading everywhere (Luke 4:31–37). Jesus entered
a synagogue less and less, each occasion wonderful for the ones
he healed—a man with a paralyzed hand, a woman with a bent
back, a man who was blind and could not talk—but rife with the
anger and jealousy, the scribes and Pharisees plotting retaliation.
Halfway through the Gospels, any reference to synagogue visits
abruptly ends. Jesus continued to refer to synagogues, but to warn
against their hypocrisy and lament their cruelty, and he repeatedly
encounters the religious hierarchy who pursued him relentlessly.

Had the "Jewish strategy" failed as well? In chapter after chapter, Jesus taught on hillsides and by the seashore, in private homes
and in the marketplace, wherever a crowd gathered, often teaching
as he walked. He talked with demoniacs, engaged with foreign-
ers and sat with lepers. He defied law and custom, cutting grain
and healing the sick on the Sabbath, talking alone with a woman
at a well. He sat at table with prostitutes and tax collectors and
touched the unclean. He spent more and more of his time with
the "crowds"—appropriately translated, in the vernacular of the
day, as riffraff, outcasts, outsiders, the mob.

Jesus's calling remained crystal clear: his mission focused, his
message resounding, and his movement unstoppable. There were

people to love, heal, encourage, and empower. That is why he came. But the tradition and institution that gave him his identity proved an inadequate venue to carry forth his work. With a sadness he did not hide, he stepped away from that institution, its religious professionals not only unwilling to support his ministry, but unyielding in their opposition.

A SAD IRONY

So, however unfortunate, it comes as no surprise that those who seek to carry forward the message and movement of Jesus today may experience a similar irony. The church has branch offices in every city, town, and rural village around the globe. A network of seminaries, across the Christian traditions, has trained and deployed thousands of religious professionals. Thirty percent of Earth's population name themselves as Christian. We are graced with a powerful text, the voice of Jesus and the prophets. There are people to love, heal, encourage, and empower. That is why we are here. But is a "church-based strategy" bearing fruit? Indeed, is a "Christian strategy" emerging with authority? Are faith-motivated people joining to speak and act the message and movement of Jesus in the face of what threatens our global family?

I must speak more directly and personally. I trust that my commitment to the church speaks clearly through each essay that has come before. But a trend, unnoticed at first, has begun to establish a trajectory in my life. I heard myself articulate it near the beginning of a sermon a year or so ago, a spontaneous and unscripted line. "There is an awesome challenge before us, we who inhabit this planet," I heard myself say. "Rising to this challenge is no longer an option but an urgency," I went on. *I do not expect government or church to give it leadership,* "words that startled me as much as anyone in the pews. "I do hope my government and my church will catch the spirit, contribute and collaborate, 'tag along' and join the flow. I surely hope they will not resist or impede, though I fear

they might. This movement belongs to the people, the whole human family," I concluded. Wherever these unplanned, unrehearsed
words came from, I believe them and trust them.

A FUTURIST'S HAUNTING QUESTION

I have become intrigued by the writing of futurists, representatives
from a broad spectrum of disciplines—physicists and cosmologists,
evolutionary biologists and mathematicians, philosophers and theologians, economists and social critics, poets and journalists—who
project and predict, discern trajectories and their pace, create
plausible scenarios in the near and distant future. They gather at
conferences, meet electronically in virtual reality, write books and
scholarly papers, and appear in television documentaries.

The Arlington Institute specializes in anticipating global
destiny, suggesting that "Humanity has never lived through the
convergence, in some cases the collision, of global forces of such
magnitude and diversity, one foreseeable outcome being global
instability, and another planetary renaissance."[2] There are deeply
troubling scenarios and breathtakingly hopeful ones, these a small
example:

- It is *unnerving* to note that the average temperature in
  Antarctica is continuing to rise, 4.5 degrees since 1940;
  soon the summertime average will be above 32 degrees
  Fahrenheit. The ice cap is disintegrating at 3,000 square
  kilometers per year, and tsunami-driven sea levels could
  rise 100 feet with devastating results.[3]
- It is *hopeful* to anticipate that scientific breakthroughs
  might create an energy revolution—cold fusion, zero-
  point energy, hydrogen-based fuels—making fossil fuels
  obsolete and causing rapid improvement in ecosystems
  and the biosphere.
- It is *troubling* to note that food and water shortages could
  cascade into a global crisis—mass starvation, monumental

scarcity, diseases the result of new viruses and antibiotic-resistant infections becoming epidemic—prompting desperation, hysteria, and massive unrest.

- It is *thrilling* to anticipate nanotechnology, a process by which molecular-sized machines build human-scale products, totally transforming manufacturing and resulting in positive environmental transformation, solving worldwide food shortages, resolving pollution-producing energy problems, and increasing the human life span.[4]

What Is Enlightenment? magazine produced an oversize issue in the summer of 2003 focusing on the work of futurists, a pithy and provocative title blazoned across the cover: *Can God Handle the 21st Century?* The issue posed a clear and focused question to which dozens of scholars from a broad continuum of disciplines and backgrounds responded: *Can our existing spiritual and ethical structures, both traditional and contemporary, equip us to handle the enormity, the speed, the complexity, and the overwhelming nature of the changes we are undergoing?*[5]

Such a disarming, beguiling, disconcerting question! I choose to use it to give structure to the balance of this essay. But don't leave all the work to me. I have completed an exercise that I challenge you to undertake for yourself. Feeling a surge of audacity, I further propose that all pastors and congregational leaders; bishops, denominational executives, and their staffs; priests, monsignors, and cardinals; national denominational officers and presiding bishops, anyone of influence in or having concern for the church complete the exercise as well. That question the magazine proposed could prompt lively discussion, stir controversy and debate, become its own inspiration for articles and books in response, but that would stall the process in the realm of the merely theoretical and hypothetical and fail to mobilize a response that issues in action.

This exercise has three phases:

1. Identify those dynamics which most threaten Earth and the human family in the next quarter-century: I will

name twelve, then focus on three, offering enough detail
to profile the threat and substantiate its choice as urgent,
even dire.

2. Identify faith resources—biblical teaching and historic
    traditions, the words of Jesus and the prophets—that speak
    with relevance and could inspire responsibility-taking.

3. Identify your own personal activist agenda, that which you
    commit to say and do, those with whom you will covenant
    to work in collaboration.

My Threat List—Long, and Still Open-ended

The focus of my concern—thus the focus of study and prayer, thus
the focus of choosing assertive, biblically based action—includes
the following:

1. Environmental degradation and ecological systems col-
    lapse.
2. The broadening gap between rich and poor.
3. Technology gone awry: accelerating experimentation and
    invention with unpredictable or irreversibly negative ef-
    fects.
4. The collision of global fundamentalisms.
5. An epidemic of consumerism, accumulation, and greed.
6. Increasing violence and militarism.
7. Growth of global terrorism and access to weapons of mass
    destruction.
8. The continuing threat of nuclear holocaust.
9. The hegemony of transnational corporations.
10. Antibiotic-immune bacteria that lead to global disease
    epidemics.
11. Increasing desperation that accelerates global uprisings,
    chaos and anarchy.

12. The failure of the major religions to respond to new realities.

"But I thought the focus of faith and the church was on spiritual matters," a voice within me insists, perhaps joining a similar voice within you. I am no stranger to being confronted with that complaint, variously expressed in various settings. And I never want my response to be glib or simplistic. These are issues in a world Jesus tells us God loves, to which God sent a Son not to judge but to be its savior (John 3:16–17); thus, I assume, they are issues of concern to God, and those who address them work with God. The promise of salvation, forgiveness, and heeding the call to faithfulness must be at the heart of whatever seeks to be healing, redemptive, and saving. I have chosen three of these issues to apply my proposed threefold exercise: the broadening gap between rich and poor, increasing violence and militarism, and the hegemony of transnational corporations. I plan to continue my research, reflection, and activism to address the others. I take each issue with utter seriousness. I will not shy from the awesome threat each presents, but I remain grounded in audacious hope and trust in a God who "works all together for good."

1. The Broadening Gap between Rich and Poor

From the end of World War II to the mid-seventies a "rising tide lifted all boats"; robust macroeconomic trends were realized at the micro-level. At differing trajectories all segments of the U.S. economy, each household across the socioeconomic spectrum, shared in expanding prosperity, experiencing financial gain. The gap between rich and poor actually narrowed. From 1975 to the present that trend dramatically changed.[6]

It is easy to "numb out" in the face of statistics, forgetting that human faces peer from beneath the data. The rich/poor divide widens at a staggering rate, increasing threefold during those last thirty years.[7] Across that span annual income for 90 percent of us increased just 2 percent, while the top 1 percent saw a 57 percent increase (to an average annual income of $940,000), the top .1 percent an 85 percent increase ($4.5 million per year) and the top .001 percent a 112 percent increase ($20 million per year).[8] One in six of our children is poor, and 37 million of us live below the poverty line.[9] CEO-to-worker income ratio, the starkest of contrasts, expanded from 43-to-1 in 1975 to 344-to-1 in 2008.[10] A chief executive, who once had to work ten days to match a worker's annual income, can leave the office by midafternoon on any given day and match that worker's yearly salary.[11]

Fifty percent of our global neighbors are undernourished, 80 percent living in substandard housing, while 50 percent cannot read.[12] They outnumber us. The life expectancy differential between low- and high-income nations is a mind-boggling nineteen years,[13] nearly 60,000 women die every year in Nigeria from preventable pregnancy-related causes,[14] and the child death rate in sub-Saharan Africa rose from 13 times to 29 times higher than in richer countries in the last 25 years.[15] Two billion people live on less than two dollars a day, another billion on one dollar a day.[16]

Getting closer to home, perhaps uncomfortably so: if I have assets of $2,200 (my checking account balance, the value of my car) I am among the global population's top 50 percent; assets of $61,000 (the equity in my home) put me in the top 10 percent. I went to *www.globalrichlist.com* and punched in my annual income (my pension, Social Security checks, and investment income providing a modest total, most people I know earning more than me) to discover that I am in the .93 percentile globally, and the top 1.7 percentile in the United States.

Sit quietly and take in the following scene. The sermon title was *Whatever Happened to Outrage?* Before the preacher began, he placed a small table in the center aisle and turned the small key that activated a metronome he'd carefully placed there. Tick . . . tick . . . tick. The ticks occurred just under three seconds apart, he explained, the interval at which somewhere on the planet a child dies of a preventable or easily curable disease. Tick . . . tick . . . tick.

Twenty ticks a minute, four hundred during this sermon, twelve hundred during this worship hour, 30,000 by this time tomorrow. I don't remember a lot of what he said, but that ticking remains indelible in my memory.

Supreme Court Justice Louis Brandeis warned, "We can have democracy, or we can have great wealth concentrated in the hands of a few—but we cannot have both."[17] A U.N. human-rights inspector in an informal report on the racial poverty situation in the U.S. asserted that the situation was tantamount to a human-rights violation under international norms.

Consider a last thought, though hardly the last word, about poverty. People are increasingly, understandably concerned about global terrorism, especially the prospect of weapons of mass destruction in rogue hands. The ranks of radical ideologues swell and acts of violence are becoming disturbingly widespread, desperate acts of desperate people. A War on Terror, amply armed and funded, seems imperative. But unless coupled with a just as ardent an assault on poverty, such a war may prove unwinnable. The futurist-oriented Arlington Institute describes a catastrophic scenario, "Africa Unravels," where population growth, famine, environmental degradation, and lethal epidemics spawn massive upheaval, large-scale rebellions and anarchy which erupt as a spontaneous, continent-wide northward migration toward developed countries with colossal destruction of basic equilibrium.[18]

My closest personal exposure to widespread poverty is Mexico. While the macro numbers appear promising, it is the immense new wealth in the hands of a few that creates a statistical illusion of increased national prosperity (if Bill Gates walked into any gathering, the average income would spike, even as actual incomes remained the same!). Seventy percent of Mexico's population is losing ground economically and thousands fall each week into desperation.[19] *Desperate people do desperate things.* If driven only by prudence and self-interest, an assertive response to global poverty is critical.

A WORD FROM JESUS AND THE
PROPHETS ON POVERTY

Talk about unhesitant and unbridled apocalyptic language, explosive forecasts of cataclysmic events. Read the prophets. They did not warn of periodic military setbacks, significant but cyclical economic downturns, occasional political and social unrest. They predicted utter and absolute collapse, the physical destruction of a civilization, ultimate and crushing defeat. Isaiah did not warn that Assyria posed merely a military threat, but that Samaria would fall to their advancing armies (Isa. 10:5–6). Jeremiah did not prophesy a damaging, even crippling assault on Jerusalem, but predicted the unthinkable, the surely impossible, that the city would fall, its surviving inhabitants exiled to Babylon (Jer. 21:2–7). Jesus standing in the shadow of the magnificence of the Holy City, tears in his eyes, predicts a day in a not-distant future when the city would be surrounded, besieged, and crushed to the ground, and there would not be left "one stone upon another in you" (Luke 19:41–44 RSV).

If we are to learn lessons from history and fathom the depths of the prophetic mission, we must discern what inspired their penetrating perceptions and confident predictions, what one core issue, deeper than any other, animated them. Isaiah was disturbed by militarizing the quest for security, Amos and Micah challenged political and judicial corruption, Jeremiah railed against idolatry and immorality, but a single issue lay at the heart of their message—*failure to respond to the poor*. And, just as tragic, complicity with the forces that create and exacerbate poverty.

It is literally impossible to read the prophets, even a cursory reading, and not have your eyes fall frequently on verses that make the point with abrupt and fierce directness: "They do not defend the rights of the needy. Shall I not punish them for these things?" (Jer. 5:28–29). "Woe to those . . . [who] rob the poor of my people . . . . What will you do on the day of punishment?" (Isa. 10:2–3 RSV).

"Hear this you rulers...who abhor justice and pervert all equity . . . Jerusalem shall become a heap of ruins" (Micah 3:9, 12).

The same prophetic message permeates the New Testament: "Just as you did not do it to one of the least of these, you did not do it to me. And these will go away into eternal punishment" (Matt. 25:45–46). "He has filled the hungry with good things, and the rich he has sent away empty" (Luke 1:53 RSV). "There was a rich man who was dressed in purple . . . at his gate lay a poor man . . . Father Abraham I am in agony in these flames" (Luke 16:19–20, 24). A well-known author a generation ago read James 5:1–5 to a group of ministers, but attributed the passage to Emma Goldman, a controversial and flamboyant agitator and activist. The ministers were incensed, insisting that she should be immediately deported![20]

Is there such a thing as biblical economics? The consistent and unrelenting prophetic offensive against those who ignore or actively intensify the plight of the poor must be sounded anew, but are there at least contours of a biblically based economic theory and practice? Hoping these paragraphs will inspire your own research, my biblical exploration yields three foundational elements or principles that I must note are resonant with those of biblical scholar and activist Ched Myers and others involved in developing what some call Sabbath Economics.

First, the creation is bountiful and abundant, with more than enough for everyone. God looked out on the unfolding creation declaring it "good" (Gen. 1:25) and then, brimming with exuberance and delight, declares it "*very* good" (1:31). As is often the case in the biblical languages, apparently simple words are often rich and multi-textured, "good" defying precise translation in a single word—incredible, magical, extraordinary, and astonishing all just touch the surface. The earth is generous, lavish, and awesomely bountiful. Food experts say the planet at this moment can feed seven times its population and that every nation is potentially food self-sufficient.[21] The issue is distribution, not production; a matter of will, not capability.

*Second, the creator does not intend a broad disparity between rich
and poor.* We must call it sin, Ched Myers insists.[22] No prophet
railed at the shocking extremes of wealth and poverty like Amos,
and archeology supports his picture. Excavations of the earliest settlements in Canaan suggest that the land was distributed
equitably among the tribes and then among families, each enjoy-
ing similar standards of living. As late as the tenth century BCE,
homes were about the same size. However, archeologists working
at eighth-century sites found a dramatically different picture with
bigger, better built, more ornate homes on large tracts of land and
smaller, less sturdy houses tightly clustered in other sections.[23]

*Third, people of faith, inspired by biblical models, are called
to strategies of wealth redistribution.* Trust me, you venture onto
homiletical thin ice if you dare to utter the word "redistribution"
in a sermon, let alone in more casual conversation about biblical
themes related to economics. Yet if you extract all pages of Scripture
that address the theme of redistribution, that enumerate its theory
and practice, the Bible becomes seriously thinner. As the Hebrews
sojourned in the wilderness, manna, a thin and flaky nourishment
that tasted like honey and coriander, appeared each morning when
the dew had dried—Moses named it "bread from heaven" (Exod.
16:4) and "bread that the LORD has given" (16:15). Instructed to
gather only as much as they needed (16:16), what they attempted
to hoard became worm-infested and foul. The manna story appears
to have taught the Hebrews in the wilderness the "economics of
enough," first glimpses of a new paradigm, counter to the Egyp-
tians' "economics of accumulation," the only model they had ever
known.

Yahweh, being a rather practical and earthy deity, knew inevitable inequalities would emerge among those who settled the
Promised Land, and did not want the gains or losses of one generation to become the blessing or burden of the next, so every seventh
year was a "Sabbath Year" and every fiftieth a "Jubilee Year"—each
with precise and detailed provisions about, yes, redistribution.

Jesus's first sermon appears to announce a renewal of these
redistribution practices, which evidently lapsed, likely when those

with accumulated wealth and power successfully vetoed their application. His parables, once saved from the domesticating influence of prevailing scholarship and typical sermons, seem to speak clearly about everyday issues of economic injustice in an advanced agrarian society, with emphasis on redressing the plight of the poor. The early church pooled their communal resources, giving and receiving each according to ability and need (Acts 2:42–47, 4:32–37). At the heart of Paul's invitation to *charity*, most clearly stated in 2 Corinthians 8–9, is the deeper challenge to *justice*, the prime motivation for giving and sharing being, yes, redistribution.

Finally, the foundational themes of structural injustice and institutional evil, essential to understanding biblical teaching on poverty, must be reclaimed. Amos denounced dishonest judges and a corrupt judicial system. Jeremiah deplored dishonest businessmen and a fraudulent economic system. Is there a more powerful statement of God's work to dismantle unjust structures than the Magnificat of Mary, pulling the "mighty from their thrones" and exalting "those of low degree" (Luke 1:52)?

2. Increasing Violence and Militarism

Violence happens in our *homes*. Domestic violence accounts for 35 percent of emergency room visits by women, a half million a year,[24] with three women murdered each day by boyfriends or husbands.[25] Thirty percent of women will experience domestic abuse across their lifetimes, and 50 percent of abusing spouses also abuse their children,[26] resulting in increased incidence of depression, post-traumatic stress disorder, and other psychological manifestations.

Violence assails our *children and youth*. Ten percent of children will experience inappropriate sexual advances by an educator.[27] The leading cause of death of African American males age 15–24, usually by a handgun, is homicide. The annual homicide rate for children and youth in the United States is 22 per 100,000, four times higher than Scotland at 5 per 100,000, Austria the lowest at less than 1 per 100,000.[28]

Violence erupts most dramatically in our *cities*. Half of the global population will live in cities by 2020, and urban violence has increased 3.5 percent a year for two decades, ranging from muggings to drug-related gangland shootouts. There is a direct relationship between urban population increase and incidence of violence.[29] Half of the homicides in most Latin American countries are committed in the single largest city—Buenos Aires, Medellin, Caracas, Lima, and Mexico City as examples.[30] At the same time, rural violence is also increasing, massive displacement and whole population migrations prompted by political and social strife, warfare, or environmental degradation, an experience they share in common with city dwellers.

Violence assumes its most awesome magnitude and brutality in "ethnic cleansing" and genocide: Darfur, Rwanda, Bosnia, Chechnya, and Congo are anguished examples in recent years of a phenomenon which, though overwhelming in its magnitude since World War II, has blighted history from its beginning. Whether it is orchestrated by governments, paramilitaries, marauding ethnic hordes, or spontaneous and explosive eruptions of ancient racial or ethnic rivalries, the numbers exterminated by killing or the fall-out of massive displacement are staggering, the focus on civilians unconscionable.

A PATTERN BEGINS TO EMERGE

Across these widely varied contexts, I discern a pattern emerging with increasing clarity—with distinct steps and stages that appear common to all, startling but perhaps illuminating parallels.

1. *Migration and displacement:* People form an identity, feel rooted in history and heritage, and are supported by networks of family and friends in a locale called home, on a rural farm or a crowded city street. Familiarity, consistency, and stability create basic security and confidence. But displacement and forced migration have uprooted vast

populations on every continent, whether into a city or to some strange and unfamiliar rural terrain. Family members and lifelong friends may go in opposite directions.

2. *Dislocation, disorientation, and isolation:* Overwhelmed by isolation, wrested from sources of support and encouragement, struggling, often unsuccessfully, to find shelter or a means of income, life edges toward despair. Local populations may resent and marginalize newcomers. Structures and norms that gave order and guidance are gone.

3. *A rapid slide into poverty:* Regional governmental agencies mandated to respond to social concerns and to assist with assimilation become inundated and ineffectual, unresponsive to the needs of the newly displaced people. Discouragement leads to frustration, edges into anger, ready to burst into violence. Things go from bad to worse.

4. *Dissatisfaction and radicalization:* They gather at first on street corners, pool their discontent, march in spontaneous demonstrations, and organize direct political action. They create or join protest movements and align with opposition political parties, often with little success. When struggle tumbles into desperation, desperate people ready to do desperate things become susceptible to recruitment into extremist political movements. The ranks of the terrorists swell.

5. *Violence becomes a movement:* Now the violence has become institutionalized, a coherent movement, a target for a war on terrorism that fails to see the poverty that lies at the heart of the narrative.

Opportunities for creative and assertive intervention by governments, nongovernmental organizations, or faith-based initiatives lie at each juncture of the stages I have named. Concerted and collaborative effort by public and private sector partnerships formed out of shared concern might well address these issues before they coalesce into such an immense threat.

A Militarized World

Of all the enemies of public liberty war is, perhaps, the most
to be dreaded because it comprises and develops the germ of
every other. War is the parent of armies and from them proceeds
debt and taxes . . . institutions for bringing the many under the
domination of the few. No nation could preserve its freedom
in the midst of continual warfare.

James Madison
"Political Observations," 1795

Global military spending together with the arms production in-
dustry has become the largest single worldwide expenditure, just
over $1.47 trillion. After the Cold War, aggregate military budgets
steadily declined. That trajectory has shifted upward, a 10 percent
overall increase since 2001, 80 percent of that increase created by
the United States. Of this $1.47 trillion global expenditure, just
fifteen countries expend 83 percent, the United States comprising
48 percent of that total, with Europe at 20 percent (Britain, France,
and Germany 4–5 percent each), China 8 percent, and Russia 5
percent. Our military budget has more than doubled since 2001,
from $330 to $700 billion. By comparison, the total United Nations budget is $20 billion ($3 per global inhabitant),[31] a budget
it struggles to subscribe, the United States a reluctant financial
partner. In the aftermath of the invasion of Iraq, its advocates
insisting the world would become safer, other countries, both our
allies and adversaries, are increasing their military expenditures and
renewing their quest for nuclear weapons. Finally, a pie chart of
our total national budget indicates 43 percent for military, while
only 20 percent goes to health research and services, 12 percent
for poverty-focused projects, and 3 percent for social programs.[32]
Meanwhile our Food Foreign Aid Budget has remained the same,
an effective decrease with the cost of food shipped having increased
30 to 40 percent, many countries eliminated from the list and all
receiving dramatically reduced amounts.[33] Of twenty-two Western

aid-giving nations, comparisons adjusted by percentage of GNP, the United States ranks twenty-second.[34]

There are still 25,000 active nuclear warheads, built at a cost of $12 trillion, 95 percent controlled by Russia and the United States at a cost of $11 million a day, 2,500 on high alert, able to be launched within fifteen minutes. Congress has authorized the development of a "comprehensive nuclear weapons strategy for the 21st century" which prompted Vladimir Putin to announce a similar plan in Russia. Kofi Annan, former secretary general of the United Nations, has said, "The world is sleepwalking toward a nuclear catastrophe."[35]

The rationale for war can be persuasive. We must not take the threat of terrorism with anything less than utter seriousness. As the single superpower in a world where national, economic, and religious ideologies collide, able to explode without warning, the United States has an arguably vital peacemaking role to play, and sometimes peacemakers wear guns. Pure pacifism may be an impossible ideal, though I personally edge ever more steadily in that direction. I do know this. It is disturbingly easy to cast up scenarios where a global conflagration erupts and explodes with power to annihilate the planet. It seems oddly ironic that we are so disturbed contemplating weapons of mass destruction in the hands of rogue states and terrorists, yet so little disturbed with similar firepower in the hands of the so-called free world. Pacifist A. J. Muste put it succinctly, "If you arm yourself, you arm your enemy,"[36] while William Blake put it more poetically: "They looked at each other and became what they beheld,"[37] and elsewhere, "The iron hand crushed the Tyrant's head and became a Tyrant in his stead."[38]

A WORD FROM JESUS AND THE PROPHETS ON VIOLENCE AND MILITARISM

I have favorite verses of Scripture, biblical characters to whom I feel strangely drawn, and scenes most indelibly imprinted in my mind. I offer a most compelling scene, with some context, which speaks powerfully to the theme at hand. Once Jesus "turned and set his face toward Jerusalem," he walked inexorably toward a defining moment, a public confrontation he had carefully chosen to avoid during his itinerant ministry. He appears to have carefully planned those final days: a password uttered, his instruction precisely worded, and a donkey is released . . . a man with a jar of water on his head leads Jesus and his disciples to a room where the feast has been prepared . . . access has been arranged for a private garden outside the city wall after that supper. Utilizing what some call prophetic theater, he acts a message in a visible and symbolic way, riding that donkey through a screaming throng on what we call Palm Sunday.

The suspense is gripping as Jesus approaches the brow of the hill from which he will first see the golden gate through which his parade will enter the city. Imagine you have already reached the pinnacle and are chatting with a disciple, the chanting thunderous as thousands dance and wave palms. Awaiting Jesus's arrival, you expect a broad smile to splash across his face. He rides into view . . . and weeps!

Why weeping? What does he see or hear that the others miss? Why is he not delighted? Some scholars speculate that words we sing with exuberance on Palm Sunday, words those pilgrims sang so enthusiastically, may be different in both content and tone than we thought. Those palms may have been raised with clenched fists, not simply innocent celebration. "Alleluia" may be a revolutionary slogan, not unlike "right on to the revolution." Jesus, with Zechariah in mind, came as the peaceful king riding on a donkey's foal, but the people may have seen instead a projection of their hopes and expectations, a son of David on a mighty steed, sword drawn, ready to sound a call to arms to liberate the city.

Jerusalem was located at a distant corner of the Roman Empire, its occupying forces often depleted by deployment to other locations. Rome had granted the Hebrew hierarchy unusual power of self-governance, with the clear understanding that occupation would remain benign only if firm and steady control were maintained. Ready when the moment came, arms caches were secretly and strategically located among the population. Insurrection was always a threat, awaiting a bold and charismatic figure to lead the charge. Was their exuberance, their clenched fists, their loud shouts appealing to Jesus to seize the moment to be that leader?

I heard years ago about some biblical scholars who invited some special guests to help them more deeply assess the Palm Sunday phenomenon—a team of high-ranking military officers, several with expertise in assessing battle readiness and planning strategies of attack. The scholars asked a clear and specific question: did Jesus refuse to lead an armed revolt on *principled* or *strategic* grounds? That is, did he reject the armed option because he believed it could not succeed, resulting in crushing defeat, a strategic blunder? Or did he reject it on principled grounds, as morally wrong, because he had a different kind of kingdom in mind?

After careful study and vigorous deliberation the military experts concurred that Jesus could have led a successful uprising, powerful enough to defeat the Roman army. During the Passover the Jews outnumbered the occupying force by hundreds to one. Not unlike guerilla warfare that prevails against enormous odds, they knew more intimately the terrain where the fight would occur and they had an informal but vast and effective communication system typical among oppressed people. *Nonviolence, rejecting the militarized strategy, was a matter of principle for Jesus, a principle that must characterize those who would reside in the kingdom he announced to be at hand.*

SAYS IT ALL—AS IT HAD BEEN SAID ALL ALONG

I rest my case. This picture does speak a thousand words. That face drenched with tears wants to launch, if not a thousand ships, a movement toward a peaceable kingdom. Jesus the prophet stood in a long line of those who came before, echoing the same theme. Before the first king was anointed, God had argued through Samuel of the dangers of monarchy, the desire to "become like other nations," the initial warnings related to warfare—soldiers, a cavalry, and war chariots—which will lead to depending on military might over God's protection (1 Sam. 8:10–22). Isaiah warned that expanding the military and forming military alliances with neighboring countries would hasten the momentum toward defeat by the Assyrians: "Woe to those who go down to Egypt for help and rely on horses, who trust in chariots because they are many and in horsemen because they are very strong, but do not look to the Holy One of Israel or consult the LORD!" (Isa. 31:1 RSV).

BE NOT AFRAID

No words of comfort are offered in the Bible more directly and frequently (no less than forty times, thirty-four in the Old Testament and twelve in the New) as variations on "Be not afraid," and one can argue that nothing provokes violence, whether it be a schoolyard fistfight or a world war, like fear. "Be not afraid" does not suggest "there's nothing to be afraid of," and it offers courage, not bravery, as the antidote. The psalmist receives divine comfort and assurance in the face of fear-laden, even terrifying circumstances—poverty and disease, loneliness and rejection, enemies poised to pounce like lions, depression and desperation, oppression and unjust imprisonment. Comforted, the psalmist is able to forego retaliation, to set aside the bow and spear (Ps. 46:9). Reassured, the psalmist is freed to praise God and to respond to human need with generosity and justice. Isaiah 10 offers the prophet's most emphatic warning against letting fear of the Assyrians prompt those unwise alliances and military buildup, yet offers the secret to living with trust, "Be not afraid" (Isa. 10:24 RSV). Jeremiah and Ezekiel quickly learned that a prophetic call, given with divine assurance, an invitation to be unafraid (Jer. 1:8, Ezek. 2:6) does not mean protection from inner turmoil and discouragement or bodily harm inflicted from without.

Jesus frees us to be peace*ful*, and then calls us to be peace*makers*. The peace he promises us is "not as the world gives," it is a peace only he can "breathe" on us. Only as we become personally peaceful, mindful of and being steadily healed of our personal capacity for hatred and retaliation, beginning with relationships close at hand, can we dare to be peacemakers. What people more than Christians, what organizations more than the churches, are better called, trained, and deployed by faith and hope for this peacemaking work?

3. The Hegemony of Transnational Corporations

I visited the studio of an artist friend and became immediately curious about a large, unfinished canvas on his easel. Three-quarters of the painting appeared complete, but the final part near the middle was only beginning to take shape. "It's been rather odd," he said quietly, "an experience I've never had before. I had planned to paint a particular figure there, fully complementary, I thought, to the total composition. But the canvas refused to receive it!" He went on, my expression now as perplexed as his. "While I was standing there confused," he explained, "a figure seemed to arrive from behind the canvas, the canvas 'inviting' me to paint her in that spot. That's what I was doing as you arrived."

I had a different selection from my list of twelve primed for this spot, and had struggled through several paragraphs to give it shape. But the page refused the words! My thoughts jumbled, each sentence more awkward than the one before, I was constantly shading and deleting, each new effort more frustrating than the one before. I sat here confused, like my artist friend, until the page seemed to announce its choice! Well aware of having artfully avoided even considering this issue, I chose to accede to this unorthodox leading.

Challenging a person's behavior as deviant, harmful, illegal, or immoral does not make one *anti-people*. Calling the church to accountability for letting trivia and a propensity for conflict distract and mute its mission and ministry does not make one *anti-church*. Confronting a school board, a teachers' union, or parents for lack of responsibility-taking for their school and its students does not make one *anti-education*. Unmasking a country's lack of political transparency, skewed budgeting priorities, failure to address the needs of its poorest citizens, and allowing its corporations undue power and privilege does not make one *anti-American*. Rest assured, that accusation lies near at hand when one dares, Christian or not, to address this issue, their patriotism in question, their national loyalty suspect. Welcome back onto the thin ice!

Hegemony is defined as "control or dominating influence by one person or group, especially by one political group over society, or one nation over others."[39] Like the word *empire* it has been used sparingly in reference to the United States and its economic global reach, except by radical social critics, until more recently, when even conservative commentators and media personalities began to employ these terms.

I am personally most familiar with Latin America, having visited a number of countries in Central and South America, which has prompted my focus of personal reading and research, and will be the focus of the following paragraphs. Though populated by people of varying racial and ethnic heritage, a common story line characterizes the national history of many of these countries, a common lineage: thousands of years of indigenous rule, the rise of dominating civilizations such as the Mayas and Incas, the Spanish conquest beginning in the sixteenth century, and then the hegemony of the United States and large corporate interests beginning early in the twentieth century.

High-school students in Latin America know the following names well—Chile's Allende, Guatemala's Arbenz, Venezuela's Andres Perez, Ecuador's Roldos, or Panama's Torrijos, democratically elected presidents overthrown by coups with documented CIA involvement—while many North Americans do not recognize the names. More familiar to our citizens are corporate names from recent or present history—United Fruit, Bechtel, Shell Oil, Brown Brothers, Harriman Bank—but those same high-school students would connect those corporations to Guatemala, Bolivia, Ecuador, and Nicaragua, respectively, and could tell you the story in greater detail. They would argue that political and military history in Latin America is driven largely by corporate economic self-interest. The ice only gets thinner!

Author and activist John Perkins is controversial, his writings stirring a storm of avid interest and angry retort. He makes
compelling claims about the devastating impact of an unsavory
partnership of corporations, the World Bank and International
Monetary Fund, the U.S. government, and the compliant governments of developing countries at the expense of the poor and the
environment. Framing the narrative in a half-dozen Latin American
countries around a common story line, Perkins names the recurrent
sequence: Initial proposals, made by firms that broker transnational
corporate involvement, promise a given country modernization,
solid economic development, and benefit to the poor, with financial
gain assured to the already wealthy and powerful in that country.
Huge loans are secured from the World Bank, large engineering
and construction companies commence ambitious infrastructure
projects, companies intent on harvesting natural resources from oil
to precious metal arrive creating an economic boom that typically
busts, leaving crippling national debt, a savaged environment, and
the poor in even more untenable conditions.[40]

I know why I kept pushing aside Perkins's books, though each
one is now dog-eared and heavily underlined. What I don't know
I can remain silent and passive about. What I read but can successfully rebut I can set aside with a sigh of relief. What I hear or
read and come to believe is significantly, if not completely, true
obligates me to speak and act. So, I am speaking and acting.

Each Sunday that I vest to lead worship, I slip a cross necklace
over my head—the cross painted in indigenous Salvadoran style
by Moises and Gloria, refugees from El Salvador and friends who
lost most of their extended family to paramilitary incursions into
their rural village, accused of being communists because they
worked cooperatively with other peasant farmers inspired by local
priests and their weekly Bible study group. I then settle a brightly
colored stole over my shoulders, the fabric woven by Macario and
Elena, Guatemalan refugees who fled when death squads placed the
infamous white handprint on their cottage door, indicating their
execution was at hand. I wear a tightly woven bracelet made by an
Andean woman from Ecuador, whose village life became unsus-

tainable after the environmentally disastrous drilling practices of oil companies in the rain forest. Their stories are not unconnected from the stories I have been recounting.

A high-school friend was the daughter of a mafia don, though we didn't know it at the time, including those Friday nights when we gathered at her home, her father and his friends in dark suits sitting in front of the fireplace speaking in hushed tones. He told her what a mafia don tells his kids: You have nice clothes, a lovely home, a house at the shore, a father who takes good care of you—don't ask a lot of questions. Just enjoy the good life. I live a long way from Central America, have no family or friends employed by a transnational corporation, have no dealings with the World Bank and no friends in high places in this or any other country. Maybe I should enjoy life and not ask questions. That no longer seems to be an option—as a citizen or a Christian.

A WORD FROM JESUS AND THE PROPHETS ON CORPORATIONS

The Genesis story offers a place to start, our misunderstanding of "dominion" of particular importance with *stewardship*, the better translation. Psalm 24 lends a corrective in the simple phrase, "The earth is the Lord's," together with God's words to Job, "Whatever is under the whole heaven is mine" (Job 41:11 RSV). One can argue that the Bible supports the concept of private property—"steal" and "covet" in the Ten Commandments implies ownership, and Peter owned a home where Jesus frequently stayed. But ownership in the Bible—unlike the Roman concept of unconditional and exclusive ownership, which has guided its definition throughout Western history—is *relative* and not absolute. Dominion-as-stewardship is trusteeship, guardianship, faithful management of a creation that belongs to God. Jeremiah warns against accumulation and ostentatious use of the earth's resources, as does Jesus as he speaks of a successful but foolish farmer building bigger barns.

Author and activist Ron Sider offers delightful counsel, inspired by Jesus's words about the anxiety-free life of birds and lilies (Luke 12:22–31), urging a "carefree attitude toward possessions."[41] Unless we can muster some "holy nonchalance" about possessions— unlike that foolish farmer who lost distinction between *me* and *mine*, a self-definition based on *being,* not *having*—we remain in the unrelenting grip of transnational corporations.

TOWARD A THEOLOGY OF CORPORATIONS

The territory where Jesus conducted much of his public ministry, north and east of the Sea of Galilee, was an economically active region, a crossroads of transportation routes where caravans conducting international trade passed. Peter and Andrew were fisherman, but John and James had a fishing business. Jesus seemed keenly aware of networks of economic enterprise in Jerusalem. He stood in the tradition of the prophets who focused their discerning and challenging words to the structures of their society—the political, judicial, military, and economic institutions—as well as to individuals. Is it a stretch, or are there at least basic contours for a Theology of Corporations in Scripture?

Return to Jesus's tumultuous visit to the temple just after his arrival in Jerusalem that begins the last week of his life. Counter to prevailing assumptions, the temple, though housing a place of worship, was fundamentally an economic institution and dominated the city's commercial life.[42] More than simply a cluster of small, independent merchants, there was a substantial, inter-connected mercantile establishment. This was big business, first-century Palestine style. According to contemporary historian Josephus, a dominant economic monolith quietly linked political, economic, and religious players.[43] The money changers were local vendors representing banking interests of substantial power. There is evidence of priestly collusion with those who sold doves, the principal cultic commodity, a price-fixing scheme. Corporate interests made inordinate profits on the backs of the poor. Biblical scholar Ched

Myers argues persuasively that the "overturning" refers, beyond just tables, to an exploitive economic system, and calling architects of the system "thieves" hearkens back to Jeremiah's warning that economic exploitation in the temple will lead to its destruction.[44] The dramatic response by the religious establishment observing the event, plotting Jesus's murder, suggests more than a demonstration of outrage, but evidence of personal economic threat. Had Jesus threatened their corporate hegemony?

I hasten to add that transnational corporations are not by definition evil. If we are to read Colossians 1:16–20 as Paul's addendum to the creation story, as I do, "thrones, dominions, principalities, and powers" as the component parts of structural, institutional reality, then, as Walter Wink summarizes it, "the Powers are good, the Powers are fallen and the Powers will be redeemed."[45] As with individuals, the Powers are not evil by nature, yet, as fallen, become inevitably evil. And, like persons, unable to redeem themselves yet partners in the redemptive process, the Powers need divine redeeming.

THERE ARE HOPEFUL SIGNS

The tide may be turning. A grassroots, bottom-up, worldwide people's movement, joining hands across much that often divides the human family, may be making an impact. Though late to this phenomenon, people of faith, from local churches and denominational hierarchies, across the theological spectrum, have joined the movement, lending energy and momentum.

The slogan "going green" not many years ago would have likely evoked quizzical looks: some inexplicable odd reference to a color; maybe Kermit the Frog coming to mind; or a favorite team with green uniforms. Environmentalists a decade ago were dismissed as "tree huggers," as "grandmothers in sneakers," as the latest "cause" of the garden-party, society-page set. Social justice advocates viewed them as a distraction from more urgent and pressing issues, and the provocative acts of Greenpeace, their tiny boats blocking shipping lanes of oil tankers and transport ships, prompted cynicism.

Today that phrase has virtual universal recognition. More and more people are aware of the threat to the environment, many making conscious, if modest lifestyle changes. Though some might dismiss it as cosmetic and public-relations-driven, many automobile manufacturers and oil companies have made environmental concern a dominant advertising theme. A major newsmagazine that had changed the familiar red border on its cover only once in fifty years chose a green border for an issue on the environment and decided, counter to its editorial policy, to write from an advocacy position.

Christians bring a unique contribution to this rising consciousness and growing movement. Facts about corporate abuse might inspire and motivate a Christian, and the force of conscience can energize action, but I am convinced we have a particular and singular contribution to bring. I am at my best when my perception and analysis, my truth-seeking and action-taking, are rooted in Scripture. We bring biblical resources to mold and mobilize a Christian response to corporate hegemony.

Joined with the People of God ... and a Church Member Too

I want to be a tree known by its fruits. What I have seen and heard, I want to do. Resistance always close at hand, I want to be able to say "Send me." I want to be numbered among "who we've been waiting for." Flawed as my effort may be, I want to "be the change" that is needed. I want my faith to be a resource for a people made well.

In the course of writing these essays, no insight coaxed forth in the process seems more cogent than this. For years I have used two phrases as if they were synonyms: *the people of God* and *the church*. My perspective has dramatically shifted. Defining the *church* is simple, as I am now using that word: those who are part of faith communities—Roman Catholic, Orthodox, Protestant, or independent churches—however official their membership or active their participation. This is a finite number that minimal research could produce.

But what of *the people of God?* I have named and profiled the risks facing the human family, issues that must be identified, understood, and addressed with immediacy and resolve. I do not hesitate to assume that, to the degree discernment of these issues is accurate and their urgency appropriately assessed, God sees them as urgent as well. Yes, I am daring to conclude that this work, when it is aligned with divine will, always, of course, partial, flawed and incomplete, is the work of God. Those who respond to these issues, by definition, partner with God, are *the people of God.*

In a broad variety of settings—drawn together by mutual concern, gathered by a shared urgency, animated by a common compassion—I stand beside and walk with a broad slice of the human family: when I march in a demonstration at the Federal Building downtown, serve food at a soup kitchen, or attend a workshop on nonviolent civil disobedience. When I attend a Pachamama Alliance seminar, lead an Awaken the Dreamer/Change the Dream symposium, or serve on a panel reflecting on creative response to pressing social issues. When I preach a sermon, lead a Bible study or teach a seminary class. I name them all as *the people of God,* when our shared intention is to do faithful work. Some may name themselves as Christian, as I do—or Buddhist, Jewish, Muslim, or Baha'i, or have no faith at all. I call them all, often silently, *the people of God.* I name Jesus as my teacher, guide—they may name Moses, Mohammed, Buddha, or Baha'u'ullah, or have no one who plays that role. I call them all, with delight, *the people of God.* I name the Holy Spirit as the divine presence that animates me—their names are often unfamiliar, nearly unpronounceable for me, if they offer a name at all. I call them all, joyfully, *the people of God.*

How do *the people of God* and *the church* relate? Maybe this will work: My township has created sidewalks on one side of each road, and painted bike paths along the side of the road surface, for safety and environmental reasons and to promote the camaraderie made possible by foot and bike traffic. On Memorial Day we have a town parade, a throwback event if there ever was one, only in small-town America. It's the covered-dish supper of village parades. No planning committee recruits marching bands and fire departments or announces an order of march. It's a spontaneous make-it-up-as-we-go-along affair. Kids decorate their bikes, veterans don often ill-fitting uniforms, women wear their most festive hats, and families make banners. What it lacks in formality it makes up in festivity. The crowds in the street swell with each block; marchers pull reluctant spectators into the fray, though some choose just to watch.

Maybe we have a metaphor. This is a parade with a purpose, walking together for a peaceful, safer, more just world. Imagine those walking in the roadway as *the people of God*, with those in the bike path, within *the people of God*, the Christians, those from *the churches*. Imagine other Christians walking on the sidewalk, also part of *the church*, but not part of the parade. Some may be willing to be coaxed into the parade, others not. I want to be in this parade walking with *the people of God*, my preference to walk in the bike path with the *church* folk.

There's No Such Thing as Too Small

Betsy and I are evolving a covenant together, a shared commitment, however small and seemingly insignificant. We want to lower our carbon footprint from 4.9 to 3.5, *carbon footprint* being a scale that measures the impact of human activities on the environment in terms of the amount of greenhouse gases produced, measured in units of carbon dioxide. Completing a simple questionnaire provides a number reflecting that household's environmental impact, the number representing the number of earths, the resources extracted, and the waste to be absorbed it would take if everyone on the planet lived as we do.[46] Encouraged by our church, which has become innovative and assertive in affirming environmental responsibility, we are changing to low-energy appliances and light bulbs, collecting the water that flows waiting for hot water, unplugging the clothes dryer, composting, supporting the regional economy, increasing our use of public transportation, and better insulating our home to prevent heat loss. These may seem to be small steps, but they may ready us for the next steps. As we live more simply we seem to be living more joyfully.

The mission statement of the Pachamama Alliance, to which I have referred with some frequency, has inspired us: *To call forth on this planet an environmentally sustainable, spiritually fulfilling and socially just presence as a guiding principle for our time.*[47] We lead daylong symposiums to raise consciousness and promote action, and we speak on these issues as biblically based Christians.

We have struggled over the years with an abiding quiet anxiety about money, how to plan a financially secure future. Knowing it to be difficult to face such issues alone, inspired by a small support group, we made a decision a year ago that seemed unlikely, though it has been surprisingly life-giving—to give away $50,000 each of the next ten years, carefully calculated to spend down our assets across that decade. We have had increasingly comfortable conversations with our sons about an anticipated inheritance of unknown amount, sharing our ambivalence about the justice of inheritance and now working together to plan its distribution. How wonderfully incongruous—a decision that has "on paper" increased financial insecurity resulted in dramatically greater inner security.

Hey, you on the sidewalk . . . join the parade!

Notes

Preface

1. Lyall Watson, *Lifetide: The Biology of the Unconscious* (New York: Bantam Books, 1980), 147–48.

2. Ken Kesey, *The Hundredth Monkey* (St. Mary, Ky.: Vision Books, 1982).

3. Walter Wink, *Engaging the Powers* (Minneapolis: Fortress Press, 1992), 251–52.

4. Irfan Habib, "Civil Disobedience 1930–31," *Social Scientist* 25, nos. 9–10 (September/October 1997): 43–66.

5. Mahatma Gandhi and Dennis Dalton, *Mahatma Gandhi: Selected Political Writings* (Oxford: Oxford University Press, 1996), 72.

6. Richard L. Stanger, "Václav Havel: Heir to a Spiritual Legacy," *The Christian Century,* April 11, 1990, 368–70.

7. "Franciscan Benediction," quoted by Phillip Yancey in *Prayer: Does It Make Any Difference?* (Grand Rapids: Zondervan, 2006); lifebrook.wordpress.com/2008/03/24/a-franciscan-benediction.

I

1. Paolo Freire, *Pedagogy of the Oppressed* (New York: Seabury, 1970), 186ff.

2. Morris West, *Shoes of the Fisherman* (New York: St. Martin's, 1963, 1991).

2

1. Adapted from Polly Young-Eisendrath, *The Resilient Spirit* (New York: Addison-Wesley, 1996), 5.

2. Adapted from Howard E. Friend, Jr.: *Recovering the Sacred Center*, copyright © 1998 by Judson Press. Used by permission of Judson Press, 800-4-JUDSON, *www.judsonpress.com.*

3. John Sanford, *The Kingdom Within* (New York: J. P. Lippincott, 1970), 97.

4. Adapted from Friend, *Recovering the Sacred Center.* Copyright ©1998 by Judson Press. Used by permission of Judson Press, 800-4-JUDSON, *www.judsonpress.com.*

5. Baba Ram Dass, *Be Here Now* (San Cristobal, N. Mex.: Lama Foundation, 1971), Preface.

6. *www.edits.net/POI.html.*

3

1. Karen Armstrong, *Battle for God* (New York: Random House, 2000), xv–xvii.

4

1. From an informal talk by Henri Nouwen at Church of the Savior, Washington, D.C., March 1989.

2. Told to me by a dancer in the Philadelphia Ballet.

3. From a sermon, Nova Nada Hermitage, Spiritual Life Institute, June 1985.

4. Henri Nouwen, *Out of Solitude* (Notre Dame, Ind.: Ave Marie Press, 1974), 14.

5. Adapted from Tim Hansell, *When I Relax I Feel Guilty* (Elgin, IL: David C. Cook, 1979), 146–47.

5

1. Roy M. Oswald and Robert E. Friedrich, Jr., *Discerning Your Congregation's Future* (Herndon, Va.: Alban Institute, 1996), 148.

2. Ibid., 149.

3. Eugene Peterson, *The Message: The Bible in Contemporary Language* (Colorado Springs: NavPress, 2002).

4. Arlin Rothauge, *Sizing Up a Congregation for New Member Ministry* (New York: The Episcopal Center, 1985).

5. Stephen Covey, *Principle-Centered Leadership* (New York: Firestone, 1991) 170–71.

6

1. Covey, *Principle-Centered Leadership*, 164–65.

2. Summarized from Charles M. Olsen, *Transforming Church Boards* (Herndon, Va.: Alban Institute, 1995).

7

1. David A. Roozen, "Oldline Protestantism: Pockets of Vitality within a Continuing Stream of Decline," Hartford Institute for Religion Research Working Paper 1104.1, Hartford Seminary, 2004. *http://hirr .hartsem.edu/bookshelf/roozen_article5.html.*

2. Summarized from Elisabeth Kübler-Ross, *Death and Dying* (New York: MacMillan, 1969).

3. Building on a thought from Ched Myers, *Binding the Strongman* (New York: Orbis Books, 1988).

8

1. Excerpt from T. S. Eliot, *Four Quartets* (New York: Harcourt Brace, 1971), 59.

2. Reinhold Niebuhr, *The Nature and Destiny of Man* (New York: Charles Scribner and Sons, 1941), I: 112–22, 164–66; II: 47–52, 287–321.

3. Václav Havel, *Disturbing the Peace: A Conversation with Karel Huizdala* (New York: Knopf, 1990), 181–82.

4. Summarized from Adam Hochschild, *Bury the Chains* (New York: Houghton Mifflin, 2005).

5. Tracy Apple, ed., *Awakening the Dreamer, Changing the Dream Symposium Presenter's Manual* (San Francisco: Pachamama Alliance, 2007), VI-2.

6. There are many versions of this story in Native American lore available on numerous websites.

7. Randolph Byrd, "Positive Therapeutic Effects of Intercessory Prayer in a Coronary Care Unit Population," *Southern Medical Journal* (July 1988): 826–29.

8. R. Rosenthal and D. Rubin, "Interpersonal Expectancy Effects: The First 345 Studies," *Behavioral and Brain Science*, 1978, 377–415.

9. Larry Dossey, *Healing Words* (New York: HarperCollins, 1993), 49–50; quoted from Robert G. Jahn and Brenda J. Dunne, *Margins of Reality: The Role of Consciousness in the Physical World* (New York: Harcourt Brace Javanovich, 1987).

10. I began using these illustrations long before Malcolm Gladwell's use of them, but which I must acknowledge: Malcolm Gladwell, *The Tipping Point* (New York: Little Brown, 2000), 11–19.

11. Quoted in Tracy Apple, ed., *Symposium Presenter's Manual*, V-8; a metaphor originating with Norie Huddle, quoted in Keith Thompson, "What the Butterfly Knows/Wired for Wings," *Institute of Noetic Sciences*, June–August 2000.

9

1. Marcus Borg, *Meeting Jesus Again for the First Time* (San Francisco: HarperCollins, 1995), 47–50.

2. See John Perkins, *Confessions of an Economic Hit Man* (New York: Penguin Books, 2004).

3. Noam Chomsky, *Turning the Tide* (Boston: South End Press,1985) 221–53.

4. Summarized from Howard Zinn, *People's History of the United States* (New York: HarperCollins, 1995).

5. Riane Eisler, *The Chalice and the Blade* (New York: Harper & Row, 1987), 44–46, 58, 94–95.

6. The National Priorities Project, "Cost of War," *http://www .nationalpriorities.org/costofwar_home*.

7. Paul Solman, "Five Years In, Cost of Iraq War Far Exceeds Early Estimates," March 26, 2008, *http://www.pbs.org/newshour/bb/military/ jan-june08/warcost_03-26.html*.

8. *http://www.nationalpriorities.org/costofwar_home*.

9. GlobalSecurity.org, "U.S. Casualties in Iraq," *http://www .globalsecurity.org/military/ops/iraq_casualties.htm*.

10. "For amputees, an unlikely painkiller: mirrors," March 19, 2008, *http://www.cnn.com/2008/HEALTH/03/19/mirror.therapy/index.html*.

11. IraqBodyCount.org, "Documented civilian deaths from violence," *http://www.iraqbodycount.org*.

12. National Coalition on Health Care, "Facts on Health Insurance Coverage," *http://www.nchc.org/facts/coverage.shtml*.

13. Bruce Vladeck, "Universal Health Insurance in the United States: Reflections on the Past, Present, and Future," *American Journal of Public Health* 93, no. 1 (2003), *http://www.pubmed.central.nih.gov/articlerender .fcgi?artid=1447684*.

14. Center for Disease Control, "Eliminate Disparities in Infant Mortality," *http://www.cdc.gov/omhd/amh/factsheets/infant.htm*.

15. Administration on Aging, "AOA Information for African American Elders," *http://seniorhealth.about.com/library/news/blafa.htm*.

16. The Urban Institute, "Fast Facts on Welfare Policy," *http://www .urban.org/UploadedPDF/900703.pdf*.

17. "The Wealth Divide: The Growing Gap in the United States between the Rich and the Rest," *The Multinational Monitor* 24, no. 5 (2003), *http://multinationalmonitor.org/mm2003/03may/may03interviewswolff .html*.

18. Tracy Apple, ed., *Symposium Presenter's Manual*, II-6.

19. Jim Wallis, *God's Politics: Why the Right Gets It Wrong and the Left Doesn't Get It* (New York: HarperCollins, 2005), 279.

20. Awakening the Dreamer Initiative, "Social Justice—Is Our World Fair?" *http://awakeningthedreamer.org/content/view/109/145/.*

21. Anup Shah, Global Issues, "Poverty Facts and Stats," September 3, 2008, *http://www.globalissues.org/article/26/poverty-facts-and-stats.*

22. Children's Defense Fund, "Over 13 Million Children Face Food Insecurity," June 2, 2005, *http://www.childrensdefense.org/site/DocServer/foodinsecurity2005.pdf?docID=482.*

23. United States Census Bureau, "Poverty: 2007 Highlights," *http://www.census.gov/hhes/www/poverty/poverty07/pov07hi.html.*

24. Elizabeth C. McNichol and Iris Lav, Center on Budget and Policy Priorities, "29 States Faced Total Budget Shortfall of at Least $48 Billion in 2009," August 5, 2008, *http://www.cbpp.org/1-15-08sfp.htm.*

25. Tracy Apple, ed., *Symposium Presenter's Manual*, 22.

26. National Aeronautics and Space Administration, "Mississippi Dead Zone," August 10, 2004, *http://www.nasa.gov/vision/earth/environment/dead_zone.html.*

27. Greenpeace, "The Trash Vortex," http://www.greenpeace.org/international/campaigns/oceans/pollution/trash-vortex.

28. Awakening the Dreamer Initiative, "Social Justice—Is Our World Fair?" *http://awakeningthedreamer.org/content/view/109/145/.*

29. Tracy Apple, ed., *Symposium Presenter's Manual*, 19.

30. David Gutierrez, "Supporting World Population at U.S. Consumption Rates Would Require Five Earths," *Natural News*, March 26, 2008, *http://www.naturalnews.com/022890.html.*

31. C. S. Lewis, *The Screwtape Letters* (London: Collins, 1942), 64.

32. Ibid, 40.

10

1. Adapted from Howard E. Friend, Jr., *Recovering the Sacred Center;* copyright © 1998 by Judson Press. Used by permission of Judson Press, 800-4-JUDSON, *www.judsonpress.com.*

2. Arlington Institute, "Mission," *http://www.arlingtoninstitute .org/tai/mission.*

3. Weather Underground, "About Antarctica," *http://www .wunderground.com/climate/Antarctica.asp.*

4. John L. Petersen, "Visions of the Future," *What Is Enlightenment?* 23 (Spring-Summer 2003), *http://www.wie.org/j23/visions.asp.*

5. Ibid.

6. Tracy Apple, ed., *Symposium Presenter's Manual*, II-5.

7. Ibid.

8. Ibid., VIII-7.

9. United States Census Bureau, "Poverty: 2007 Highlights," *http:// www.census.gov/hhes/www/poverty/poverty07/pov07hi.html.*

10. United for a Fair Economy and the Institute for Policy Studies, "Executive Excess 2008: How Average Taxpayers Subsidize Runaway Pay: 15th Annual CEO Compensation Survey," August 25, 2008. Available online at *http://www.faireconomy.org/files/executive_excess_2008.pdf.*

11. Tracy Apple, ed., *Symposium Presenter's Manual*, II-6.

12. Donella H. Meadows, "If the World Were a Village of 1,000 People," from Doug Aberley, ed., *Futures by Design: The Practice of Ecological Planning* (Philadelphia: New Society Publishers, 1994).

13. CIA World Factbook, "Field Listing - Life expectancy at birth," *https://www.cia.gov/library/publications/the-world-factbook/ fields/2102.html.*

14. Center for Reproductive Rights, "Broken Promises: Human Rights, Accountability, and Maternal Death in Nigeria," June 2008. Available online at *http://www.reproductiverights.org/pdf /pub_nigeria2.pdf.*

15. Associated Press, "Global Mortality Rates Slow to Drop, U.N. Reports," *Washington Post*, October 8, 2004.

16. Meadows, "If the World Were a Village of 1,000 People."

17. Quoted in Tracy Apple, ed., *Symposium Presenter's Manual*, II-6.

18. Petersen, "Visions of the Future."

19. Rev. Kim Erno, lecture at the Lutheran Center of Mexico City, January 15, 2008.

20. Ronald Sider, *Rich Christians in an Age of Hunger* (Dallas: Word Publishing, 1997), 137.

21. Statement by a Hunger Project workshop leader at a seminar at Gladwyne Presbyterian Church, Gladwyne, PA. Learn more about The Hunger Project at *www.thp.org*.

22. Ched Myers, "It is an Issue of Equality, Biblical Reflections on Wealth and Poverty," *Priests and People* (London, England: Tablet Publishing, May 1999).

23. John Bright, *History of Israel* (Philadelphia: Westminster, 1957), 240–41.

24. U.S. Department of Justice, *Violence Related Injuries Treated in Hospital Emergency Departments*, August 1997.

25. Callie Marie Rennison, U.S. Department of Justice, NCJ 197838, *Bureau of Justice Statistics Crime Data Brief: Intimate Partner Violence,* 2003.

26. Murray A. Strauss, Richard J. Gelles, and Christine Smith, *Physical Violence in American Families; Risk Factors and Adaptations to Violence in 8,145 Families* (New Brunswick, NJ: Transaction Publishers, 2003).

27. C. Shakeshaft, U.S. Department of Education, 2004.

28. National Vital Statistics Reports, vol. 47, no. 19, National Center for Health and Human Services, 1999.

29. Graham Dwyer, "Violence and the Poor," Asian Development Bank, 2003, *www.adb.org*.

30. Caroline N. Moser, "Urban Violence and Insecurity," *www .brookings.edu*.

31. Anup Shah, Global Issues, "World Military Spending," March 1, 2008, *http://www.globalissues.org/article/75/world-military-spending*.

32. Ibid.

33. Samuel Loewenberg, "Bush in food aid fight with Congress," Politico.com, February 6, 2008. *http://www.politico.com/news/stories/0208/8378.html*.

34. Ron Sider, *Rich Christians in an Age of Hunger* (Dallas: Word Publishing, 1997), 31–33.

35. *Sojourners,* March 2008, 29.

36. A.J. Muste, *Gandhi and the H-Bomb: How Nonviolence Can Take the Place of War* (Nyack, NY: Fellowship Publications, 1983), 11.

37. William Blake, "Jerusalem," *The Complete Works of William Blake,* David V. Erdman, ed. (Berkeley: University of California Press, 1982), 177.

38. Blake, "The Gray Monk," *The Complete Works of William Blake.*

39. Encarta Dictionary Online, "Hegemony," *encarta.msn.com.*

40. John Perkins, *The Secret History of the American Empire* (New York: Penguin Group, 2007), 2–3.

41. Sider, 117.

42. Joachim Jeremias, *Jerusalem in the Time of Jesus* (Philadelphia: Fortress, 1969), 251.

43. Ibid., 49.

44. Ched Myers, *Binding the Strong Man* (New York: Orbis Books, 1988), 300–301.

45. Walter Wink, *Engaging the Powers* (Minneapolis: Augsburg, 1992), 65.

46. Earth Day Network Footprint Calculator, *http://www.earthday .net/footprint/index.html.*

47. Tracy Apple, ed., *Symposium Presenter's Manual,* I-4.